ENGLISH RECUSANT LITERATURE
1558—1640

Selected and Edited by
D. M. ROGERS

Volume 205

JOHN HEIGHAM
A Devout Exposition
of the Holie Masse
1622

JOHN HEIGHAM

A Devout Exposition
of the Holie Masse
1622

The Scolar Press
1974

ISBN o 85967 188 7

Published and printed in Great Britain by
The Scolar Press Limited, 59-61 East Parade,
Ilkley, Yorkshire and
39 Great Russell Street,
London WC1

1819628

A
DEVOVT EXPO-
SITION, OF THE
HOLIE MASSE.

VVITH

An ample declaration of all the
RITES & CEREMONIES
belonging to the same.

COMPOSED,

By IOHN HEIGHAM.

The more to mooue all godly people, to the
greater veneration of so sublime
a Sacrament.

The second edition, reuiewed and aug-
mented by the Author.

AT S. OMERS,
With licence of the Superiors.
Anno Dom. 1622.

THE PREFACE
TO THE CATHOLIKE
READER.

FOure caufes there were (right courteous Reader) which firft mooued mee to explicate vnto thee (according vnto my fmall capacitie) the myfteries and Ceremonies of the holy Maffe. The firft was, the incomparable dignitie, and moft excellent fublimitie, of this diuine and dreadfull facrifice: which although it be fuch, that neither the tongue of man nor Angel, can worthelie magnifie, as it deferueth, yet the verie excellencie of the thing it felfe, inuiteth euerie one, with what praifes he can, to fet forth, extoll, and celebrate the fame.

2 The fecōd was, the moft fingular honor, refpect, & reuerence, which the deuout & Catholike people, of al places, of al ages, &

A 2

of

*of all callings, the greatest Doctors them-
selues, and most learned diuines of all the
worlde, Emperours, Kinges, Princes, and
Commons, haue euer borne and carried to
this Sacrifice: whose example it behoo-
ueth euery good and godly man to follow.*

*3 The third was, the deepe, mortal, and
cankered malice of wicked heretickes,
their most execrable blasphemies, together
with manie most feareful, vylde, and
damnable facts, done and committed by
them, in hatred and contempt of this diuine sacrifice: and what good Christian is
there that will not, to the vttermost of his
power, defend a treasure so inestimable,
from the sauage assaults of such wicked
miscreants?*

*4 The fourth was, the great and long
want of a full and perfect exposition, of
this so diuine a mysterie in our English
tongue, by reason that none of our nation
haue purposel.e written of the same (for
ought that euer I saw) these fourtie years:
which foure motiues, seemed vnto me ma-
ter more then sufficient, to explicate vnto
thee*

thee, this vnexplicated secrete, and to vn-
folde vnto thee, a mysterie of such maiestie.

5 Of the supereminent dignitie, as
also of the great & singular respect, which
Catholikes doe beare to this ineffable misterie, I haue amplie treated and discour-
sed vnto thee, in the third, fourth, fifth,
and sixth chapters of this ensuing Treatise. I beseech the infinite mercie and good-
nesse of God, that thou mayest receaue a-
boundant consolation, and edification, for
thy paines in perusing of them. But touching the deadly hatred and malice of our
aduersaries, or of their blasphemies, and
other abuses of this blessed Sacrifice, I
haue no where made any mention of them;
and would to God there were no cause at
all, euer to'defile the paper of my Preface,
with their execrable enormous and filthie
facts.

Now against this most singular Sacrament, pearle of inestimable price, ada-
mant of Angels, rose of our religion, only
life, only lawrell, only tryumph, only treasure

sure, onely glorie, onely beautie, and onely crowne of all Christianitie; the hereticks of our age, doe beare so rabide a rage, so mischieuous a minde , and so spiteful a spleane, ioyned with such audatious attempts , barbarous abuses , and insolent outrages, as neuer the like were heard of before our dayes, yea, and in a maner is incredible, could euer enter into the heart of a Christian.

For some rushing violently into the Church, where the Priest was celebrating this vnbloodie Sacrifice, stamping vnder their filthie feete, the sacred Host, and spilling vpon the ground, the blessed blood, vsed the consecrated challice, insteed of a pisse-pot: and hauing compelled the Priest to drinke off the pisse, next presently hung him vp on high, fastened and bound with cordes, vnto an image of Christ crucified, and then with many shots of gunnes and pistols, pierced quite through, both the Priest and the picture, as witnesseth Laynay in his Replique Christien. lib. 2. cap. 16.

Another

Another, seeing the Priest at Masse, to hold vp the sacred Host that it might be adored of the people, tooke vp a dogge by the legges, and helde him ouer his head, shewing him vnto the people, in mockage and contempt of the Priest, and of his sacrifice, Fox Act. and Mon. pag. 1033.

Another (as witnesseth the same Foxe) finding a Priest administring the blessed Sacrament to the people with great deuotion, offended to see them so deuoutly and reuerently vpon their knees, presently pulled out a whyniard or wood-knife which he wore about him, and very grieuouslie wounded the Priest in diuers places, both of his head, arme, and hand, wherwith he held the holy Challice, full of consecrated Hosts, which were sprinckled with the blood of the Priest: nor would haue left him, til he had killed him out-right, if hee had not bene preuented by the people preset.

10 *But least thou (gentle Reuder) maist thinke that God, who is the iust reuenger of all such villanyes, hath permitted these men to escape vnpunished, let this example*

next enſuing ſatisfie thee, and ſerue for a warning to all the aduerſaries & malitious enemies of the Maſſe. After that the holy Maſſe, was by publike proclamation of the late Queene, commãded to ſurceaſe in all places of England (by Midſommer day immediatly following) ſower men of Douer, *in the countie of* Kẽt *(beſids others which aſſiſted at the ſame actiõ) wẽt into the Church of the ſame towne, and tooke foorth the copes, veſtmẽts, & other Prieſtly Ornamẽts belonging thereto, giuing forth and boaſting abroad, that they would goe fetch the Pope frõ* Canterburie. *And the verie next day after Midſomer day, theſe companions came to* Canterburie, *put on the ſaide Copes and other Ornaments vpon their backs, and in a Pix (made to reſerue the bleſſed Sacrament of the bodie of our Sauiour* Ieſus*) they put a dogs-turde; and then beginning at* S. Georges *gate, rode in forme of Proceſſion quite through the Citie, til they came to* Weſtgate; *which done, the very ſame night they poſted backe againe to* Douer.

11 One

11 *One of these foure, was Captaine* Roberts, *who presently after carryed all the Copes, Vestments, and other ornaments, ouer the seaes to* Dunkerke, *where he sold them. His miserable and wretched ende was, that there leaping out of one smal boate into another, to goe to his ship, the boate he was in, slipping away, he stepped short of the other, and so falling into the water, pitched his vnhappie head vpon an Anchor, where he beate out his braines.*

12 *The second, shortly after running madde, cast him selfe off, from* Douer Peere *into the sea, and so was drowned.*

13 *The third, dyed of* Iohn Caluins *disease, that is to say, he was eaten vp with lyce, being yet aliue.*

14. *The fourth (who afterwardes became* Minister *of* Maidstone) *falling grieuously sicke, indured Gods terrible iudgements; for he stunck so abhominablie, that none (no not his owne wife) could indure to come neere him, so that when they gaue him meate to eate, they were forced to put it vpon the ende of a long Pole, and so to*

A 5 reach

reach it vnto him through a window. For
confirmation whereof, there are right cre-
dible and worshipful persons yet aliue,
who can testifie the same for a certaine
trueth.

15 These are some fewe, though not
the thousand parte, of the malitious dea-
lings of heretickes against the Masse, and
of the most remarkable iudgements of Almightie God against them, for their horrible abuses of the same. O immortal God,
what is there in all this diuine and dread-
ful misterie, which may mooue any reasonable man to such height of mallice, furie, mischiefe and manifest madnesse! Doth
the sacred Psalmes of thy seruant Dauid
(for from them the Masse doth take its beginning) the humble acknowledgement of
our humaine frailtie, the asking of mercie
for our dailie offences, the song of Angels,
pronounced at thy Natiuitie, petitions vnto thee for obtaining of graces, the lecture
of thy Prophets, the Gospells of thy Euan-
gelists, the Creed of the Apostles, the Sanctus of thy Seraphines, supplications for
all

all sorts of persons, the Commemoration
of thy Passion, the prayer of all prayers,
both made by thy selfe, and taught by thy
selfe to thy disciples. And which is more to
be lamented then all the rest, doth thy precious bodie & blood realhe present in this
holy sacrifice, deserue to be dealt with all,
in so sauage a sort? Surely no, for such de-
meanors as these are most sathanical, nor
so much as beseeming any Christians in the
world saue ouely Caluenists.

16 Thou therefore, ô Lord, who art
the sole protector of that which thou thy
selfe hast instituted, protect thy selfe in
this blessed sacrifice against thy persecu-
tors. Thou Lord of hosts, defend thy selfe
in this holie Host, against thine enemies.
Permit not, I beseech thee, thy pretious bodie & blood, any longer to be so barbarous-
lie abused. Reestablish the same in our Ilād,
mauger the mallice of thine enemyes.
And grant that after fourty years, wherein thou hast bene grieued with this wic
ked generation, at the last this noble sacrifice may be publickly celebrated by vs,

to

to thine euerlaßing and perpetual praiſe.

17 *And you (religious Fathers and re-*
uerend Prieſts) to whom is committed the
care of this our deuaſted vyniard, & who
are vnto vs in this our diſtreſſe, the ſole
diſpenſers of this diuine ſacrament, ven-
ture ſtill I beſeech you (as hetherto you
haue done) the loſſe of your liues, to di-
ſtribute vnto vs this diuine foode, and te
breake vnto vs this celeſtial bread. For
in your handes only it is, to giue vnto men,
this heauenly Manna. In your hands onely
it is, in this time of dearth, to preſerue the
liues of your brethren, leaſt they perish by
famine.

18 *And we againe (my Catholike bre-*
thren) let vs as boldly aduenture our liues
to giue them harbour and entertainement.
Imitating herein our noble Patron and
Protomartyr of England, bleſſed S. Alban,
who preſented himſelfe, yea and gaue his
owne life, to preſerue the life of his Prieſt
Amphibolus. Imitating alſo (in ſome ſort:
herein) the glorious virgin S. Catherin
of Sienna, who beating and afflicting her
bodie

bodie so seuerely that she drew the blood; the deuil appearing vnto her, and perswading her that it was both foolish & needlesse deuotion; she made him answere, that her Lord and Sauiour had giuen his blood for her, & that she would requite and repay him againe, with blood for blood. Euen so, whē either foolish heretickes, or tiimorous friendes, shall condemne you of follie, for loosing your goods, or exposing your liues, for to harbour Priests, consider with your selues, that you harbour him, who bringeth vnto you, the bodie and blood of Iesus Chrisl: and, that if you shed your blood, to receaue him who consecrateth in your houses the blood of Christ, what else doe youbut render blood for blood, & spend your blood for the blood of Christ?

19 Comfort your selues likewise with this consideration, that when our Lord and Sauiour instituted his last supper, and consecrated this misterie, in the house of a friende, euen a fewe dayes before, did the traytor Iudas, betray and sell the same most innocent blood for thirtie pence. You therefore

therefore, right Honorable and Worshipful of our English nation, which haue
bought this holie sacrifice at a hundreth
marks: and such as were poore, with the
vtter depriuance of all the poore little they
had in the world: and further, such as
haue not so much money as heretick s haue
asked for the price of this sacrifice, nor no
worldly goods at all to giue them, and insteede of money, haue layde to pawne their
verie carcasses, into sundrie prisons, iayles,
and loathsome dungeons, O with what
great and vnspeakable reward, will our
Lord and Sauiour one daye repay and requite your charitie!

20 Neuer was there any acte in the
world so vyle and abhominable, as that of
Iudas, to sel to the Iewes for money, the
blood of his master: nor neuer can there be
amongst Christians any acte more honorable, then to buye with such sommes of money, with such losse of landes and liuings,
the blood of Christ. That cursed creature
sold the blood of his master, but onely for
thirtie pence, and yet how hatefull is he to
all

all the worlde, as also to heauen? you paye
for the same aboue threescore poundes, ô
howe gratefull shall you be, both to God
and his Angels! Surely this sacrifice cannot
be esteemed by you that loue it at any lowe
price, sith those that hate it, doe value it
vnto you at so heigh a rate: for that thing
must needes be pretious, which both the
Marchant doth set so heigh, and the Chap-
man is côtented to buy so deare. In a word,
all the sufferings, all the ignomynies, al
the iniuries, all the dammages, and all the
detriments which you shall indure for the
defence of this sacrifice, wil minister matter to all ensueing posteritie of your most
noble, and heroical acts: which though you
dye, will euer liue to future memorie, re-
sound to your owne immortal glorie, and
the euerlasting renowne of our English
nation.

11 Finallie, for as much as I may haue
iust occasion to feare, least I haue offended,
for offering to touch, or support with my
penne, this sacred Arke, I therefore here
from the bottome of my hart, right humbly
craue

craue pardõ of the blessed Trinitie, the maker of this ineffable mistery, of Iesus Christ
reallie present in this mysterie, of all the
blessed Angels which assiste at this misterie, of all Catholike Priests the consecra-
tors of this misterie, & of al Catholik people the true worshippers of this ineffable
misterie. And in further satisfaction for
this my presumption, I am, and euer wil be
ready so long as I liue, to cast my selfe vnder the feet of the meanest Priest in al the
world, and to serue him as his foote stoole,
whilest he celebrateth this sacrifice.

22 And lastly if peraduenture there be
any thing cõtained in this Treatise, which
in the iudgemẽt of the Catholike Church
(the onely elected Spouse of Iesus Christ)
shal seem cõtrary ether to the faith, or good
maners of the same Church, I vtterly ab-
iure, damne, condemne, and detest the same
protesting my selfe to be the man, that
with the same handes wherewith I writ
it, with the selfe-same handes, to be the
first that shal throw the same into the fire.

Thy hearty wel willer and most
affectionate contryman
IOHN HEIGHAM.

A VVOORD OR

two concerning Cere-
monies.

THose which make pro-
fession of learning, cō-
monly and with verie
great reason doe complaine, that
arts and sciences, haue no greater
enemie, then the ignorant man.
And euen so, wee at this day, may
iustly complaine & say the same,
that touching the affaires of Religion, we finde no greater enemies
and mockers thereof, and principally of the religious rites and
Ceremonies belōging to the same,
then those who are most of all ignorant of their sense & meaning.

2 And

2 And whereas we see in this our cursed & execrable age, a great number of Christians so easilie contemne, & so impudētly mocke at such godly Ceremonies; so if they rightlie vnderstood the rea-son of them, they would certain-ly receaue them with singular re-uerence and deuotion.

3 Now amongst all the fiue sen-ces of nature which God hath gi-uen vs, two especiallie (to wit, our Eares, & our Eies) are principallie called, *Sensus doctrinæ, aut disci-plinæ.* Sences of doctrine, or disci-pline: that is to saye, whereby wee are made capable to receaue in-structions & discipline: For with-out these two, it is impossible e-uer to learne any thing, and by the meanes of these two principal sences

fences , we come to vnderstande and learne all maner of fciences. All the Ceremonies therefore of the Maſſe, are inſtituted by the Church, principally to inſtruct the people by the fence of Seeing And euen as they who would take away preaching out of the church do as much as if they should ſtop the peoples eares : euē ſo they who would take awaye thc Ceremonies out of the Church, doe as much as in them lyeth, to hide, or cleane put out the peoples eyes.

4 What then may we thinke or ſaye , of the pernitious practiſes of the Arch heretickes of our age? Yea, and howe iuſte occaſion haue thoſe which are of their owne religion (as well as we) to cry out againſt them ? For

firſt

firſt theſe malitious Maſters, haue quite caſſierde a greate number of godly Ceremonies, frō amōgſt the Chriſtian people , in all citties and countries where ſo euer they haue liued. And next, euen of thoſe few which ſtill they retaine, they as vtterly depriue them of their ſenſe and meaning , as if there were not ſo much as any one vſed, in all their religion.

4 But what ſuppoſe you to be, the drift and legierdemaine of theſe deceiuers ? Forſooth, becauſe knowing full well, that in our Catholike Ceremonies, there are comprehended and lye hid, ſo manie notable myſteries , they plainely foreſee, that if they ſhould truely explicate and manifeſt vnto the people , the ſenſe & meaning

ning of fome of their owne, they
should prefently giue thē a light,
& inflame their hearts with the
loue of ours. For which caufe (as
by a fubtle & craftie deuice) they
for the moft part, either conceale
them from them, or fpeake in cō-
tempt and hatred of them.

6 To make this poyπte the
more apparant; Of howe manie
thoufands of them may you aske
thefe queftions, before you shall
meete with one that can make
you aunfwere ? For example, aske
them, why, to the accomplishmēt
of their cōmon feruice, the Clarke
& Minifter muft be clad in white,
rather then in black, blew, or yel
low, or in a coate, or garment of
any other collour ? Aske thē, why
in faying the fame feruice, the
leffon

leſſon is read out of the olde teſtament, and not out of the new? &
why not all ſcripture out of the
olde, or all out of the new ? Aske
them why the olde teſtament is
read before the newe : & why not
the newe before the old, ſeeing it
is of farre greater dignitie as thē-
ſelues doe freelie confeſſe ? Aske
them, why they kneele at the ſaying of the Lords prayer, and riſe
vp at the Creede, rather then riſe
vp at the Lords prayer, & kneele
downe at the Creed, Aske them,
why they ſet the Fonte neere the
Church doore, and the Communion table within the Chancell :
& why not as wel thē Cōmunion
table at the Church doore, and the
Font within the Chancel? I omit
for breuities ſake, the churching
of

of women. The marrying with a ring. Goodfathers and Godmothers in the Sacrament of Baptifme. The confirmation of childrē, &c. All which, with a hundred more which I might name, the Proteftant Cleargie doe ftill retaine, whereof the people no more vnderftande the meaning, then the mau in the Moone.

6 Now therefore, for as much as all Ceremonies (vfed for the better, & more folemne fetting foorth of the deuine feruice) are of one of thefe two forts, that is to fay, either Commoditatiue, or Significatiue, it followeth, that to weare a white Surpleffe, rather then a blacke, or to reade for the firft Leffon, rather parte of the old Teftament then of the newe : or
to

to set the Fonte at the Church doore , rather then within the Chancel (or in the bottome of the Bel-frie) are nothing Commoditatiue, neither to the Prieſt, nor yet to the people; ergo they are Significatiue, that is to ſaye, ſignifying ſome ſpeciall myſterie, wherein the Chriſtian people, ought to be inſtructed.

8 The holie Ceremonies therefore of our Religion, if they were explicated vnto thee, gentle Reader (if thou be a Proteſtant) as they are vnto Catholiques, they would aſſuredly yeelde thee moſt ſingular comfort; wherein I will report me to thine owne experience, after thou ſhalt haue firſt peruſed , the explication onely of theſe which appertaine to the holy

Maſſe

Maſſe (whereof thou haſt here ſet downe, euerie word, ſentence, and ſillable that is in the ſame.) Nothing doubting, but that in the ende, thou thy ſelfe, wilt freely conteſſe, that the hearers and beholders of the holy Maſſe, enioye, and receaue, a moſt incredible comfort, by occaſion of the Ceremonies which are handled therein: which thou being a Proteſtant, canſt neuer enioy, by aſſiſting or being preſent, at thy morning prayer. Trye, and then truſt, and ſo farewell.

B   *CHAP.*

CHAP. I.

Of the Etymologie, Deriuation, and Sig-
nification, of the word Masse: *and from*
what tongue the same was first deri-
ued.

O proceede orderly, in the exposition of the holie Sacrifice of the
Masse: it is conuenient that we begin at the Etymologie, or signification of the word.

First therefore it is very probable, that the
word Masse, is neither Greeke nor Latine,
but pure Hebrew; the Apostes who were of
the Hebrew Nation, hauing promulgated the
same in that language; and named it *Missah*,
drawen and taken of this Hebrew worde,
Mas, which signifieth Oblation, Taxe, or
Tribute, as is manifestly to be gathered out
of Deut. 16. and 20. and 3 Reg. 8. and Esay 13.
And in many places of holy Scripture, it signifieth the Sacrifices, and Oblations, of the

old Lawe, made of Lambs, Oxen, Turtles, Pigeons and the like. Num. 6. Iudg. 6. Ezech. 45. &c. For which caufe the Catholike Church, doeth moft willingly retaine this name, as finding none other more conueniēt and proper, to fignifie this moft excellent Oblation and Sacrifice, reprefenting that other, which was the Taxe or Tribute, paide by Iefus Chriſt, vnto God his Father, for the price and ranſome of our redemption.

2 Others will haue it to be of the Latine word, *miſſa, ſent*, becauſe in the Maſſe, principally we fende vp our prayers and oblations to almightie God, Hug. Vict. l. 2. de Sacram p. 9. cap. 14. which fome explicat in this maner: that this Hoſte was firſt fent by God the Father, when he fent vs his onely Sonne, to be incarnate, and to take fleſh in the wombe of the B. Virgin Marie, and afterwardes to offer vp that bloodie Sacrifice vpon the Altar of the Croſſe, for our Redemption; in remembrance whereof, this Sacrifice is celebrated, and is by vs againe, fent and prefented to the eternal Father, for as much as wee daily offer it vp to his diuine Maieſtie. Innocent. 3. lib 3. de Sacrificio Miſſæ, cap. 12. & Bon. op. de miſterio Miſſæ.

3 Againe, others thinke it to be fo called of difiniſſing the people, and fo to fignifie the fame that *Miſſio*, which fignifieth, a fending away, or diſniſſion. as Bellar lib. 1. de Miſſa,

Missa. But howsoeuer this be, and whether the word be Hebrew, Greeke or Latine, or whether it be contained in the new Testament, or in the olde : it is sufficient for vs, that in the Scripture is expressed,that which this worde most truely signifyeth. As in the like case and difficultie, S. Aug told the Arrian heretike Pascentius, Epist, 194.that he was not to grounde his disputation, vpon the bare word *Homusion*, which the Catholikes onely vsed, thereby to giue to vnderstand,that God the Sonne was consubstantiall, with God the Father, but that he should argue against that which it signifyed And the like may be said' of many other tearmes still retained by Catholikes, as Trinitie, Humanitie, Person, Incarnation, Transubstantiation, and the like.

C H A P. II.

Of the diuers parts of the Masse: and by whom the holy Masse was first ordayned.

THE holy and dreadfull Sacrifice of the Masse, hath two essential parts. The one is. Consecration: the other is, the Receauing of the Priest, or Communion. Touching these two principall and essentiall parts of the holye Masse, it is most certaine, by the Euangeliste-

them-

felues, Matt. 16. Marc. 14. Luc. 21. and likewife by S. Paule 1. Cor. 11. that they were inftituted by Iefus Chrift himfelfe, and by no
other, neither man nor Angell: our Sauiour
contenting himfelfe, to inftitute fo much as
was of the nature, necefsitie, and effence of
the thing, leauing other ceremonies and rites
requifite to celebrate the fame, to the iudgement and prudence of his Apoftles and of
their fucceffors, to whom he committed the
care of his Church, and of all his faithfull
and Chriftian flocke: In which refpect, hee
faid vnto his difciples: *Yet many things I haue
to fay to you, but you cannot beare them now:
but when he, the Spirit of trueth commethe, he
shall teach you all trueth: and the things that
are to come, he shal shew you.* Ioh. 16. 12.

2 We fee the like alfo performed in other
points of our Religion, as when or Lord ordained that we fhould faft, he contented him
felfe to inftitute only, fo much as was of the
effence of the thing, faying, *ieiunate*, Faft yee.
Mat 17. prefcribing neither how, when, nor
how oft, his holie pleafure was to haue it
performed: but left all thofe circumftances
to be ordered and accommodated, according
to the care and difcretion of his difciples.
The like he did and performed, concerning
prayer, willing, & ordaining that men fhould
praye, faying: *Orate*, Praye yee. Marc 13. and
Luc. 18. and added thereto, this worde,
fem-

*semper,*euer: but that *euer,* I feare m by many,would be turned into *neuer,* if his fpoufe
the Catholike Church, had not decreed,and
ftreightly commanded and prefcribed the
time,the place,the Ceremonies,and the manner howe the fame fhould be accompli-
fhed.

3 Hence therefore it is, that we affirme &
fay with very good reafon, the holy Maffe to
haue bene inftituted and ordained by our
Lord himfelfe , for as much as hee inftituted
and ordained the moft effential and principal
parts thereof,to wit,Confecration and Communion,referring the Ceremonies,and other
circumftances, to the care and difcretion of
his Apoftles, and their fucceffors: who in
this behalfe, haue taken fuch order, as might
beft reduce his death and pafsion, into our
memories, according to that which he commanded, that fo oft as they fhould doe it,
they fhould doe it in remembrance of him.
But of all this , wee fhall fpeake hereafter
more at large.

4 Nowe, in a worde I may faye , that
thefe Ceremonies , or additions , may bee
reduced to thefe heades , to witte, to giuing of Thankes , Confefsion of finnes,
Prayer, Doctrine , Profefsion of faith, and
and fuch other parts of our deuotion : which
albeit they be no effential parts of this holy
Sacrifice, yet are they very requifite & con-
　　　　B 4　　　　　uenient

uenient to induce vs, the more to reuerence
and contemplate , the Maieſtie and excellencie of ſo great a myſterie, to ſtir vp & mooue
our hearts, being preſent at the ſame, and to
prepare and diſpoſe our ſelues, befoie wee
come to receaue ſo great a Sacrament.   For
which cauſe, we ought to holde for very laudable, theſe other parts of the holy Maſſe, annexed to the former, all tending to the greater ornament, reuerence, and maieſtie of ſo
ineffable a myſterie.

CHAP.   III.

Of the excellencie and dignitie of the holy
Maſſe: and of the great worthi-
nes of the things, that are
handled therein.

A Mongſt all the things that giue teſtimonie of the ſweetnes, benignitie, and
loue of God towards man, one of the chiefe
and principal, is, this moſt diuine , and moſt
excellent Sacrament of a'l Sacraments. The
which, becauſe of the great and ſuper abound-
dant grace, which it containeth, is therefore
worthelie called Euchariſt , or good grace.
For this moſt ſacred and holy action, is of it
ſelfe, and by it ſelfe , both a Sacrament, and
Sacrifice; and that the moſt noble, diuine, and
most

moſt worthy that euer was offered , nor can there poſſiblie be a greater, it being no other then the onely, true, and eternal Sonne of God himſelfe.

2 To preſigure vnto vs the dignitie of this Sacrifice, our Lord in the olde Teſtament, would, that the Prieſt entring into the Sanctuarie, ſhould be attyred with moſt rich and pretious ornaments : and thoſe moſt coſtly and artificiall wrought : to the ende, that the people ſeeing him to enter ſo venerablie, ſhould know the greatnes of God, to whom he went to ſpeake, and to render due honour.

3 In like manner , the riches and diuers Ornaments, the magnificent Churches, the Altars ſo ſumptuouſly adorned , the great nūber of lights,& al other ceremonies which the Catholike Church doth now vſe in celebrating this Sacrifice, were ordained to this ende, to declare the greatnes,ſanctitie, & vertue of this miſterie. For euen as he who entring into a great Pallace,ſeeing the walles of the chambers hung with Arras, or Tapeſtry, commeth to know the greatneſſe,the noblenes, and the riches of the Perſonage that dwelleth therein(for as much as poore folks, or people of meane eſtate, cannot be fitted with ſuch coſtly furniture:)euen ſo,& no otherwiſe happeneth it vnto him,who entreth into the Church , and ſeeth Maſſe to be celebraſed

B 5 braſed

brated with fuch curious ornaments : for as
much as wife and vertuous men would neuer be at fo great expences , nor euer labour fo much for the performance thereof, if they knew not fulwell, this worke to
be the greateft, that pofsiblie a man can practife in the world.

4 An other thing, which doth moft fingu-
larlie demonftrate vnto vs the dignitie of this
Sacrifice , is, that it is a perfect Epitome, or
abridgement, of all the workes of Almightie
God , and of the whole olde and new Teftament, comprifing brieflie and fummarily,
all that which is contained therein , The
Trinitie, Vnitie, Eternitie, Omnipotencie,
Glorie, Maieftie, Infinitie, and Excellencie,
of Almightie God The creation of Heauen,
Earth, Angels,Men,and of all Creatures. The
Incarnation, Natiuitie, Preaching, Miracles,
Life,Death,Pafsion,Refurrection, and Affen-
tion of our Sauiour Iefus : and confequently,
our Redemption , Vocation , Iuftification,
Sanctification , and Glorification , together,
with what foeuer elfe concerneth the glorie
of God,or faluation of man.

CHAP.

CHAP. IIII.

Of the great worthineße of Priestes, who offer this Holy Sacrifice.

THis Sacrifice being so excellent a thing, as hath before bene shewed ; it was conuenient , that the diuine Maiestie of Almightie God, should ordaine in his Church, an order of men , which should be aboue others, who should both consecrate, and offer the same : which thing, he performed in his last supper, instituting the order of Priesthood, vnto which, hee gaue power and authoritie, to consecrate, receaue, and distribute to others , his most pretious Bodie and Blood, veiled vnder the formes, of bread and wine.

2 By which, it is most manifest , that the Maße, is a woike, the most great, the most worthie, and most excellent, that possiblie a man can vndertake or enterprise , seeing the Priest , who sayeth it , excelleth in dignitie, all the Kings, Emperours, and Priests, either of the writte law, or of the law of nature. And furthermo e, he surpasseth in this power, the Patriarkes , the Prophets, yea, and the Angels themselues, who neither can consecrate , receaue, nor distribute to others, the Bodie , of our bleſſed Sauiour:

where

whereas the Prieft hauing confecrated it, holdeth it in his hands, receaueth it, keepeth it, and imparteth it to others.

3 Rightlie therefore doe wee faie, that this noble dignitie of Prieſthood, can with no pompe, eloquencie, or ornament of wordes, be ſufficiently extolled. For it ſurmounteth and ſurpaſſeth the tongues of the moſt ſubtle Philoſophers, yea the top and height of all excellencie of euery creature. If you compaꝛe it to the glorie of Kings, or to the ſplendor of Princes Diadeams, theſe are as farre inferiour thereto, as if wee ſhould compare the baſeſt lead, to the pureſt and fineſt gold that is.

4 But what neede I ſtand vpon earthly cõparifons, when the celeſtiall citizens, the Angels themſelues dare not aſpire to Prieſtlie authoritie. For to which of the Angels, hath God at any time ſaid? *whoſe ſinnes you ſhall forgiue, they are forgiuen them: and whoſe ſynne ſhal retaine, they are retained.*Io.20.yea, which is much more: *Doe this for the commemoration of me* Cor.11,24. In a word, they admire and tremble to beholde, that which the Prieſte may bouldly touch, handle, and deuide in pieces, as being warranted by Chriſt himſelf.

5 But to paſſe yet further from the Hierarchies of Angels, and to come to the Ladie of Angels, and Queene of all the worlde, euen ſhee, I ſaie, albeit ſhee farre ſurpaſſed
all

all creatures, in the plenitude and abundance of heauenly grace, yet euen shee her selfe, also giueth place to the orders and Hierarchies of the militant Church. For hauing all other honor, giuen vnto her by her Sonne in the highest degree, yet she arta ned not to this dignitie of consecrating or offering this dreadfull Sacrifice. True it is, that shee in pronouncing eight humble words. *Ecce ancilla, &c.* once onely, corporallie conceaued the Sonne of God, the Sauiour and Redeemer of all the world. But Priests as his instruments, are daily the cause that the se fe-same Sonne of God, and of the Virgin. is truelie and reallie present in the Blessed Sacrament.

6 The heigh King of Heauen, being incarnate in our blessed Ladie, shee brought foorth to the world, a Sauiour, mortall and passible: the Priestes offer to God, and giue to men the very same Sauiour, now impassible and most glorious. Shee gaue sucke to the new borne babe, with hir virginal breasts, handled him with hir hands, bare him in hir armes, and performed such other seruiceable offices to Chrifts litle members. These Priests receaue him with their mouthes, carrie him, and giue him in meate to others; who is the bread and food of Angels. O venerable sanctitie of holie hands ! O high and happie dignitie! O great and only wonder of the world?

7 Not

6 Nor any of thefe comparifons, either arrogant, or hyperbolicall, but true and iuftifiable, in all proprietie & rigour of fpeech. For as in al rigour of fpeech, it muft of neceffitie be confeffed, that God is far aboue his Creatures, the foule, much more noble then the bodie, & fpirituall things more excellent then temporall: fo in all rigour of fpeech, it muft needes be granted, Prieftlie dignitie to be the higheft dignitie, and degree of this life, for as much as it is immediatly exercifed about the honour of God, and adminiftration of diuine and fpiritual affaires: whereas the dignitie of Princes (though in their ranck, moft to be refpected) yet their functions and affaires, are chieflie touching temporal things.

CHAP. V.

Of the ende, for the which Maffe is faid or heard. And of the great deuotion and attention, wherewith the Prieft is to celebrate the fame.

THE end, for which the Maffe is to be faid or heard, is moft heigh and excellent: yea, fo heigh, that a heigher or greater cannot poffible be inuented or imagined. The chiefe & principal end, is only one the other
are

arediuers. The firſt is, the honour of God. who being the laſt and finall ende of all things, of good right, willeth and ordaineth, that all things, be done and referred, to his honour.

2 The better to vnderſtand this point, it is to be noted, that Sacrifice is, an acte of Worſhip, adoration, or honour, the which is due onely to God, with paine of death to all thoſe who ſhall attribute the ſame to any other. *Sacrificium Diis erudicabitur, niſi Domino ſoli. Exod.* 22. Hee that ſhall ſacrifice to gods, but onely to our Lord, ſhall be rooted out. The Maſſe therefore is, and ought to be both ſaid and heard, chiefly to honour God, by, and with ſo diuine a Sacrifice.

3 The other endes, are diuers, for the which the ſame may either be ſaid, or heard. As for the preſeruation, of the vniuerſall Church : the propagation of the Catholike Reiigion: for the Popes holines : for all Biſhops, Paſtors, and religious Perſons, for peace and concord, amongſt Chriſtian Princes, for our parents, friends, and benefactors, for thankſgiuing to God for all his benefites, for the preſeruation of the fruits of the earth, and for our temporal ſubſtance, and generally for all manner of neceſſities, either of ſoule or bodie.

4 In ſaying of Maſſe, there is required of the Prieſts parte, a ſingular attention and deuotion:

uotion: be it either in regarde of the thinge
that is offered, or in regard of him to whom
the fame is offered, which is almighty God
himfelfe, who is *Rex regum, & Dominus Do-*
minantium, King of Kings, and Lord of Lords.
Before his prefence, euen the heighest powers of Heauen do fhake and tremble.

5 This S.Chrifoftome, ferioufly pondering
and weighing with himfelfe, faith: He who
is a Legate to treate for a whole Cittie, what
fpeake I of a Cittie? yea of the whole world,
and is an intercefor to almightie God, that
he may become propitious vnto all men, not
onely to the liuing, but alfo to the dead, what
manner of man I praye you ought he to be?
Truely I cannot thinke the confidence of
Moyfes or Elyas, to be fufficient to difpatch
fuch an embaflage or fupplication lib. 6.de
Sacerdotio, And againe, in the fame place, he
further faith: what hands ought they to bee,
that doe adminifter it? what the tongue that
pronounceth fuch deuine wordes? How pure
and cleane, ought that foule to be, that doth
receaue fo worthy a Lord? Thus S. Chrifoft.

6 For further proofe and confirmation
hereof, the holy Scripture recounteth a feare-
full example, of the two children of Helie
the Prieft, who were punifhed by death for
that they did not performe the office of
Priefthood, duely as they ought: what then
may we thinke, fhall be the punifhment of
                                        fuch

ſuch Prieſts, as ſhould now approach vnwor-
theiy to the Altar of our Lord?

7 It is written of S. Marke the Euangeliſt, that hee had ſo great reuerence of this
holy Sacrifice, and ſo greatly feared his owne
inſufficiēcy, that he cut off his owne thombe,
to the end he might be vncapable, and vnfit
to be made a Prieſt, which yet was afterwardes reſtored vnto him by miracle, as is
to be read, Canon ſi quis à med. diſt. 55.

8 It is alſo teſtifyed, of the glorious Father S. Francis, that being onely a Deacon, &
purpoſing to be made Prieſt, one appeared
vnto him, houlding in his hand a violl of water, of moſt admirable cleannes, and ſaid vnto
him: Francis, ſeeſt thou this water? And the
bleſſed Father hauing anſwered, that he did.
He further added. He that will be a Prieſt,
muſt be like vnto this in purity: which words
ſtrooke into the Holie man ſuch a deepe im-
preſſion, and ſuch a feare and reſpect, of that
ſacred function, that he neuer afterwardes
would permit himſelfe to be made a Prieſt.

CHAP.

CHAP. V.

Of the attention and deuotion of the afsi-stants. And how the same may be obtained by hearing of Masse.

FOr as much as vpon all festiual dayes, a man must either saie Masse, or at the least, heare Masse, by the expresse commandement of the Church: it is great reason, that this worke, should be well and orderly performed, according as is conuenient, and as the weight and importance of the thing it selfe requireth.

First then, we must procure to haue an ardent and inflamed desire to heare the same with fruite, and with the greatest attention that possible we may: which desire ought to be accompanied, with a liuely faith, of the presence of Iesus Christ our Sauiour, who with such exceeding loue, vouchsafeth to come to visite vs.

2 Secondly, it will helpe verie much, to thinke vpon the wonderful greatnes and dignitie, of this most holy Sacrifice, whereof I haue spoken a little before.

3 Thirdly, to remember our owne vilenes and abiectnes, reputing our selues most vnworthie, to be present at so excellent and diuine a mysterie, in the presence whereof, the verie Angels doe humble and bowe downe

                    them

themselues with moste diuine reuerence:
wherefore, with farre greater reason ought a
wretched sinner to doe the same, and after
the example of the Publican, holding downe
his head for shame, to knocke his breast, say-
ing· *Deus propitius esto mihi peccatori.* God be
merciful to me a sinner.

4 Fourthly, it is also requisite, that a man
goe to Masse, out of mortal sinne, for as much
as this greatly hindereth, both deuotion and
due attentio̅, as also the fruit which he might
otherwise draw from the same. Yet, if a man
be fallen into any great sinne, he ought not
therefore to leaue to heare Masse: for albeit
it serue him not then to merite eternall life,
yet it serueth him neuertheles, to satisfie the
commandement of the Church, which is, to
heare Masse on the festiual dayes: which if he
performe not, he doth adde another mortall
sinne to his former.

5 Fiftly, that our end, or intention be right:
which is, that we purpose to do that which
our holy mother the Church doeth, who in
the Sacrifice of the Masse, maketh an offring
and present, to the eternall Father, of his only
Sonne, of his most holie Passion, and of his
merits, in satisfaction of the sinnes of hir
children. Whereupon we ought to accompa-
ny and ioyne our desires with those of the
Priest, and to beseech the diuine Maiestie,
that it would please him to heare vs, and that
he

he would mercifully pardon both our owne offences, and those of our nieghbours, and that hee would gratiouslie assist vs in all our necessities, and that in the vertue of this most holie Sacrifice.

6 Sixtlie, to endeauour to conceaue within our selues, a holy feare, and a wonderfull reuerence, considering that we are present in a place that is holie, and specially dedicated to the seruice of God: remembring howe God commaunded Moyses to put off his shooes, for reuerence of the place whereon he stood. Deut.

7 Seauenthly, besides the sanctitie and holines of the place, we ought to consider, the presence of our Lord, and Sauiour himselfe, who at that time, causeth his blessings and graces to raine downe in great plentie and aboundance vpon all those, who are there present, with pure, vnfained, and profounde deuotion.

8 Eightly, when we see the Priest comming towardes the Altar, wee ought to lift vp our eyes (especially those of our vnderstanding) to heauen, and to imagine, that wee see descend, as by Iacobs ladder, a multitude of Angels, who come to present themselues at this most holy Sacrifice, & with their presence to honour it, in such wise. that all the Church is filled with Angels, which busie themselues here, and there amongst the people, inciting them

them all to modeſtie, denotion, and reuerent
behauiour in the preſence of this moſt holy
and dreadfull Sacrament.

9 Ninthly, the great and louing deſire, that
our Sauiour himſelfe hath to come vnto vs,
and therefore, to lift vp a new our eyes to
Heauen, and with a liuely faith, to behold the
Sonne of God, ſitting at the right hand of his
Father, being readie and prepared, to be preſent (ſo ſoone as the wordes of conſecration
ſhall be pronounced) in the handes of the
Prieſt, in the ſacred Hoſte, and with a longing
deſire, waiting and attending (in ſome ſorte)
the time and oportunitie to come vnto vs.

10 Tenthly, conſider the cauſe, and ende
of our Sauiours comming, & ſo contemplate
the greatnes of him that commeth, who is
infinite. The ende for which he commeth,
which is, to be offered vp for vs, to his heauenly Father. Whether he commeth, into
earth (the place and habitation of beaſts.) The
maner wherein he commeth, hidden vnder
the formes of bread and wine.

Finallie, to maintaine the honor of this holy Sacrifice againſt all enemies, and to vſe the
ſame aright as wee ought to doe, we muſt e-
uery day aſſiſt thereat, without diſtraction
of ſpirit, in ſilence and decent compoſition,
and be perſwaded this to be the principall &
chiefeſt of all our actions, and which deſer-
ueth, that we dedicate vnto it the beſt and
moſt

moſt conuenient hower of the morning. And
in ſo doing, our merciful Lord wil doubtleſly
ſende downe his bleſſing vpon vs, in great a-
boundance, and the better, proſper all our affaires and buſines, in the day following.

CHAP. VI.

Of the fruite and profite which commeth, and is reaped, by hearing of Maſſe.

THE fruites, which a man may gather
by hearing of Maſſe are great, and many
in number.

1 The firſt is, that a man is admitted vnto
the inwarde familiarity of our Lord Ieſus
Chriſt, and to be neare to his perſon, as his ſe-
cretarie, or chamberlaine, where he both heareth and ſeeth, ſo many diuine ſecrets: which
places and roomes in the courts of earthlie
Princes, are ſo much ſought after, euen by the
greateſt Lords and Nobles of this world, and
are ſo heighly eſteemed, that oftentimes they
are content to ſerue their whole life for them,
without any recompence at all in the ende:
whereas our Lord Ieſus Chriſt, the King of
Heauen and Earth, doeth neuer (vnleſſe he be
forſaken) forſake him who hath done him
ſeruice, nor leaueth him without reward and
recompence.

2 Se-

2 Secondly, he who is present at Masse, do th participate, so much the more of this diuine Sacrifice , for as much as in the same, more particuler prayer is made for him, then for the abset, the Priest saying, *&t pro omnibus circumstantibus*. And for all that are standing about. He profiteth also more by the attentio and deuotion, caused by the real presence of our Lord Iesus Christ : euen as the Sun doth more heate the cuntries neere vnto it , then those that are further from it : and the fire doth more warme those that approach vnto it, then those that stand a far off from it. And hence it was, that the Apostles receaued so manie graces and priuiledges, becaufe they were continually in the presence of our Lord Iesus Christ. S. Chrisostome also saith, that grace is infused into sundrie persons in the presence of the bodie of Iesus Christ.

3 Thirdly, in hearing of Masse deuoutly, wee receaue pardon of our veniall sinnes, & obtaine remission (at the least in part) of the temporall paine, which remaineth after the fault or guilt of our sinnes is forgiuen vs, and for the which a man is to endure, either in this life, or in Purgatorie: which is truely a most wounderful benefite, seeing that the verie leaft paine in Purgatorie , is greater then all the paines, of this world together. Infomuch that S. Anselme; doubteth not to affirme , that one Masse, heard by vs with deuotion

deuotion in this life, is of greater value, then a thoufand faid for vs by others, after our departure.

4 Fourthly, in hearing of Maffe deuoutly, a man difpofeth himfelfe, to receaue, pardon of his mortal finnes: for as much as he hath occafion by the memorie, of the Paffion of Iefus Chrift; and of his great loue and benefites. and of this facrifice, offered vp for our finnes, and with the reall prefence of Iefus Chrift, to haue repentance, and to be mooued to contrition for them.

5 Fiftly, it doth bring vs encreafe of grace, to refift all our euill paffions, and to vanquifh all forts of temptations: wherefore well is he that may heare it daily. S.Hier.lib. .in Ioan. S.Aug. cont. Petli.4.cap.10.

6 Sixtly, it is a ftrong, and affured buckler againft all euill fpirits, and a fingular meanes, to obtaine of God, fafegarde againft all dangers, together with many bleffings, euen corporall, as health, & fuch other like; it maketh vs more capable , of the vifitation and protection, of our good Adgel, yea, and more readie for death , how foone foeuer it fhall affaile vs. Clemens.can Apoft.li 8.Cyril.Cath. 3, Chrifoft.hom. 13.ad Heb.

7 Seuenthly, it is a fingular remedy againft all fuperftition : & a moft peculiar and effectuall meanes, to conferue all faithful Chriftians in perfect loue, charitie, peace, and concord.

cord, as being particularlie inftituted to that intent. S. Aug. Lib. 22. de ciuit. Dei. c. 10. Sozo. hift. Ecclef lib 9. c. 8. 1. cor. 10.

8 Eightly , by hearing of Maffe, commeth an other fpeciall fruire (to wit) the fruit of in-ftruction, which is had and obtained, in the doctrine , which a man heareth and learneth, by being prefent at the fame.·· Wherein he is taught, at the Confiteor , to aske pardon of his offences. At the Mifereatur , to pardon the faultes of his neighbour. At the Introite, to laude God. At the Kyrie eleifon, to aske mercie of God. At the Gloria in excelfis, to magnifie God. At Dominus vobifcum, to be vnited with his neighbour. At the Collectes, to prefent his prayers.   At the Epiftle , to thinke of the contempt of the world. At the Gofpell, to follow Iefus Chrift. At the Credo, to profeffe that , which he ought to be-lecue. At the Preface, attention. At the Canon, deuotion. At the fifth Memento , to pray for the liuing. At the fecond Memento, to pray for the departed. At the Eleuation, to adore Iefus Chrift. And at the Communion, to communicate fpiritually.

C   *CHAP*

CHAP. VI.

Of the faults and abuſes, which may be committed in hearing of Maſſe.

FIrſt, it were an intollerable abuſe, if any (which God forbid) ſhould goe to Maſſe, to content their eyes, with wanton and diſhoneſt ſights, making the church a ſhop of their diſordinate appetites, not hauing anie reſpect, either to the preſence of God, or of his Angels, nor to his deuine ſeruice, nor to the time, in which is repreſented the greateſt benefite that our Lord hath done for man.

2. The ſecond abuſe were, to heare Maſſe onely for faſhion, and much more to ſpende the time in idle talke: without any attention or deuotion, for this were not onelie to depart without fruite, but to looſe much by that, they might gaine exceedingly. For euen as you paye not, but thoſe who labour in your vineyeard (not thoſe who goe thither to ſee and beholde it) euen ſo our Lord doth not giue his hyre, but to thoſe who are attentiue to the worke of his diuine ſeruice, but eſpecially vpon holy & feſtiuall dayes, ſuch perſons ſhould ſinne moſt grieuouſlie

3. The third abuſe, were to be preſent with ſuch diſtraction, and vagation of ſpirite,
that

that insteede of thinking vpon the holie mysteries of the Masse, one should call to minde
his worldlie busines , bethinking him selfe
of the meanes where with hee should haue
profecuted some negotiations, which therefore came not to so good effect and issue, as
he desired : and discoursing of the circumspe-
ction which he must vse for the time to come
in some other busines, which he hath yet to
doe, and so as we may say, build castles in the
ayre. Surely the spindle, of wheele or a mille,
doth not turne so much as doeth the spirite
of such a man, being present at Masse, suffe-
ring himselfe to be carried without bridle,
whether so euer his wandring fancie shall
please to mooue, or to transporte him. And of
these, I say, as of the former, that they should
offende in the same degree, and loose the fruit
and merite, which they might reape by hearing of Masse deuoutlie.

4 The fourth abuse were, to seeke for the
shortest Masses, and to thinke the time long
that we are present at this diuine sacrifice. For
surely this sheweth, that our mindes are more
set vpon earthlie, then heauenly things, since
that we finde no such yrksomnesse in corporal
bankets, playes, or other vayne sightes. But we
should rather confider, how our B. Sauiour
thought not the time of three houres long to
hang vpon the Crosse for our fakes: in which
respect, their deuotion is verie commendable,

who

who vfe to heare more Maffes then one euery
day, according as their other neceffarie buſy-
neffe will permitte them. Yea, if the fire of
the loue of God, were perfectly enkindled in
our hearts, all the while that the Maffe ſhould
laſt, would ſurely feeme vnto vs verie ſhorte
and little: like as the Scripture faith of Iacob,
that he ſerued the ſpace of 14. yeares to haue
Rachael in mariage, and that he eſteemed all
thofe yeares but as a few dayes, in reſpect of
the loue he bare vnto her.

5. The fifth abufe were, to be ouer curious in adorning our felues, when wee goe to
Church, and in this women, eſpecially of
young yeares and good calling, muſt be more
warie, becaufe they may otheiwife, not onely
hinder their owne deuotion, but that of others
alfo. It is ſtrange what caueats S. Paule and
the holie Fathers giue them in this kind : For
furely when they goe to Church, they ſhould
rather feeke to p eafe God, then men. Neither can they eaſilie excufe themfelues, if they
doe otheiwife. To conclude, when we repaire
to the Temple of God to pray, we ought to
laye awaie all toyes and vanities, which any
waie may hinder our deuotions, and carefullie recollect our ſpirits, and driue away all
diſtractions, that wee may without anie perturbation, freelie lift vp our hearts to God, and
deuoutlie employ the time, in holie, pious,
and holefome meditations, according as ſhall
                                        hereaf-

hereafter is declared. And now to ſpeake of the Altar it ſelfe.

C H *A* P.   VII.

Of the Altar, whereon the ſacrifice of the Maſſe is celebrated, and of the furniture and ornaments, belonging to the ſame.

How the Altar (made of ſtone) repre-ſenteth Chriſt.

1 IRST, the Altar, whereon this moſt diuine Sacrifice is celebrated, is made of ſtone : to ſignifie vnto vs , that Ieſus Chriſt, is the head corner-ſtone of the Church, as witneſſeth the Apoſtle S, Peter. 1. Pet. cap. 2 7

How vnitie of faith.

2, The ſame Altar compacted and made of manie ſtones cleauing together: doeth repreſent the Church of God, gathered together of diuers nations, all coupled and linked in one faith, in one profeſſion, and exerciſe of Religion.

C 3   How

How Charitie.

3. Both in the old law, and now also in the new, some Altars were made of beaten gold: to signifie, the inestimable and pure loue wherewith our Lord loued vs, and the inestimable and pure loue, wherewith we ought to loue him againe.

How our Lords table.

4. This Altar also, representeth vnto vs, the table whereon our Lord, instituted and celebrated his last supper, with his Disciples. Mat, 26. 26.

How the mount Caluarie.

5. Also the mount of Caluarie, wheron he suffered his death and Passion, for the saluation and redemption of all the world.

How the Altar-stone, rep. the graue.

To the adorning of this Altar, diuers mysterious ornaments are belonging. First, there is placed thereon an Altar-stone : which representeth the graue or monument, wherein the bodie of our Lord was buried or entombed. *And there was nigh the crosse a new monument* Iohn, 19.

How the linnen clothes, rep. the sindon.

The white linnen cloathes, where-with the Altar and the Altar stone are couered, do betoken, the white sindon, wherein Ioseph of Arimathia, did wrap and enfould the body of
our

our Sauiour. *Et inuoluit ſindone.* And he put it
in a cleane ſindon. Luc.23.

Hovv the Croſſe, repreſenteth the hiſtorie of the Paſsion.

There is a Croſſe ſet vpon the Altar, to
ſignifie, that the hiſtorie of our Sauiours
Paſſion, is there to be handled. Againe to
ſignifie, that the Sacrifice of the Altar, is the
ſame in ſubſtance, which our Lord accompliſhed vpon the Altar of the Croſſe.

Hovv the Chalice, repre. the Cup.

The Chalice repreſenteth the Cup, wherein
he conſecrated his moſt precious Blood. *And
he tooke the Chalice, ſaying: This is my Blood.*
Mat.26.

Hovv mortifycation and martyrdome.

Likewiſe, by the Chalice, is betokened
mortification. and a minde alwaies readie to
ſuſſer martyrdome, for the loue of Ch iſt. *Can
you drinke the chalice, which I am to drinke?*
(to wit, ſuffer death for my ſake:) *and they an-
ſvvered we can* Mat.20.

Hovv the Paten repreſenteth the ſtone.

The Paten layde vpon the Chalice: repreſenteth the ſtone which was rowled againſt
the doore of our Sauiours ſepulcher. *And
they rowled a ſtone to the doore of the ſepulcher.*
Mar.15.46.

Hovv

Hoᵂ the shining of the Corporall, repre. Chriſts reſurrection, and immortalitie.

The Corporall (the which is moſt white and ſhining:) ſignifieth , that Chriſt by manifould paſſions, was brought to the brightnes of his reſurrection : who as the Apoſtle ſaith, *entred not into glorie, before he had ſuſtayned the ignominie of the croſſe.*

Hoᵂ puritie and chaſtitie.

Againe, the brightnes and ſhining of the ſame Corporall, admoniſheth, that to receiue the bodie of Ieſus Chriſt , a man ought to ſhine with all Angelical puritie and chaſtitie, both of bodie and ſoule. And that as it ſhineth with brightnes, ſo the intention of the offerer, ought to ſhine with ſimplicitie, before our Lord.

The ſignification of the Candles.

1. Candles are lighted and ſet vpon the Altar. For by Candles is ſignified, ſomtimes the Law : ſometimes the Church: and ſometimes Chriſtian conuerſation. *Let your light ſo ſhine before men, that they may ſee your good workes, and glorifie your Father which is in heauen.* Matt. 5. 17.

Hoᵂ Candles ſignifie the light of faith.

2 Againe, by the two Candles (for commonly

monly there are so manie) is signified, the
light of faith, reuealed to two seuerall people,
the Iewes, and the Gentiles. Or the two testa-
ments, wherewith mankinde is illuminated,
Or the two wtnesses, of the resurrection:
Moyses, and Elias.

How they are a signe of ioy.

3 Also, Candles are lighted in signe of ioy, as
testifieth Alcuinus: and in respect of our B. Sauiours presence, whose diuinitie is likewise
signified by the same. As also to signifie the
giftes of grace, and the light proceeding from
the holy Ghost, wherewith the Church is illuminated.

How the fyre of Charitie.

4. And not vnaptly, are there fire-lights, placed vpon the Altar to burne : because hee is
there, who came to sende fire into the world,
and desireth nothing more, then that it burne
and be kindled, in the heartes of all his faithfull. Luc. 12.

Of the Curtaines.

Lastly, for the better adorning, both of the
Church, and Altar, there are rich Hangings,
and Curtaines, of diuers and sundrie colours,
answerable to the diuersitie of Feasts through-
out the yeare.

Of the significayation of the red.

Vpon the feastes of the holy Crosse, whereon Christ shed his pretious Blood for vs: and

C 5   vpon

vpon the Apoftles, and Martirs, Red is vfed:
to fignifie the bloodie Martirdome, which
they indured for the loue of Chrift: for they
are thofe which are come out of great tribu-
lations, and haue wafhed their Stoles, in the
blood of the Lambe. Apoc 7.

Of the White.

Vpon the Feaftes of Angelles, Confeffors,
and Virgins, we vfe White, to fignifie their
holines, chaftitie, and puritie. As alfo vpon
the Dedication of the Church, which is called by the name of a Virgin. *For I haue defpou-
ed you to one Man, to prefent you a chafte virgin vnto Chrift.* 2.Cor 11.2.

Againe, by the White, which is of excellent
purenes, and cleanes : may be fignifyed, the
fplendor and integritie, of good name and
fame. efpeciallie requifite in any Ecclefiafti-
call Magiftrate. *That a Bifhop haue a good teftimonie* (according to the Apoftle) *both of thofe
whith are within, and of thofe which are without* 1.Tim.3.

The fignification of the Blacke.

Vpon the dayes of prayer, for the foules
depart, is vfed Blacke : to fignifie the dolo-
rous and mournefull eftate of their foules. Of
whom it is faid, *they fhall be faued, yet fo as
by fyre.* 1.Cor 3.15.

The fignifycation of the greene.

Vpon other common dayes, greene is
vfed:

vſed: for greene is a colour in the midſt, betwixt white & black,& ſignifyeth the Church
militant,ſtill liuing in this worlde, which is,
ſometimes in ioye, and ſometimes in ſorrow:
and as it were, but yet *in herba*, that is greene
growing,and not ripened, for the harueſt of
the Church,is in the world to come.

The ſignification of the purple.

Sometimes is vſed Purple: to ſignifie the
ſpirituall power and dignitie, which reſideth
in the chiefe biſhop,and other Paſtors of the
Catholike church, who ought to behaue and
comport themſelues in their places, like kings,
not to decline to the right hande , nor to the
left: not to binde the worthie , nor to pardon
or vnbinde the guiltie.

The ſignification of the Scarlet.

Sometimes Scarlet is vſed, which is of the
colour of fire: by which is ſignifyed, pontificall, or Prieſtlie doctrine , which like vnto
fire , ought both to ſhine, and to burne To
ſhine, by giuing light to others. To burne,
by reprehenſions, excommunications,and o-
ther cenſures. *Euerie trſe , that yeeldeth not
good fruit,ſhall be cut downe, and ſhall be caſt
into the fyre* Mat.7.19.

The ſignification of the hiacinth.
Sometimes,Hiacinth, or skie colour is vſed:
by

by which may be vnderftood, the ferenitie
of confcience, which a Bifhop or Priefte
ought alwaes to haue, both in things pro-
fperous, and things aduerfe. According to
the fame Apoftle: For our g'orie is this, the teftimonie of our Confcience. 2 Cor. 1£. As alfo
that hi though.s ought not to be on earthlie,
but on heauenly thinges, according to the
fame Apoftle faying: *onuerfatio n ft a in ca-*
li. ft. Our conu rfaion is in heauen.

To conclude, touching the Ornaments
of the Church and Altar, Sozmon. l 6 cap.
16. and Nicephcru l 11. cap. 18. recounte,
howe the Arrian Emperour Valens, a great
perfecutor of Catholikes, once vppon a
Chriftmas day, entred into the Church of
S. Bafill, whi'eft he was at the Altar celebrating Maffe, affifted by all his Cleargie, and
the people ound about, with fuch deuotion
and reuerence, as the qualitie of the Feaft &
place required. And that he comtemplating
the goodly order, which was in euery thing,
was fo aftonifhed with admiration, that hee
wel nigh fell downe in extafie. Loe here the
proper wordes of Nicephorus, as they were
tranflated out of Greeke into Latine. *Quod ibi*
omnia maro ordine gererentur, ad ftuporem de-
lapfus, & totus mutatus in folum concidiffet, nifi
quidam ex primoribus tunica correpta, impera-
torem iam ruentem retinuiffet. Aftonifhed in
admiration, and altogether altered or changed

ged, for that hee fawe all things gouerned
by fo admirable an order, hee had fallen
downe, vnleff. one of the Princes taking him
by the Robe, had helde him vp, being nowe
readie to fall to the ground. Thus he.

But in this poynt, fo bare and naked, are the
churches of Heretickes, & fo vtterlie deftitute
of all hangings, & other coftlie ornamentes,
yea, fo emptie and quite disfurnifhed, that to
enter into them is much like, as to enter nto
fome emp ie grange or barne, after all the
corne, hay e, and ftrawe, is carried out of it,
Which is the caufe, why fome Heretickes,
comming ouer the feas, and contemplating
the ornaments, riches, and beautifull Ceremonies of the Catholike Church, doe fo greatlie
wonder and admire thereat, that when they
do depart, they finde themfelues fo maruei-
louflie delighted and comforted thereby, as
if they had bene for the time, in fome earthly
Paradife. Yea, to fome, this hath bene a chiefe
motiue of their change, and conuerfion to the
Catholike Faith. Much more might be faide,
concerning this matter, but I will leaue it to
the Readers better confideration, and proceed
to that which is to follow.

CHAP.

CHAP. IX.
Of the ornamētsbelōging to the Pꞃieſt

And firſt of the Amice.

INnocentius the third, ſpeaking of the ornaments, belonging to the Pꞃieſt, ſaith, that
the Veſtments of the Euangelicall Prieſt, doe
ſignifie one thing in the head, (to wit, our Sauiour) and another in his members

And for as much, as both head and mēbers,
are vnderſtood, in the perſon of the Prieſt,
therfore, theſe ornamēts haue ſometimes, re-
latiō to the head, & ſomeimes tothe mēbers.
*Hoꝟ by the Amice, is ſignifyed, the cloath
that hid and couered our Sauiours eyes.*

According hereunto, the Prieſte puꞅting
the Amice before his face: repreſenteth vnto vs, the mockeries, which the Sonne of
God ſuſtained, when his ſacred eyes were
blindfoulded, & the perfideous Iewes, buffe-
ted him on the face, ſaying, *Prophecie vnto vs
ô Chriſt,* who is he that ſtroke thee: Mat. 26.68.

Hoꝟ the croꟃne of Thornes.

2. The putting the ſame afterwardes vpon
his head: repreſenteth vnto vs, the crowne of
Thorns, which thoſe moſt wicked miniſters,
planted vpō the head of our Bleſſed Sauiour.

Hoꝟ recollection and attention.

3   Morallie, the Amice admoniſheth, that
as the Prieſt couereth his head and face there-
with

with, so ought we to be very vigilant (during the time of this diuine Misterie:) that neither our eyes, nor vnderstanding, be carried awaye, or busied about any vaine cogitations.

How fortitude of good workes.

4. The spreading of the same abroad, vpon the Priests shoulders: doth signifie, the fortitude of good workes. For as the shoulders are made strong, to performe hard works: so a mã (specially a Priest) ought neither to be idle, nor faint in working, but to insist & labour painefully, in well doing, according to that of the Apostle. Labour thou as a good souldier of Iesus Christ. 2. Tim. 2. 3.

How Faith.

6. Lastly, the Priest putting on this ornament, prayeth, saying: *Impone Domine, &c.* Put, ó Lord, the Helmet of saluation vpon my head, that I may ouercome all diabolicall incursions. So that by the Amice, is also signifyed Faith, which is indeede, the first and chiefest thing, that a christiã ought to bring, cõming to preset himself, at so great a Sacramet.

CHAP. X,
Of the Albe.

And how by the same is signifyed the most pure humanitie, of our B. Sauiour.

THIS garment is called the Albe, of this Latin word *Albedo*, whitenes; wherby

by the pretious Humanitie of our Sauiour
is fignifyed vnto vs , the which was formed
by the holy Ghoft, of the moft pure fubftance
of the Virgin Marie , which was moft pure,
(that is to fay) without all fpot of finne, either
Originall, or Actuall.

How the Incarnation.

2. The putting on of the Albe, ouer the head
of the Prieft (wherewith hee is all couered)
may put vs in minde of the Incarnation of
our Sauiour, in the wombe of the bleffed Virgin, according to the wordes of the Angell,
fpoken vnto her   *The holy Ghoft shall come
vpon thee , and the power of the moft heighest
shall ouershadow thee* Luc. 1. 35.

How the garment of Innocencie.

3. Next, this garment may fignifie vnto vs,
the garment of Innocencie, giuen vnto vs by
Chrift , in the Sacrament of Baptifme.   And
may put vs in minde , of our promife made
therein , to leade continual y, a pure, holie, &
innocent life. *Laye away the olde man, and put
on the new man ; which according to God, is
created in iuftice* Ephef. 4 23. 24.

How the garment of mockerie.

4. It likewife reprefenteth, the white garment , which Herod put vpon our B. Sauiour, reputing him for a foole and fo mock-
ing, and deriding him, fent him backe to
Pilate. Luc. 33. 12,

It

5. It also signifieth, the White garment of glorie, wherewith we shal be gloriouslie cloathed in the Kingdome of heauen, where wee shall shine more bright, then the beames of the sonne, as saith S. Iohn. *I sawe a great multitude, cloathed in white robes* Apoc. 7.9.

How Penance and Mortification.

6. Againe, this garment admonisheth vs, that euen as silke, or fine cloath, getteth that whitenesse, by often beating, or knocking, which it hath not by nature : euen so a man (especially a Priest) should by workes of Penance, and corporall castigations, attaine to that sanctitie by grace, which he hath not by a.u re.

How spirituall puritie.

7- The Priest, in putting on this garment, prayeth saying, *Dealba me Domine, &c.* Make mee white, O Lord, and cleanse my hearte, that I being whitened in the Blood of the Lambe, may enioye eternall gladnesse. So that the Albe also, by its whitenesse, representeth spirituall puritie, and cleannesse of soule, which is most requisite in him, that is, to administer before our Lord.

CHAP.

CHAP. II.

Of the Girdle.

*And how by the ſame is ſignifyed, the in-
diſſoluble bond, betwixt Chriſts diuinitie, and his humanitie.*

BY the Girdle, wherewith the Albe is
ſtreightly bounde, and girded together,
is ſignifyed the indiſſoluble bond, betwixt the
diuinitie of Chriſt, and his humanitie, which
(after the Incarnation) were neuer ſeperated,
neither according to his bodie, nor according to his ſoule ; notwithſtanding, that his
ſoule deſcended into hell, and his bodie remained in the ſepulchre.

How his vndertaking our humaine frailty.

2 The Girdle bringing together, the am-
pleneſſe of the Albe, doth ſignifie, that Chriſt
as it were, ſtraightned his heigh and diuine
conuerſation (after our manner of vnderſtanding) by taking vppon him our humaine
fralitie. And euen as the Albe, is not made
leſſe, by the ſtraigh-neſſe of the Girdle, but only infoulded within the ſame: euen ſo the
immenſitie of Chriſt, remained moſt entire,
and perfect in him, although for our example,

ple, hee ſeemed to ſtreighten and narrow the
ſame.

How the virtue of Chaſtitie.

3. This Girdle hath three properties : to
girde, to binde, and to mortifie : betokening
the care and circumſpection belonging to a
Prieſt, leaſt the virtue of chaſtitie, which the
white garment repreſenteth in him, be remiſsly
and negligently garded. And that therefore
as hee girteth the raines of his bodie , ſo
ſhould he girt and reſtraine, the raines of his
minde , which are his thoughts and deſires: to
which virtue, our Sauiour himſelfe exhorteth
ſaying: *Sint lumbi veſtri præcincti, &c.* Let
your loynes be girted, &c. Luc. 12. 35.

How faſting and prayer.

4. The two endes of the girdle, that are
turned in, the one vnder the right ſide, the
other vnder the left: doe ſignifie, the two
meanes , requiſite to conſerue the virtue of
chaſtitie, to wit, faſting, and prayer: the one
to debilitate and ſubdue the fleſh : the other
to ſtrengthen and eleuate the ſpirit: Pray, leaſt
ye enter into temptation Luc. 22 40.

How the cordes wherewith our Lord was bound to the Pillar.

5 The Prieſte in taking the Girdle , putteth both his handes behinde him at his back,
whilſt he that ſerueth , giueth the ſame into
them : repreſenting thereby , howe the moſt
inno-

innocent Sonne of God for our offences, had
his bleffed handes faft bounde behinde him,
whileft he was moft lamentablie whiped and
fcourged at the Piller.

The Prayer.

6. In putting on the Girdle, he prayeth faying, *Præcinge me Domine, &c.* Girte me, ô Lord
with the girdle of puritie, and quench in my
loynes, the humour of luft, that there may remaine in me, the vertue of continencie and
chaftitie.

CHAP. XII.

Of the Maniple.

And by how the fame is fig. perfecution for the faith of Chrift.

1. THE Prieft putting the Maniple vpon his left arme, doeth kiffe the fame:
to put vs in minde, of the reddines of heart,
wherewith we ought willingly and gladly to
fuffer perfecution, for the faith of Chrift: becaufe, *Bleffed are they that fuffer perfecution
for iuftice, for theirs is the Kingdome of Heauen* Mat. 5. 10.

How

How the contempt of earthly things.

2, By the putting thereof, vpon the left arme, we are admoniſhed, that wee ought to be ſtrickt and ſparing, in ſeeking after earthlie thinges, but free and diſcharged in ſeeking after Heauenly. According to the councell of our Sauiour, ſaying, *Seeke firſt the kingdome of God, and the iuſtice of him , and all theſe things ſhall be giuen you beſides.* Mat.6.23.

How Chriſtes Humilitie , combate for iuſtice, and tender affection towards vs.

4. According to ſome others, the Manuple put vpon the left arme, ſignifieth the humilitie of Chriſt in this life. As alſo his continual combate for iuſtice, according to S. Bonauenture. And becauſe the left arme is the neareſt to the heart, it may likewiſe ſignifie the great loue and tender affection, which our bleſſed Lord and Sauiour, carried towards vs.

How ſorrow and contrition for ſinne.

5. The putting of the Manuple vpon the left arme, may likewiſe put vs in minde of ſorrow and contrition for our defectes. For as ſinnes are committed by ſiniſter actions, ſo may they be ſignifyed, by the left arme. And euen as in the ſoule of a ſinner, there ought to be continuall ſorow and griefe for his offences, committed againſt the maieſtie of Almightie God: ſo is it alſo good reaſon, that

that on his left arme, the Prieſt (who needeth dailie to offer Sacrifice, not onely for his owne, but alſo, for the ſinnes of the people) ſhould carrie ſome externall ſigne, of the internall ſorrow, which both he and they, ought to haue, for this occaſion, imitating herein S. Peter, whoſe aboundance of teares, which iſſued from his eyes, in the bewailing of his offences, was ſo great, that he had markes of them, like little gutters in his cheekes and for this cauſe, continuallie carried in his hand or boſome, ſome napkin wherewith to wipe them away.

How the cordes wherewith our Lord was violently bound.

6.   The ſame being applied to the inſtruments of our Lords moſt holy Paſſion, moſt properly repreſenteth, the hard, rough, and boyſterous cordes, wherewith he was rudely and cruellie bound, when he was ledde from place to place, and from one Iudge to another. Luc. 21. 3.

The Prayer.

7. The Prieſt, in putting on this Manuple, prayeth, ſaying: *Mereor Domine portare, &c*. Let me merit, ô Lord, to beare the Maniple of weeping and ſorrow, that I may receaue the recompence of my labour with exultation.

CHAP

CHAP. XIII.
Of the Stole.

And how , by the same is ſignifyed, the yoke of Obedience.

1 BY the Stole, is ſignifyed the yoke of o bedience, whereunto our meeke Lorde ſubmitted himſelfe for our ſaluation. Take vp my yoke vpon you Mat. 1 29. Which thinge the Prieſt , ſheweth himſelfe readie to performe by kiſſing the ſame, both when he putteth it on, and when he putteth it off: expreſſing by this ceremonie, the deſire and reſignation, wherewith he willingly ſubmitteth himſelfe, vnder the yoke of our Sauiour Chriſt.

How meekenes and humilitie.

2. In that it extendeth or reacheth to the knees (whoſe office is to bende and bowe) it admoniſheth vs, of meekenes and humilitie. *Diſcite à me quia mitis ſum & humili corde.* Learne of me, becauſe I am meeke and humble of heart. Mat. 11.29.

How Perſeuerance.

3. The ſtole, by the length thereof, doth put vs in minde of the vertue of perſeuerance: For hee that perſeuereth vnto the ende, ſhall be ſaued Mat. 10.

How

How prudence in profperitie, and patience
in aduerfitie.

4. It is foulded before the breaft, in forme of
a Croffe, from the right fide to the left: to
admonifh vs, that wee muft vfe prudence in
profperitie, and patience in aduerfitie, and that
we be neither puffed vp by the one, nor deie-
cted by the other.

How the carrying of the Croffe.

5. The refting thereof vpon the fhoulders:
may put vs in minde of the Croffe, which,
with other inftruments of the Paffion, our
Lord was forced to carrie to the place of execution, vpon his foare, and weatie fhoulde.s.
Or the rope or corde, wherewith they hafte-
lie drew and haled him forwardes, to the
mount of Caluarie.

The Prayer.

The Prieft, in putting on the fame prayeth,
faying, *Redde mihi Domine ftolam immortalita-*
tis, &c. Render vnto me, ô Lord, the Stole of
immortalitie, which I haue loft in the preuarication of our firft parent: and although I approach vnworthelie to thy holie myfterie, I
may neuerthelefle, deferue to attaine euerlafting ioy and felicitie.

CHAP

C H A P. XIIII.

Of the veſtment, or Caſula.

And how by the ſame is ſignifyed , and re-
preſented the vertue of Charitie.

1   His veſtment, couereth both the bodie,
     & al the other habits, & in Latine is cal-
led *Caſula*, of this word *caja*, a houſe becauſe
it couereth the whole man, like vnto another
little houſe: by which is vnderſtood the vertue
of Charitie, which, as the Apoſtle ſayeth, couereth the multitude of ſinnes.

How *charitie towards God, and*
our neighbours.

2. This garment, being diuided into two
partes: doth put vs in minde of a double , or
two-foulde charitie. The one towardes God,
to loue him aboue all things. The other, to our
neighbour, to loue him as our ſelues. Thou
ſhalt loue the Lord thy God, from thy whole
hart, and with thy whole ſoule, and thy neighbour, as thy ſelfe. Deut. 6.5 & Leuit. 19.18.

How *charitie to our friends, and*
to our enemies.

3. This garment is large, ample, and o-
pen, neither tyed nor girded, as the other ornaments are: to giue vs to vnderſtande, tha

        D   cha

charitie extendeth it felfe farre off, not only in doing good to our friends, but alfo to our verie enemies, neuer ceafing to doe well to all perfons, whenfoeuer time and occafion is offeted. If you loue them, who loue you, what rewaid fhall you haue, doe not alfo the Publicans this? Mat. 5.46.

Hovv the Church, before and after Chrift.

4. Likewife, the forepart (which is the leffer) reprefenteth the Church, before Chriftes Paffion, and the hinder part (which is the larger and bigger, and hath the Croffe on it:) fignifyeth, the increafe of Chrifts Church, fince his Paffion.

Hovv the vniting, of the Iewes & Gentils.

5. The vniting thereof aboue, fignifieth the vniting of the two people (the Iewes and the Gentiles) in the confeffion of one faith, as it was foretolde, faying: And there fhall be one Paftor, and one fiocke.

Hovv the Veftment of fundrie vertues exercifed in the Catholike Church.

6. This garment, is commonly rich, and curioufly wrought with golde: infinuating that which the royall Prophet fayth, in the Pfalme: *Aftitit Regina à dextris suis.* The Queene (to witte, the Church) ftood vpon thy right hand, in a golden Veftment, compaffed about with varietie. Pfal. 44.

Hovv

How the purple Veſtment.

7. It likewiſe repreſenteth the Purple Veſtment, where with, the Iewes cloathed our Lord in ſcorne, and diuers and ſundrie waies, abuſed his holy perſon. Mat. 27. 10.

How vnitie, againſt ſchiſme and hereſie.

8. This garment of our Lord, the Souldiars would not deuide, becauſe it was without ſeame: to fore-ſhew, how great an offence it ſhould be in thoſe, who ſhould preſume to rent, or deuide, the vnitie of Chriſts Church, by ſchiſme, or hereſie. Iohn. 19, 23.

The Prayer.

The Prieſt, in putting on the ſame, prayeth, ſaying: *Domine qui dixiſti,* &c. Lord who haſt ſaid, my yoake is ſweete, and my burthen is light: graunt that I may ſo beare the ſame, that I may obtaine thy grace.

How, by the two Croſſes vpon the Stole, and Maniple: is ſignifyed, the Croſſes of the two Theeues. And by that vpon the Veſtment, the Croſſe of Chriſt.

And note, that vpon three of theſe ornaments, belonging to the Prieſt, there is commonlie made the ſigne of the Croſſe. Vpon the Stole, and the Maniple, there is made

D 2 two

two little Croſſes ; and the third vpon the Veſtment, more larger then the reſt: whereby is ſignifyed vnto vs, a double myſterie.

Firſt, by the two leſſer Croſſes, vpon the Stole and Maniple , is vnderſtood the croſſes of the two theeues, who were crucifyed, one on the left-ſide, and the other on the right ſide of our bleſſed Sauiour, and he himſelfe in the middeſt , ſignifyed by the Croſſe made vpon the Veſtment, which is greater then the other , as his Croſſe was greater then theirs.

How more perfection in the Prieſt, then other men.

Secondly, by theſe three Croſſes, is giuen to vnderſtande, that the Prieſt ought to be of much more perfection, then other men; and that he ſhould not onely beare the Croſſe of Chriſt , ſignifyed by the Croſſe on the veſtment: nor his owne Croſſe, ſignifyed by the Croſſe vpon the Stole : but alſo his neighbours Croſſe, ſignifyed by the Croſſe on the Maniple, which he beareth on his left arme.

CHAP.

CHAP. XV.

Of the comming of the Prieſt out
of the Veſtrie, attyred and reueſted, with his holy Ornaments.

*How the Prieſt repreſenteth our
bleſſed Sauiour.*

BY the Prieſt (as the Doctors ſay) is vnderſtood, our bleſſed Sauiour. By the people:
the world. And by the Altar: the mount of
Caluarie, whereon he was Crucifyed, for our
redemption.

*How his comming out of the Veſtrie, repre-
ſenteth, our Sauiours comming from
heauen*

The Prieſt comming foorth of the Sacriſtie,
thus reueſted with his holie habits: ſignifieth
our Sauiour comming forth of the boſome of
his heauenly Father, and entring into the
world, to take our nature vpon him.

*How his hands, ioyned vpon his breaſt, re-
preſent the affection where-with our
Sauiour prayed for vs.*

He proceedeth with his handes reuerently,
ioyned before his breaſt: to repreſent vnto vs
the great deuotion, & feruent affectiõ, wherewith

with our Sauiour alwaies prayed vnto his heauenly Father for vs. *Exauditus eſt enim pro re-
uerentia ſua.* For he was heard for his reuerence. Heb 5.8.

How his holy veſtments, repreſent our Sauiours holy vertues.

His holie veſtments and ornaments: do fignifie, the holie vertues, gracés and other perfections, which moſt glorioufie fhined in our
Sauiour. Of whom it is written, ſaying, And
the word was made fleſh and dwelt in vs (and
we faw the glorie of him, the glorie as it were
of the onely begotten Sonne of the Father)
full of grace and veritie. Ioh. 1.14.

The diuerfitie of ornaments, doe not onely
fignifie, the diuerfitie of vertues and perfections, which were contained, in our Sauiour
Chriſt, but alſo, the diuerfitie of paines and
torments, which he fuſtained for vs: as hath alreadie bene declared.

How honour and reuerence, in thoſe that receaue and handle the bodie of Chriſt.

And for as much as Almightie God gaue
expreſſe commandement, to the Prieſtes of
the ancient law, that they ſhould not approach
to his Altar, to offer vnto him, but firſt to be
waſhed & inueſted, not with their prophane,
but with their holy ornaments, is it not then
moſt conuenient, that the Prieſts of the new
Law

Lawe, ſhould be peculiarlie adorned, and
thereby diſpoſe themſelues with much more
reuerence, to handle and touch, the moſt pretious bodie, of our redeemer and Sauiour Ieſus, then the olde Prieſts and Prophets did, the
fleſh of ſheepe and oxen, or the bodie of a
bruit beaſt?

Our Prieſts therefore, going to the Altar,
thus apparrelled, doe ſet before our eyes, our
Sauiour Ieſus, as he was at his Paſſion, and
conſequentlie, thoſe that ſcoffe at the Prieſt,
thus repreſenting Chriſt vnto vs, doe nothing
elſe, then with the wicked Iewes, ſcoffe and
deride at Chriſt himſelfe. And euen as thoſe
Iewes, put all theſe ornaments vpon our Sauiour, for deſpite, and the more to diſhonor
him, yet Chriſts holie mother, and his bleſſed
Apoſtles, did both loue him, and reuerence
him ſo much the more entyrelie, for endu-
ring ſuch reproaches and ſhames, for our
ſakes: ſo theſe men, now a dayes, whoſe
mindes are wholie ſet againſte the Catholike
Church, will mocke perhaps at the Prieſt, ſtan-
ding at the Altar in ſuch apparrell; but contrarie wiſe, the true Chriſtian and Catholike
people, doe eſteeme and honour him ſo much
the more, who is, by the ordinance of God,
exalted to ſo high a dignitie, as to preſent vnto
vs, ſo great myſterie.

To conclude, Prieſtlie habits (ſo much
offenciue to the heretikes of our age) were

ſo

fo heighly refpected by Alexander the great,
(although a Panim & Idolater) going to Hierufalem, with deliberatiō to ruine it, that with-
houlden , by the onely fight of the Pontificall
veftments of the heigh Prieft, and touched in-
ftantly with the feare of God, did caft himfelfe
from his horfe, vpon the ground, as it were to
craue pardon for his finifter defignes, & granted to the citie and countrie of Iewrie, all the
priuiledges, franchifes, and immunities, that
poffible they could defire: as witneffeth Iofe-
phus. lib. 11. cap. 8.

CHAP. XVI.
Of carrying the booke before
the Prieft.

And how therby is reprefented the Annun-
tiatiō of the Angel, before the Incarnation.

THE Prieft proceeding in reuerent wife
towardes the Altar, hath one to goe before him to beare the booke, which contayneth, the glad tydings of our faluation: fignifying, by this Ceremonie , that Chrift entring
into this worlde, fent firft an Angel before
him, to announce the ioyfull newes of his incarnation. Let him therefore, who fupplyeth
this place, confider well. whofe perfon he reprefenteth, and let him fee, that his carriage
be

be conformne to ſo heigh a calling.

Hoᴡ the ſame repreſenteth, the dignitie & and veritie of the Goſpel of Chriſt.

Alſo, the bocke of the Goſpell is therefore carryed before: to ſignifye, the dignitie and infallible veritie of the goſpel of Chriſt, which is ſuch, that if an Angel ſhould come from heauen, and teach vnto vs other then this, wee ought in no wiſe to beleeue him.

Hoᴡ a life conforme to the Goſpell of Chriſt.

Againe, the goſpell carried before, and the Prieſt following after, is to admhniſh: that euerie Chriſtian (eſpecia'lie a Prieſt) ought to conforme his life and conuerſation, to the Goſpel of Chriſt.

Hoᴡ the Church built vpon a rocke.

The booke brought & layd vpon the Altar, which is of ſtone: ſignifyeth, that the foundation, of the Church of Chriſt, is built vpon a rocke, againſt which, the gates of hell ſhal neuer preuayle. Luc. 16.

Hoᴡ the faith, firſt preached to the people of the Iewes.

And it is therefore firſt carried to the right end of the Altar, to ſignifie, that our Sauiour came firſt to the people of the Iewes: according to that of the Apoſtle. To you it behooued vs, firſt to ſpeake the worde of God: but

D 5   becauſe

becauſe you repell it , and iudge your ſelues
vnworthie of eternal life,beholde,we turne to
the Gentils. Acts. 13 46.

Why the booke is layde vpō the Altar ſhut.

1. Reaſon.

And it is layde vpon the Altar ſhut,vntil the
Prieſt come to open the ſame : to ſignifie, that
all thinges were cloſed vnder ſhadowes and
figures,vntil the cōming of Chriſt our Sauiour.

The 2. Reaſon.

Alſo to ſignifie , that Chriſt was he , who
firſt reuealed the myſteries of holi Scripture,
to his Apoſtles, ſaying : To you it is giuen,to
know the myſterie of the kingdome of God.
Mat. 8 9. And after his reſurrection,he opened
their vnderſtanding , that they might vnderſtand the Scriptures Luc. 24 45.

The reaſon , Why the Prieſt hath one to helpe him at Maſſe.

Laſtlie, the Prieſt hath euer, one , or more,
to aſſiſt him at Maſſe : & this for two reaſons.
The firſt is, for that he may haue great neede
of helpe and ayde: He may fall into ſome in-
conuenience or ſickneſſe , or ſome hereticke
or ſome enemie may take the hoaſt ou· of his
hande, as it happened to S. Matthew, who was
killed at the Altar: In which caſe all good Catholikes , ought to ſuccour and defend him ,e-
uen to the ſhedding of their blood;which danger was ordinary in the Primatiue Church, vnder

der the Heathen persequtors : and therefore
t e Bishops saying Masse were alwaies garded
With Deacons.

The 2. Reason.

The second is, in respect of the great Maiestie and reuerence , due to this holie sacrifice, which is such, that the greatest personage
in the worde, neede thinke it no disgrace, to
waite and attende vpon a Priest at Masse; and
further, to adde thereunto, all the humble and
respectiue seruice he is able.

An example to be noted by such as assist at Masse.

And to the ende, that each one may assist
with the greater reuerence , I will brieflie recite a Historie recounted by S. Ambrose how
a childe, which attended vpon Alexander the
great , when he was about to sacrifice to his
Idols, holding fire vnto him, by chance let fall
a coale vpon his owne arme , which he suffered to pierce through his garments, euen to
his verie flesh, rather then he would make any
noyse , or giue occasion by his crye, either to
distract the Emperour in his sacrifice, or di-
sturbe the people in their deuotions. With
what attention and reuerence then , ought a
Christian , to assist at this dreadfull and most
holy sacrifice? & that offered to no false idole,
but to the onely, true, and euer-liuing God
himselfe, S. Ambros. lib. 3. de Virg.

CHAP. XVII.

Of the Priests descending from the Altar.

And how thereby, is represented the expulsion of Adam, out of Paradise.

.1 THE Priest hauing placed the Chalice vpon the Altar, presentlie descendeth & standeth belowe at the foote of the same: representing thereby, the little space of time, wherein Adam remained, in the state of innocencie, and originall iustice. and how, for his transgression, he was presently thrust, and expelled out of Paradise.

How his wretched estate after his fall.

2. Againe, by his standing belowe at the foote of the Altar (humblie bowing his bodie towardes the earth, or falling on his knee) it signifyed, the wretched estate of man, after his fall, and the heauy displeasure of God conceiued against him for his grieuous sinne.

How the time before the Incarnation.

3- Mystically also it signifyeth, the time before the Incarnatiõ of the Sonne of God: who for a long season, and for the selfe-same occasion of sinne, stood a farre off, as it were, from
                                                                  all

all mankinde, and would not for ſome thou-
ſands of yeares appoach vnto him, to take his
nature an i ſubſtance vpon him, or to open the
gates of heauen vnto him.

How a ſoule in mortall ſinne.

4. Alſo, that God ſtandeth a farre off, and is
greatly alienated and eſtranged from euerie
ſoule in mortall ſinne.

How the deuout Publican and
S. Peter.

5. It alſo repreſenteth, the deuout Publican: who entring into the temple to praye,
ſtood a farre off, ſaying: God be merciful to me
a ſinner. And that of S. Peter. Goe from mee,
ô Lord, for I am a ſinnefull man. Luc. 18. 13.
ibid 5. 8.

Why the aſiſtants kneele below.

6. Laſtly, the people likewiſe kneele be.
lowe : to declare the great honour and reuerence which they beare to this Holie Sacrifice.
For God himſelfe is preſent, to heare the ſupplications of his Church. And alſo many Angelicall ſpirits are preſent, moſt earneſtly deſiring, that our petitions may be heard, and with
all, the full and entyre remiſſion of our ſinnes
obtayned.

Of

Of the ſigne of the holie Croſſe, made at,
In nomine Patris. *And of the moſt
excellent vertues, and moſt
diuine myſteries, con-
tayned in the
ſame.*

 S the glorie of a faire and ſumptuous building is viewed & perceiued, by the fore-front thereof:
And as the honor of a well ordered armie, is diſcouered in the
comely diſpoſitiō of the foreward of the battaile: euen ſo, gentle Reader, maieſt thou eaſilie coniecture, the excellencie of this ſpirituall
building, by the onely beautie which thou be-
houldeſt, in the fore-front of the ſame.

  2. And what elſe may be expected in this
venerable repreſentation, of the death and paſſion, of our Sauiour Ieſus, but that our holie
Mother, the Catholike Church, ſhould firſt
plant in the fore-front of this excellent Sacrifice, the tryumphant banner, and moſt victorious Standard of the Croſſe, the badge and li-
uerie of her Celeſtiall ſpouſe, the enſigne of
heauen, the conſolation of earth, the confuſion of hell, and the royall armes and cogni-
zance, of our Redemption?

3. For this holie figne, is the tree of life, planted in the middeſt of Paradiſe. It is the wood of the Arke, which ſaued Noe and his family,from drowning. It is the banner, which Abraham bore, when he went to deliuer his brother Lot, from the captiuitie of his enimies. It is the wood which Iſaac his ſonne. carried vpon his ſhoulders, to the place of Sacrifice. It is the ladder, whereon Iacob ſaw the Angels deſcend, and aſcend, vp to heauen. It is the key of Paradice, which openeth, and no man ſhutteth, and ſhutteth, and no man openeth. It is the Braſen ſerpent, which healeth thoſe that are ſtrooken, with the venemous ſting of the diuel. It is the rodde of Moyſes, wherewith he cauſed the ſtony rocke, to yeeld foorth ſtreames of refreſhing waters. It is the wood, which being caſt by our true Elizeus, into the waters that were bitter, made them moſt ſweete and pleaſaunt of taſte. It is the ſtone, where-with Dauid ſtrooke Golias on the fore head and preſentlie flew him. And it is the letter *Thau*, marked on the fore-heades of all the faithfull, which keeperh and preſerueth them from all kinde of danger.

4. In a word, no mortal tongue, is able ſufficientlie to expreſſe the wonderful vertues of this figne For it is the ſtaffe of the lame, the guide of the blinde, the way of them that erre, the Philoſophie of the vnlearned, the Phiſitiõa of the ſicke, and the reſurrection of the dead.

dead. It is the comfort of the poore, hope in
defpaire, harbour in danger, the bleſſing of
families, the father of orphanes, the defence
of widdowes , the iudge of innocents, the
keeper of little ones , the garde of virginitie,
the councellor of the iuſte, the libertie of feruants, the bread of the hungrie, and the drinke
of the thirſtie. It is the fong of the Prophets,
the Preaching of the Apoſtles, the glorie of
Martyrs , the confolation of Confeſſors, the
ioy of Prieſts, and the ſhielde of Princes. It is
the foundation of the Church, the benediction
of Sacraments, the fubuerfion of Idolatrie, the
death of herefie, the deſtruction of the proud,
the bridge of the rich, the puniſhment of the
wicked, the torment of the damned , and the
glorie of the faued.

No maruell then, that the Catholike church,
hath fo heighly honoured this heauenly figne,
as to plant it, and feate it , in the fore front of
this holy facrifice, and to adorne and beautifie
there with, this heauenly building: vfing (as I
may call it) no other keye , but that which
once opened vnto vs , fo heigh a myſterie, to
open vnto vs now againe, the heigheſt myſterie, both of heauen and earth .

Of

Of In nomine Patris, &c.

How In nomine Patris, *is a briefe Theo-gical proteſtation againſt Idolatrie.*

Irſt, it is to be noted, that the heigheſt, & moſt ſuperement honour, which any man can poſſible yeeld vnto Almightie God in this life, is principallie included in this holy ſacrifice. And as in the commandements which were giuen by God himſelfe, he firſt before all things, put a difference and exception, betwixt hie owne honour, and the honor of idols, and of all other falſe gods whatſoeuer: euen ſo the Chuch in this place, beginning in the name of her ſole and onely God, doth euidently giue to vnderſtand, that ſhe vtterlie renounceth all Idolatrie : and that neither Idol, nor any falſe god whatſoeuer, neither Man nor Angel, nor any other Creature, either in heauen , or earth, ought to be ſerued with this honour of ſacrifice, ſaue onely God himſelfe.

In nomine.

In the name In pronouncing theſe words, we ſay. In the name, not in the names: to ſignifie, and to giue to vnderſtand thereby, that we beleeue, one to be the name, and nature, one to be the vertue and power, one to be the diuinitie

diuinitie, and Maieftie, of all the three perfons
of the bleffed Trinitie.

Patris.

Of the Father. For euen as little children in
the time either of neede or danger, doe prefentlie breake foorth into no other crie, but
to call for the helpe of father or mother,
which crie of theirs, is no fooner heard, but
it foorth with, bringeth them fuccour and affiftance: euen fo, is it to be vnderftood of this
voice and inuocation, which is fo wel knowe,
and fo willingly heard of our heauenly Father,
that no fooner is it vttered by vs his children,
but he doth prefently acknowledge it, and
fpeedelie haftneth, to our helpe and fuccour.

Et Filij.

And of the Sonne After the name of the Father, wee fav, and of the Sonne. Firft, becaufe
he as willinglie, both heareth vs, and helpeth
vs, as the Father doth. Secondly, to declare, that
albeit, this bee properlie the facrifice of the
Sonne, yet that he is equal in glorie. coeternall in Maieft.e, and confubftantial in effence,
both to the Father, and the holie Ghoft.

Et ſpiritus Sancti.

And of the holie Ghoft Heere likewie, doe
we inuoke and call for the helpe, ayde, and affiftance of the Holie Ghoft: to fignifie, that
hee alfo procecdinge from both, and being equal vnto them, both in power, effence,
and

and glorie, doth concur with them to the effecting of this holy and heauenly ſacrifice.

Amen.

And this Amen, is as it were, a confident & firme aſſent of our ſoule, by which wee acknowledge the perſons named, to be our one, and onely God, and that in truſt of his ayde, wee meane to proceede, in offering vp of this ſacrifice, to his eternall glorie.

Where you ſee, that this petition, being taken, according to his moſt common and vſuall ſence, doth ſignifie, the inuocation of the ayde, grace, and ſanctifvcation, of God the Father. God the Sonne and God the Holie Ghoſt, to be infuſed from heauen, into the hearts and mindes of all the aſſiſtants.

Of the Pſalme; *Introibo.*

And how by the ſame is ſignifyed, the deſirs of the Fathers, for the comming of Chriſt.

1. IN the wordes and myſteries, of the holie Maſſe, two manner of ſenſes are vſuallie vnderſtood : the one litterall, the other myſticall. According here vnto, the Prieſt alwaies beginneth with certaine verſes taken out of the Prophets: to ſignifye vnto vs myſticallie, the vnſpeakable ſighs, & feruent deſires of

of Christ, long time promised vnto them, and long expected of them.

How the desires of all the world.

2. These verses are not rehearced of one alone, but of all the quyre together: to signifie, the desire of the Church vniuersall; and that not onely the holy Fathers, then detained in Limbo, but that all the worlde was exiled for sinne, and stood in neede, of the grace and mercie of our Sauiour Iesus.

How the excitation of their mindes, who are present at Masse.

3. According to some of our Doctors, this Psalme is saide, of all the quyre together, that the spirits and mindes, of all that are present, may be awakened thereby, and that hearing the noyse, and sound of the voices, they may vnderstand when the Priest first entereth into the Altar of God: like as in the olde testament, the royse and sounde of the Belles, made knowne, the entrie of the heigh Priest, into the sanctuarie of our Lord.

Of the Confiteor.

And how the same is a protestation, that we are sinners.

THis Confiteor, is a protestation which we make before God, that wee are all sin-
ners

ners, & that before the Priest, either say Masse,
or the people heare Masse (to receaue true
fruite to our selues thereby) wee ought first,
humblie to demaund, pardon and forgiuenes
of all our offences,which we haue committed
against his diuine Maiestie.

Why this Confiteor is called Generall.
The 1. Reason.

1.   This Confiteor is called generall, and
that for diuers reasons. First', for that it was
brieflie instituted for veniall sinnes,which are
generall and common to all, for as much as
no man liuing is so holie and iust, who offen-
deth not God,at the least veniallie For as the
scripture saith, The iuste man falleth seauen
times a daye.Pro.24.

The 2. Reason.

2,   Againe, it is called generall, for that it
is a declaration , which wee make in generall,
without specifying any thing in particular: it
being impossible for any man, to declare in
particular,all his veniall sinnes,which mooued
the holieProphet to say, *Delicta quis intelligis?*
&c. What man knoweth his offences?Frō my
secret sinnes, O Lord,make me cleane.Psa 18.

The 3. Reason.

3   Also, it is called generall, for that it may
be made generallie before all persons, and
generallie in all places : in the fieldes, in the
house.

houſe, within, & without the Church where-
ſoeuer.

How the Prieſt, in this Confeſsion repreſenteth the perſon of Ieſus Chriſt.

4. The Prieſt in this place, in the perſon of Ieſus Chriſt (the Lambe without ſpot) confeſſeth vnto his Father, the ſinnes of all the people, for the which he asketh forgiueneſſe of him: taking them all vpon him ſelfe, with deſire to ſatisfie the iuſtice of his Father for them, by his death.

How his bowing or inclination, repreſenteth our Sauiours humiliation.

5. His bowing or inclination of himſelfe in ſaying the Confiteor : ſignifyeth,how Ieſus Chriſt, humbled him ſelfe, taking vpon him the forme of a ſeruant, that we who were made the ſeruants and bondſlaues of the Diuel, by reaſon of our ſinnes, might be made the free men, of God our heauenly Father, through the merits of Chriſt,his onely Sonne.

How both shame and humilitie.

6. His enclining,or bowing his face, in ſaying the ſame;is alſo to inſinuat vnto vs,ſhame,
and

and humilitie: and that we ought to blush, and be apaled, to doe that in the presence of God, which we would be loth to doe or commit, in the sight of men.

How a conscience cleane, euen from ve-niall sinne.

7. And lastlie, this Confession, teacheth, with how great sanctitie and puritie, this most pure and most holie Sacrifice, ought to be handled, and receiued of vs : in so much, that if it were possible, we should keepe our selues cleane, euen from venial sinnes. And now to explicate the wordes themselues.

Confiteor Deo omnipotenti.

I confesse vnto Almightie God. First, wee confesse to haue sinned against God, because sinne is defined to be, Something said, done, or desired, contrarie to the law of Almightie God.

Beata Mariæ semper Virgini.

To Blessed Marie, alwaies a Virgin. Next after Almightie God, are recited the names of fiue of his especiall Saintes, for fiue special prerogatiues, wherin these fiue surpassed & excelled al other Saints: First, to our B. Ladie the Virgin,

virgin, becauſe ſhe it is, who next after God, is
the firſt in glorie, who aboue all other ſaintes,
is the great and generall Patroneſſe, of all ſuch
ſinners, as ſorrowfullie flie vnto her for ſuccour: whoſe onely merites, God eſteemeth a-
boue the merits, of all mē or Angels: whom he
eſpecialie loueth, aboue all the perſons that
euer he created: who only, among all the children of men, neuer commited, any manner
of ſinne.

Beato Michaeli Archangelo.

To B. Michael the Archangel. Secondly, to
ſuch as haue had greate conqueſt and victorie
ouer ſinne, and Sathan: and this was S. Michael the Archangel, who fought againſt Lu-
cifer, for his ſinne of pride, conquered him,
and laſtly, caſt him out of heauen.

Beato Iohanni Baptiſtæ.

To B. Iohn Baptiſt. Thirdly, to ſuch as did
both preach, and doe, great penance for ſinne:
and this was Saint Iohn Baptiſt, the firſt prea-
cher of Pennance, in the entrie of the newe
Lawe: The precurſer of Chriſt: a Prophet, yea
more then a Prophet: of whom Trueth it ſelfe
did teſtifie, that a greater was not borne, a-
mongſt the ſonnes of women. Who aboue all
other Prophets, merited to demonſtrate the
Meſſias with his finger: to lay his hande vpon
his venerable head: and in the riuer of Iordan,
to baptiſe him.

Sanctis

Sanctis Apoſtolis Petro.

To the holy Apoſtles Peter. Fourthly, to ſuch
as had chiefe power and authoritie, in the militant Church : and this was S. Peter, whom
our Lord ordained , chiefe Paſtor ouer the
ſame: and to whom for this purpoſe, he principally gaue , and committed in charge, the
powreſull keyes of the kingdome of heauen,
that is, power to remit, or retaine ſiune, as teſtifyeth the Euangeliſt. Mat. 16.

Et Paulo.

And Paule. Fifdy, to ſuch as greatly laboured, to conuert ſoules vnto our Lord : and this
was the B. Apoſtle S. Paule, who in the office
of Preaching, laboured more then they all, to
conuerte the Heathen, and vnbeleeuers, to the
faith and knowledge of our Sauiour Chriſt.
In which fiue prerogatiues , theſe fiue were
moſt notable paternes , far ſurpaſſing all other
Saints.

Why we ioyntlie confeſſe vnto S. Peter,
and S. Paule.

And therefore doe we alwaies ioyntly confeſſe, vnto theſe two Saints together. Firſt, becauſe theſe two , with their bloods, firſt fun-
ded, that inuincible Rocke , the Church of
Rome. 2. Becauſe, that theſe two Princes of
the Church , as in their liues they loued on
another moſt entirely, euen ſo in their deaths,
they were not ſeparated.

E   *Omni*

To all Saints. Next, wee confeffe to all
Saintes in generall, becaufe it is impoffible
for vs to difpleafe God, but that we muft alfo
difpleafe his Saints, by reafon of the perfecte
vnion, that is betwixt them. And further, becaufe God doth vfe to pardon finnes, at the interceffion, and for the merits of his Holye
Saints: as witneffeth Iob. cap. 5.

Of knocking our breaft, at
Mea culpa.

In bewailing our finnes, we knocke our
breaftes three feuerall times, faying thefe
wordes, *Mea culpa.* Wherein three thinges
may aptlie be obferued: the ftroke, the found,
and the feeling: to fignifye three things, very
requifite vnto perfect Penance: to wit, Contrition of heart, fignifyed by the ftroke: Confeffion of mouth, fignifyed by the found: & Satif-
factiõ of work, fignified by the hurt, or feeling.

2. We knock, or fmite our breafts: to fhew
thereby, that we are truely & inwardlie forry,
and that we could finde in our harts, to be re-
uenged of our felues for our offences.

3. Thereby to make our hard & ftonie harts
more foft, by often beating and knocking.

4. Therefore, wee now ftrike them in our
felues, that God may not ftrike thẽ in vs hereafter.

5. And Laftlie, we knocke our breaft, after
the

the example of the deuoute Publican , who knocked his breaſt, ſaying, God be mercifull to me a ſinner: that ſo we may depart iuſtifyed to our owne houſes. Luc 18.13.

Of the ancient practiſe of the repeating the Confiteor before Maſſe.

The practiſe of Confeſsion before Maſſe, is, and euer hath bene verie ancient in the Catholike Church, as appeareth out of Micrologus, who plainely eſtifyeth, that Confeſſion was alwaies made at Maſſe. And the Maſſe of S. Iames the Apoſtle, beginneth from Confeſſion. Azor. lib. 10, Inſtlt. Moral. pag 1634.

CHAP. XXII.

Of the Prayer which followeth , commonly called the Abſolution.

THe Prieſt , hauing humblie acknowledged himſelfe , before the whole Congregation , to haue offended Almightie God, and to be a wretched ſinner, the people, the more to mooue the mercie of our Lord, towardes him, heartily pray vnto God for him, that hee would fauourablie extend his mercy towards him , whome they haue choſen at this preſent, with ioynt conſent, to ſpeake vnto his Maieſtie in their behalfes, ſaying , *Miſeriatur*

Why

Why this Abſolution was or-
dained.

This Abſolution was ordained, to ſhewe, that the Prieſt is ſpeciallie ordained of God, to make interceſſion for the ſinnes of the peo-ple. And as the Confeſſion going before was cal'ed generall: ſo this Abſolution following, is alſo generall. Which the Prieſt giue h one'y by way of Prayer, and not of a Sacrament, as that of, *Ego te abſoluo*, and extendeth it ſelfe no further, but to the taking away of Veniall ſinnes.

Why the ſigne of the Croße, is ioyned with the Abſolution.

The ſigne of the Croſſe, is ioyned with this Abſolution: which being made from the head to the heart, and from the left ſhoulder to the right: may ſignifie the three wayes, how wee offende Almightie God, to wit, by thought, word, and worke: but doth chieflie ſhew, that all forgiueneſſe of ſinne, proceedeth from the Paſſion of our bleſſed Sauiour.

Of *Dominus vobiſcum.*

Our Lord be with you. This ſalutation , is ſeauen ſundrie times rehearſed in the Holie Maſſe. 1. Before the firſt *Oremus* (which is this) 2. Before the firſt Collects 3. Before the reading of the Goſpell. 4. After the Creede (or if the Creede be omitted, before the Of-fertorie.) 5. Before the Preface. 6. Before the
kiſſing

kiſſing of the Paxe. 7. Before the laſt Collects : to ſignifie (as ſome of our deuout inter-
preters ſay) the ſeauen-fould gift of the Holy
Ghoſt. Which verie wordes, with thoſe which
follow, S Paule himſelfe vſed to Timothie,
ſaying, *Dominus Ieſus Chriſtus ſit cum ſpiritu
tuo.* Our Lord Ieſus Chriſt be with thy ſpirite.
2. Tim. vlt.

How the wordes, Dominus vobiſcum, are wordes of admonition.

And they may here be likewiſe vnderſtood, as wordes of admonition, vſed by the
Prieſt to the people As if he ſhould ſay, See
that our Lord be with you.

Howe they are wordes of con-ſolation.

They may be alſo taken, for wordes of conſolation : as if he ſhould ſay vnto them. Our
Lord dwelleth in you, giuing effect to your
demandes, that with the helpe of his grace,
and by perſeuerance in the ſame, you may attaine at the laſt, to the happie rewarde of e-
uerlaſting life

Et cum ſpiritu tuo.

And with thy ſpirit. It ſtandeth with great
reaſon, that the people ſhould likewiſe praye
for him, and wiſh that our Lord be with his
ſpirite, who is their ſpeaker and Embaſſador,
in ſo important, and weightie affaire: which
Embaſſage, they know he cannot rightlie per-

forme

forme, if his minde be otherwife diftracted, and be not fpeciallie affifted by the grace of God. And for this caufe, doe they often praye, that our Lord may be, and remaine with his fpirit.

CHAP. XXIII.

Of the Prieſts aſcending to the Altar.

AS before we faide, that by the defcending of the Prieft from the Altar was vnderftood the fall of man, and the loſſe of Gods fauour, for his tranſgreſsion: euen fo, by his afcending at this prefent, may be vnderftood, the accomplifhment of the promife of our Lord, for his reftoring and faluation, according to that of the Apoftle, faying When the fulneſſe of time came, God fent his Sonne. Gal. 4.

Of kiſſing the Altar, and of ſundrie reaſons for the ſame. The 1. Reaſon.

1. The Prieft hauing finifhed the prayer aforefaid approaching to the Altar, kiffeth the fame: which hee doth, in figne of honour and reuerence, and in refpect, the thing it felfe is holie, as being fanctifyed by the word of God and prayer. 1. Tim. 4.

The

The 2. Reaſon.

2. In reſpect of the pretious bodie of our Lord and Sauiour Ieſus, which doth greatlie ſanctifie whatſoeuer it toucheth.

The 3. Reaſon.

3. In reſpect of the Saints reliques which repoſe vnder the ſame, for neuer is there Altar conſecrated without ſome reliques of Saints, which are put vnderneath the greate ſtone of the Altar, with in ſome little veſſel, which for this cauſe is called the ſepulcher. Concil. Carthag 5. cap. 15.

The 4. Reaſon.

4. Alſo by this kiſſe, is ſignifyed, howe Chriſt by his comming, hath eſpouſed Holie Church vnto him, according to that of the Canticles. Cant. 1. And that of the Epheſians, 5. So Chriſt loued his Church, that he gaue him-ſelfe for her. For as a kiſſe ioyneth mouth to mouth: ſo in Chriſt, the humanitie was not only vnited to the diuinity, but alſo the ſpouſe, the Chu.ch, wa coupled to her ſpouſe, Chriſt.

The 5. Reaſon.

5. This kiſſe alſo doth ſignifye peace : according to that of the Avoſtle. Salute one another, with a holie kiſſe. And the God of peace be with you all

The 6. Reaſon.

6. S. Auguſtin ſaith that to kiſſe the Altar, is a ſigne of Catholike cōmunion & vnitie,

E 4 *The*

The 7. Reafon.

7. Laftlie, it admonifheth,that at this prefent, we are to kill all hatred and malice in vs
towardes all perfons,be in charity with them,
and efpeciallie to pray for them. For whofoeuer is not in perfect charitie , is not fit to be
prefent,at this holy Sacrifice.

By al which fufficiently appeareth,how ancient this Ceremonie is, and what caufes and
reafons there are, both for the inftitution and
practife of the fame. Now befides the performance of this pyous Ceremonie, he ioyntlie
with the fame,reciteth the prayer and petition
which enfueth,faying.

Oremus te Domine, per merita fan-
ctorum tuorum.

We befeech thee,ô Lord,by the merites of
thy Saints. Graces & fauours,are many times
conferred , not onely, at the requeft of one
friende to another, but manie times at the requeft of a friende. to a verie enemie. Man
therefore, being become the enemie of God
thorough his finne, interpofeth the beft beloued friendes of our Lord, for his Interceffors
and Mediators.

Of the Introit of the Maſſe. And of ſun-
drie pious myſteries to be conſidered
in the ſame.

THe Prieſt hauing recommended the people to God by his prayers, and the people the Prieſt, he goeth vp to the middeſt of
the Altar (as we ſaid before) kiſſeth the ſame,
then turneth him to the right hande of the
Altar, where the Miſſall is layde and then beginneth the Introit of the Maſſe.

*Ho*ɯ *the right end of the Altar, ſignifyeth,*
the ſtate of innocencie.

The right ende of the Altar, whereunto the
Prieſt addreſſeth himſelfe ſignifyeth the life
and ſtate of innocencie, which our firſt father
Adam, loſt by his ſinne: and conſequently, all
we his children, through his tranſgreſsion.

*Ho*ɯ *the going firſt thereto, our Sauiours*
*firſt going to the Ie*ɯ*es.*

The going of the Prieſt, firſt to the right-
hande, or ende of the Altar, ſignifyeth, that
Chriſt, who was promiſed from the beginning, comming into the worlde, went firſt to
the people of the Iewes, before to the gentils.
For the Iewes, by reaſon of the Law, were
then on the right hand: and the Gentiles, by
reaſon of their Idolatrie, on the left.

E 5 *Of*

Of the fignifycation of the word
Introit.

The word *Introit*, is borrowed of the Latins,
as thofe that are but meanely learned, cannot
but know, and fignifyeth with vs. A going in,
an entrance, beginning or prœmium: And for
as much as all thofe who treat of thefe myfteries, doe commonly appoynt the Sacrifice of
the Maffe, to beginne at this place, and for that
at this time, the Prieft maketh his firft entrance vnto the Altar, and not before: therefore, for the proper affinitie of the word, with
the action of the Prieft, it is aptly called, by the
name of Introit. In which fence, both Rabanus and Conradus, lib. 1. Ceremoniarum, and
others expound the fame.

How the Introit fignifyeth myfticallie, an
earneft defire for the comming of Chrift.

This Introit, myfticallie fignifyeth the earneft defire of the people of al ages, for the
comming of Chrift which defire, he himfelfe
afterwardes witneffed, faying: Abraham your
father reioyced, that he might fee my day, and
he faw, and was glad Iohn. 8 56.

How the double repetition fignifyeth the
greatnes of the necefsitie, and the
feruor of the defire.

The double repetition thereof: fignifyeth
the greatnes of the neceffitie, and the feruour
of

of the deſire : together with the great ioye &
exultation which was in the world, when he
afterwardes came himſelfe in perſon .

The Gloria Patri, an humble
thankes-giuing.

The Gloria Patri, which is annexed vnto the
ſame Introit, is a moſt humble, and heartie
thankeſ giuing vnto the bleſſed Trinitie, for ſo
ſingular a benefite beſtowed vpon vs.

The Introit of the Maſſe confirmed
by myracle.

Almaricus Biſhop of Treues , teſtifyeth of
a myracle which Almightie God ſhewed in
approbarion of this part of the Maſſe. Who
writeth, that he heard ſung by the Holy Angels, for the Introit of the Maſſe vpon the
feaſt of the Epiphanie, in the Church of S.
Sophie, at Conſtantinople, the 94. Pſ *Venite
[exultemus], &c. Fortunatus de ord. Antiph.
cap. 21.

CHAP. XXVI.
Of Kyrie eleiſon, and of ſundrie myſte-
ries to be conſidered in
the ſame.

Three ſortes of langues vſed in the Maſſe:
and what is ſignifyed by the ſame.

IN the Holie Maſſe, haue long time bene
vſed, three ſortes of languages, ſanctifyed on
the

the Croſſe of our Sauiour Ieſus, to wit, Hebrew, Greeke, and Latine. Of Hebrew, theſe
wordes following, *Amen, Alleluia, Cherubin,
Seraphin, Oſanna, Sabbaoth.* Of Greeke, *Kyrie
eleiſon, Chriſte eleiſon.* Of Latine, all the reſidue
of the Maſſe, as being the moſt vniuerſall
tongue, in the weſt Church. Which three
languages, repreſent the title which was faſtned on the Croſſe of our Sauiour, written in
Hebrew, Greeke, and Latine.

Kyrie eleiſon, Chriſte eleiſon.

Kyrie eleiſon, are two Greeke words, which
ſignifye in Latine, *Domine miſerere,* Lord haue
mercie: & *Chriſte eleiſon,* Chriſt haue mercie.

Why kyrie eleiſon, is nine times re-peated.

The firſt Reaſon.

Theſe deuout petitions, are nine times
repeated, to put vs in minde, of nine ſortes of
ſinnes, wherewith we offend Almighty God.
The firſt three, by Original, Mortall, and Veniall. The ſecond three, by Thoughts, Words,
and Deedes. The third three, by Frailtie, Ignorance, and Malice, and particuarly in the laſt
three. Wherefore, for our ſinnes of Frailtie, we
addreſſe our prayer to the Father, ſaying, *Kyrie
eleiſon.* For our ſinnes of Ignorance, to the
Sonne, ſaying. *Chriſte eleiſon* And for our
ſinnes of Malice, to the Holie Ghoſt, ſaying,
Kyrie eleiſon.

The

The ſecond Reaſon.

Againe, theſe words are nine times rehearſed, to ſignifie the feruent deſires of all mankinde, for the cōming of Chriſt, by whoſe cōming he ſhould be aſociated, to the nine orders
of Angels: Which our Lord himſelfe doeth
deſcribe, by the nintie and nine ſheepe, which
he lefte , to ſeeke out the one loſt ſheepe,
which was man, to reſtore him vnto his nintie and nine, that is, to the nine Orders of
Angels.

Why we ſay kyrie eleiſon, both to the Fa-ther, and the Holie Ghoſt, and not to the Sonne.

To the Father and the Holie Ghoſt, we ſaye
Kyrie eleiſon, and to the Sonne, Chriſte eleiſō,
For the which, Innocentius the 3. giueth this
reaſon. If you will aske me why we ſay not to
the Sonne, Kyrie eleiſon, as well as to the Father, and the Holie Ghoſt, it is to ſignifie, that
in the Father and the holie Ghoſt there is but
one, and the ſelfe ſame nature, that is to ſaye,
onely diuine: but in the Sonne, there is a double nature, to wit, both diuine, and humaine,
for that he is both perfect God, and perfect
Man , and ſo is neither the Father, nor the
Holie Ghoſt. libro ſecundo, de myſter. Miſ.
cap. 19.

Kyrie

Kyrie eleison confirmed by miracle.

I cannot heere let passe, to speake of the great and wounderful vertue of these words. Saint Basil, by the pronunciation of these wordes, caused the doores of a Church which were shutte against him, to open of their owne accorde. And S. Gemianus, at the cry of these wordes, put fiue Kings to flight.

S. Basil, taking vnto him a man, which had giuen himselfe to the Diuel, by a writing vnder his owne hande (which the Diuel would in no wise restore) commanded a number of deuout people, and Religious persons present, to lift vp their hands to heauen with him, and to crie without ceasing, Kyrie eleison, Christe eleison, Kyrie eleison, which the people performing, with many deuout teares, in the sight of all that were present, the Diuell perforce, let fall the selfe same writing out of the ayre, into the handes of the holie Bishop. In vita S. Basilij.

And these holie wordes, haue alwaies bene vsed, and heighlie esteemed, amongst deuout christians, as words of singular force & vertue, to chase away the diuel, and all other malignant spirits that would annoy them.

To conclude, this sacred Canticle, is verie auntient, as the Liturgies of blessed S. Iames the Apostle, Saint Basil, and Saint Chrisostome, doe make manifest mention. And by the

the Counfell of Vafe, was brought in the cu-
ftome, to fing the fame, at Maße, Mattins, and
Euenfong: which Councell was holden, about
25. yeares, before S. Gregorie the great.

C H A P. XXVII.
Of the Canticle called, *Gloria*
in excelſis Deo.

Three hymmes in the Maße, firſt inuented
by the Angels.

T His Canticle, is commonly called, *Hym-
nus Angelicus*, The Angelical hymne (as
alfo Ailleluia , and Sanctus :) becaufe the
firſt inuention came frō the Angels, who haue
giuen vs example , to laude and praife our
Lord in this manner. Whereunto accordeth
Rupertus, faying: This hymne, the church hath
taken from the mouth of Angels.

But this is more manifeſt by the fcripture it
felf, for we read in S. Luke, that an Angel, with
a great light, apeared to the fhepheards, as they
were feeding their flockes, and brought vn-o
them tydings . that the Sauiour of the worlde
was newly borne, faying. Behold, I euangelize
vnto you great ioy, that fhalbe vnto all people,
becaufe this day is borne to you a Sauiour. And
fuddenly there was with th: Angel, a multitude of the heauenly army, prayfing God, and
faying. *Gloria in excelſis Deo*, &c. Luc. 2. 11.

Gloria

Gloria in excelſis, &c. *Partly com-poſed by men, and partly by Angels.*

This Spirituall Hymme, conſiſteth of two partes: the firſt whereof, as before is ſaid, was compoſed by the Angels, vnto theſe wordes, *laudamus te, &c.* Which other words with the verſes ſubſequent, are ſayde by ſome to be the wordes of Saint Hillarie, Biſhop of Poi-ctiers. Some report that he brought them with him at the returne of his exile out of Greece, As namely, *Aquinus lib de diuinis officus.cap. de celeb. Miſſ* Others, that it was receaued in-to the Church, by the inſtitution of the Apo-ſtles. Durand. lib 4 cap. 13.num.4.

Why this Hymme is omitted vpon the feaſt of Innocents.

This hymme, as alſo Alleluia, is omitted vpon the Feaſt of Innocents: to repreſent the ſorrowfull mourning, for the murther & bar-barous crueltie of King Herod, thinking in killing the Infants, to haue deſtroied & ſlaugh-tered, our Lord and Sauiour.

Why in Septuageſima, and Lent.

In Septuageſima likewiſe, and vntill Ea-ſter, this Canticle is omitted: becauſe, then is repreſented in the Chuⱼch, the time of Pen-nance, to wit, this life, wherein we cannot par-ticipate

ticipate of the ioyes of Angels, but are to lament and deplore, the miſerable eſtate of our
ruine and fall.

Why in the Maſſes for the dead.

Likewiſe, it is omitted in all Maſſes for the
dead, becauſe (as Almaricus Fortunatus,verie
well noteth) all Canticles of ioye, ought to
ceaſe in this Office , which is an Office of
teares and lamentations. lib 3 de Eccleſ.Offic.
cap. 44.

Why this Canticle was firſt com-
poſed, and placed in the
Maſſe.

This ioyfull Canticle (wherein is ſet foorth
the ample prayſes of Ieſus Chriſt) the Holie
Fathers of the church,firſt placed in the Maſſe,
to the end to refute and confound the wicked
Arrians who had compoſed ſundrie Ballets &
Songs, to diminiſh the glorie of our bleſſed
Sauiour. For which cauſe , the aforeſaid Fathers , by a holie zeale, were incited to com-
poſe a contrarie Canticle,wherein ſhould euidentlie be ſet foorth, the honorable titles, and
excellēcies of the ſame Sauiour:by the which,
publikelie in the Maſſe , thoſe Arrian Heretikes, might be confounded.

Why the Priest standeth before the midst of the Altar, rehearsing this Hymme.

The Priest, in rehearsing this Hymme, standeth before the middest of the Altar; to signifye thereby, that Christ is the mediator betwixt God and man. As also to declare, that it was first pronounced, in the honour of him, who is as it were, in the midst of the Trinitie.

Of the lifting vp of the handes of the Priest towards heauen.

Standing in the middest of the Altar, together with the pronunciation of the wordes of this Canticle, he deuoutlie lifteth vp both his handes to heauen, and then drawing them reuerently downe, with cheerefull voice pursueth on the rest of this Angelicall hymne: signifying thereby, the ineffable ioye which came from aboue vnto men, by the birth and natiuitie of our blessed Sauiour.

Of the word Amen, after gloria in excelsis.

This word Amen, is an Hebrew worde, wherewith the people make answere at euery Prayer, and benediction of the Priest, and is as much to say, as verelie, faithfullie, or so be it. See Rabauus de institutione cler. l 1 c. 33.

2. Neither is it the custome of the Greeks,

or

or Latins, to tranſlate this worde into their vulgar tongue, no more then Alleluia, and other woides, which for their Holie authoritie, and the antiquitie of the proper tongue, haue bene religiouſlie obſerued, by the Apoſtles themſelues

3. And ſo ſacred is this word, that S. Iohn reporteth, to haue heard the ſame aboue in heauen, Apoc 19. Therefore, let vs not attempt to ſaye it otherwiſe in earth, then it is ſayde in heauen, for that were not onely, to correct the Church in earth, in her doings, but to correct thoſe in heauen alſo in theirs.

Of the kiſſe of the Altar, after Gloria in excelſis.

At the ende of this Angelicall Hymne, the Prieſt boweth him downe, and kiſſeth the Altar, which he doth, in the celebration of the Maſſe, nine ſeuerall times, and that not without a ſpeciall myſterie. For this kiſſe is a ſigne of peace the which, in this holie hymne, was firſt announced by the embaſſage of Angels.

The Prieſt therefore, in vſing the ſame nine ſeuerall times, inſinuateth hereby, that hee deſireth to be ioyned and vnited, to the nine orders of Angels; as alſo, that they would aſſiſt him, to preſent his prayers and oblations to Almightie God.

Finallie, moſt Authors doe both agree and confeſſe, that the antiquitie of this part
of

ofthe Maſſe, is deduced at the leaſt, from Teleſphorus Pope, who liued well nigh 1500.
yeares agone. See Walfridus in lib. de reb.ec-
cleſc p. 22. Ruper us, Amalaricus, Rabanus,
Berno, and Innocentius tertius.

Of the turning of the Prieſt to the people, at Dominus vobiſcum, and of ſun- drie reaſons concerning the ſame.

The Prieſt turneth him on the right hande,
to ſalute the people, and on the ſame, returneth againe vnto the Altar: all which is not
voide, of ſingular myſterie and ſignifycation.

How the Prieſts turning on the right hand, ſignifyeth an vpright intention.

3.   Firſt, therefore it may ſignifye, that the
Prieſt is to haue, a ſtreight and vpright intention to heauen, both for himſelfe, & for the
people which is apily vnderſtood by the right
hand.

2.   Secondly, we alſo who are preſent, are
hereby premoniſhed, to lift vp our heartes to
him, who ſitteth on the right hand of his Fa-
ther:according as we confeſſe in the article of
our Creede.

Dominus vobiſcum.

Our Lord be with you. Hauing turned himſelfe to the people, he ſaluteth them, ſaying,
Domi-

Dominus vobiscum. Our Lord be with you: which he sayeth, that he may conioyne and lynke, the mindes of the people to Almighty God, and to make them more attent, to his diuine seruice.

What is meant by extending his armes.

And note, that together with the prolation of the wordes, he spreadeth, and openeth abroade his armes: to signifye thereby, howe Christ hath his armes alwaes open, and readie to receaue those, that are truelie penitent, and doe flie vnto him.

Et cum spiritu tuo.

And with thy spirit. In which wordes, the people pray that with the spirit of man, the spirite of God may be present, to teach, and direct him: without whose assistance, we can doe nothing acceptable to him, as himselfe hath witnessed, by his Apostle, saying, Without me, you can do nothing. So that the answere of the people, is wholie to be referred, to the action of the Priest, to wit, to the oblation which he purposeth to make in their behalfes.

Why after this, the Priest turneth him againe, to the right hand of the Altar.

The people hauing answered, *Et cum spiritu*
suo

two ,the Prieſt, turneth him againe to the right
hand of the Altar: expreſſing thereby, how our
Sauiour did not immediatly forſake the Iewes
for their obſtinacie, but often turned to them,
to haue turned them to him. As alſo, that we
his children, ſhould do the like to our bretheren, when at any time they offend, or treſpaſſe
againſt vs.

The vſe of this ſalutation is verie auncient
in the Holie Maſſe, as plainely appeareth by
the councell of Vaſe, and the Liturgies of S.
Iames, S Baſil, and S. Chriſoſtome.

Of Oremus, and how it ſignifyeth diſtruſt in our ſelues.

Let vs pray. The Prieſt diſtruſting as it
were, in his owne ſtrength, gathereth vnto
him, the prayers of all the people, ſaying, O-
remus as if he ſhould ſay, Aſſiſt me with your
prayers: For certaine it is, that our mercifull
Lord, will not denie to a multitude their petitions, who hath promiſed to heare the prayers of two or three , that are gathered together in his name. Mat. 5.

How that our Sauiour both prayed himſelfe, and exhorted others alſo to praye.

He pronounceth this worde Oremus , with
a heigh voice: to ſtirre vp, and prouoke others
to praye, and prayeth himſelfe alſo: for ſo our
Sauiour both exhorted his diſciples to pray,
and

and likewife prayed him felfe alfo.

How eleuation of heart in time of Prayer.

In faying Oremus, he lifteth vp handes . to put vs in mind , that our hearts should be ele-uated in the time of praier. For as we reade in 16. of Exodus , whilft Ifrael fought with A-malech ; Moyfes afcended vpon a Mountayne, and when he 'lifted vp his handes, Ifrael ouer-came , but if hee flacked,or with-drew them, Amalech ouercame. Wherein the Prieft ought to imitate that holie Moyfes, to obtaine the victorie, againft thofe inuifible Amalechites, the diuels.

CHAP. XXIX.

Of the firft Collects. And of fundry reafons concerning the fame.

The 1. Reafon.

THE firft prayers , which the Prieft offe-reth vp to God in the Maffe, are com-monly called by the name of Collects. which is a worde borrowed of the Latins,as the lear-ned do verie well know,and fignifyeth a ga-thering or collection:which as it may be made of diuers and fundrie things,fo hath it fundry fignifycations.

1. Somtimes it fignifyeth a collection which is made of tributes and duties, to be payde to the Prince : whereof it commeth, that the ga-therers thereof,are called Collectors.

2. Some

2 Sometimes it is taken for the collection, which is wont to be made in the Church, for the poore, as the 1. Cor. 16. *De collectis autem quæ fiunt in Sanctis*: And as touching the collections, which are made for the Saints. And againe prefentlie after.   *Né cum ver era tunc collectæ fiunt.* Leaft when I come, then collections be made.

3.   Both the holie Scripture, and the ancient Fathers, doe vfe this worde Colieft , to fignifie an affemblie of the people of God, & and yet not euerie manner of affemblie, but onely of fuch, as are great and folemne, as Leuit: 23. *Dies enim cætus eft atque collect.* For it is a day, of meeting, and affemblie. And in Deut. 16. *Quia collecta eft Domini Dei tui.* Becaufe it is the affemblie of thy Lord thy God. And in the 2. of Paralipemon. 7.   *Fecitque Salomon die octauo collectam.* And Salomon made a collection vpon the eight day.

So that by this . which hath bene alreadie faide, it is not hard to vnderftand, why the firft prayers in the Maffe, are called Collectes: the which Durandus, in the fourth booke and 15. cap. explicateth faying. Collectes properlie are prayers, which are fo called, for they are faide vpon the people affembled.

The 2. Reafon.

Againe, they may be called Collects : by reafon, that they are certaine briefe collections ,

ons, of all the prayers, requeſts, and ſupplications of the people of our Lord, which the
Prieſt (who is the ſpeaker for the people) doth
collect and gather in one, to preſent and offer
them vp to God in their behalfe.

The 3. Reaſon.

And againe, they are called Collects : to
ſignifye, that it is not enough for thoſe who
intende to offer vp prayers acceptable to God,
to be aſſembled in the ſelfe-ſame place bodilie, but that they ought principallie, to haue
their hearts vnited together, by perfect loue
and charitie, and to be recollected ſpirituallie.
For nothing is more contrarie to perfect prayer, then is diuiſion, or diſtraction of ſpirit.

The 4. Reaſon.

As touching the inſtitution of the Collects,
it is principallie for theſe purpoſes, to witte,
Either in reſpect of the time, wherein they are
recited. Or of the neceſſities of the perſons,
for whom they are recited. Such for example
are thoſe, for the moſt part, of Aduent, whe:e-
in is deſired of God, that the comming of
Chriſt our Sauiour into the world, may be to
our ſaluation . And likewiſe thoſe in Lent,
wherein we pray, that our faſting and abſti-
nence, may be profitable vnto vs, and merito-
rious for the ſatisfaction of our ſinnes. Alſo
ſometimes they are made, for certaine perſons in particular, as for the Pope, for the Bi-

fhop, for the Prince &c.

The 5. Reafon.

The matter it felfe , and fubiect of the Collectes , is commonly taken out of the holie
Scriptures . As for example, that of the three
children, the which is recited verie often, and
namely in the Maffes of all the Saturdaies, of
the four times of the yeare , and is taken out
of the 3, chapter of the prophet Daniel;
which Collect, beginneth as followeth. *Deus
qui tribus pueris &c.* O God , which to the
three children , didft mitigate the flames of
fire: graunt mercifully , that we thy feruants,
be not burned with the flames of our vices
&c. Where you fee. that this Collect is founded, vpon that wonderfull miracle, which our
Lord wrought , in affawaging the flames of
the fiery fornace, in the fauour and conferua-
tion , of thofe his faithfull feruantes: by occafion whereof, wee befeeche our Lord , to
affawage in vs , the flames of our vices , and
finfull concupifcences.

Likewife that of Sexagefima Sunday, is in
a manner the fame : wherein the Church, taketh occafion to praye vnto God , that he
would deliuer vs from all aduerfitie , by the
helpe and protection , of bleffed Saint Paul,
whom he gratiouflie preferued , from fo many perilles, faying . *Deus qui confpicis &c.* O
God who feeft , that we doe in no wife , put
our truft in our owne actions : graunt mercifullie,

fullie , that by the protection of the doctor of the Gentils , we may be defended againſt all aduerſities. Amen.

Somtimes they are taken , out of the liues and examples of the holie Saintes , whoſe feaſts are celebrated . As that on the feaſt of bleſſed S. Laurence ſaying . *Da nobis quęſu̅mus &c.* Graunt vs we beſeeche thee , ô almightie God, to quench in vs the flames of our vices, who grantedſt to S. Laurence , to ouercome the flames of his torments. And in the ſelfe ſame maner of diuers others .

The 6. Reaſon.

Concerning the different number of Collects, the Church practiſeth two , or three ſe̅uerall thinges, The firſt is, that ſhe ordinarilie v̇eth , diſparitie of number, ether of one alone, or of three, or of fiue, or elſe of ſeauen at the moſt: not for ſuperſtition, as heretiques doe ſuppoſe . but for ſignification and inſtruction, as ſhall further appeare .

How One, to ſignifie one God, and one faith.

She vſeth one alone , *propter Sacramentu̅ v ita i.* , for the Sacrament of vnitie, as ſayeth Innocentius 3. to ſignifie thereby, the vni̅tie of God, in whom we beleeue : as alſo the vnitie of faith , which we profeſſe: according to that of the Apoſtle Epheſ. 4. One God, one faith, one baptiſme.

Ho*w* Three, for the *myfterie of the*
Trinitie.

Shee vfeth three to fignifie the myftery of the blelled Trinitie: and in the honour of the three perfons. And after the example of our Sauiour, who prayed three times in the garden.

Ho*w* fiue, in the *honour of the*
fiue *woundes.*

She vfeth fiue, in honour & memorie of the fiue woundes of our Sauiour Iefus : which is a myfterie, that Chriftians ought alwaies, to haue in fingular commendation.

Ho*w* Seauen, *in honour of the feauen*
gifts of the *holy Ghoft.*

And fhe vfeth feauen, to reprefent vnto vs, the feauen gifts of the Holie Ghoft. And to confirme her proceedings herein, to our blelfed Sauiours, who teaching his difciples how to pray, comprifed all things neceflarie, in feauen petitions,

Laftlie, thefe Collects ought to be fhorte, and to comprehend brieflie, that which wee may lawfullie defire, hope, and demaunde, at the mercifull handes of Almighty God

They ought alfo, to be pronounced with fuch humilitie, attention, reuerence, modeftie of countenance, and comportment of bodie, that the afsiftants, may both be edified, and made attentiue thereby : For he that fhould pray

pray otherwiſe, looſelie, and ſwiftly, with the
onely motion of his lippes, ſhould make his
prayer barraine, & vnfruitful before Almightie God.

Of the concluſion of the Collects, and of ſundrie reaſons concerning the ſame.

Firſt, all the Prayers in the Maſſe are commonly begunne, in the name of the Father,
and concluded in the name of the Sonne: the
Church hauing conformed her ſelfe in this
point, to the doctrine of our Sauiour himſelfe,
ſaying: Whatſoeuer you ſhall aske the Father
in my name, he will giue it you, Ioh. 4.

Per Dominum noſtrum.

Th ough our Lord. The Prieſt, as wee haue
ſaid, concluding the Collects, demandeth all
things to be giuen, of our heauenlie Father,
in the name, and for the loue, of Ieſu Chriſt
his Sonne, our Lord: becauſe it is he, in whom
the Father is well pleaſed, and to whom hee
can denie nothing, for as much as he alwaies
accompliſheth his will and pleaſure. Marc. 11.

Ieſum Chriſtum.

Ieſus Chriſt. At which wordes the Prieſt
boweth or inclineth himſelfe: For although
there be manie other honorable names and
titles belonging to our Lord, yet at none of
theſe doe wee bowe our ſelues: the reaſon
whereof is, becauſe thoſe names, ſhew what
ke is in himſelfe: but this name of Ieſus, ſpeci-

allie declareth , what he is made vnto vs , to witt , our Sauiour : for what elſe is Ieſus, as S. Bernard ſaith, but a Sauiour.

Filium tuum.

Thy ſonne, Thine indeede, nether by grace nor election of creature , but by proprietie of kind , and veritie of ſubſtance. Thine trulie , not by adoption , like vnto other , but trulie, naturall, like vnto none other.

Qui tecum viuit & regnat, in vnitate Spiritus Sancti Deus. &c.

Who liueth and raigneth with thee, in the vnitie of the Holy Ghoſt , God. &c. In which wordes, the Prieſt admoniſheth the people, to beleue, that the Sonne of God liueth and raigneth for euer, with out beginning or ending, and is of the ſame ſubſtance, and equal power, togerher with the Father, & the holye Ghoſt.

Of the word Amen *, and of ſundrie things to be conſidered in the ſame.*

This word, *Amen*, is verie commonlie to be read and ſeene in ſundry places of holie Scripture , as Deut. 27. Curſed is he which abideth not in the wordes of this lawe , nor dooth them in worke, and al the people ſhal ſay, *Amen*. Alſo in Tobias. when Gabelus had ſayed the benediction , al anſwered. *Amen*.

How Amen *ſignifieth truth or veritie.*

Somtimes it ſignifieth the truth or veritie of a

of a thinge: ſo Chriſt anſwering in the goſpel
ſayed, *Amen Amen*, that is *veritatem dico vobis*
I ſay the truth vnto you, Wherfore when the
prieſt concludeth the Collects, ſaying. Who
liueth and raigneth with thee, God world
without end, the people to declare, that they
doe trulie and firmelie beleeue the ſame, anſwere *Amen*. As if they ſhould ſay, we doe truly, ſtedfaſtlie, and verilie beleeue, euen as
thou ſayeſt of the Sonne of God.

What is vſuallie ſignified by *Amen*.

But the moſt common, and vſuall ſignification thereof in all the petitions, of the Maſſe
is, that what the prieſt, hath faithfullie dema-
ded of almightie God, we hope vndoutedlie,
ſhal be giuen vnto vs, and trulie accompliſhed
in effect.

Why Amen, *is rehearced by*
the people.

And ſith in thoſe thinges which appertaine
to God, the people haue the Prieſt, as theire
ambaſſador or ſpeaker, therfore in the end of
all his prayers, they giue their conſent to his
demandes, ſaying; *Amen*. And for this cauſe
it is that al the prayers, which are made by the
Prieſt, although ſomtimes, ſome of them be
reci ed in priuat and ſilence, yet are they concluded openlie, and in the hearing of all the
aſſiſtants.

Amen,

Amen, one of the names of Al-
mightie God.

Finallie, for the greater honor of this most
holie and facred worde, S Iohn affirmeth, that
it is one of the names of Almightie God, faying: Thus faith Amen, the faithfull and true
witneffe. Apoc. 3 14. And fo heighly doth S.
Auguftine honour the fame, that he faith it is
not lawfull, to tranflate it, into any other language. Tract. 41 in Ioan.

CHAP. XXX.

Of the Epiftle.

And firft of the Etymologie, and figni-
fycation of the word.

Irft, the word Epiftle, is a word borrowed of the Greeke worde, *Epiftelin*, which
fignifyeth, to fende betwixt, as Epiftles, or
letters, which are a fpeech of one prefent, to
one that is abfent, Such was the Epiftle of S.
Paule. 1. 5. 27. Wherein he faith, I adiure you
by our Lord , that this Epiftle be read , to all
the holie brethren.

The reading of the Epiftle, reprefenteth the
reading of our Sauiour in the Sinagogue.

He which readeth the Epiftle, ftanding vpright , pronounceth the fame , the booke
being

being open. Becauſe according to the Euangeliſt, S. Luc 4. 16. Ieſus came to Nazareth
where he was brought vp, and he entred according to his cuſtome, on the Sabboth daye
into the Synagogue, and he roſe vp to read,
and the booke of Eſay the Prophet, was deliuered vnto him. And as he vnfoulded the
booke, he found the place, where it was written: The ſpirit of our Lord vpon me, for which
he anointed me: to euangelize vnto the poore,
he ſent mee, &c. Eſay 6. And when he had
foulded the booke, he rendred it to the miniſter.

Why the Epiſtle is read, next after the
Collect or Prayer.

The Epiſtle is preſently read, after the Collect or Prayer. To giue vs to vnderſtand, that
without humble prayer, firſt made vnto Al-
mighie God, neuer can we read any thing to
the profite or benefite of our ſoules.

Why onely the Scripture is read, in
the time of Maſſe.

Neuer hath the Church permitted, that the
liues of any ſainctes, nor the tractes of any
Doctors, how learned, or holie ſo uer they
were, be read in the Office of the Maſſe, but
only the moſt holy Scriptures themſelues, either of the Law of the Prophets, of the Euangeliſts, or of the writings, or Epiſtles, of the
B. Apoſtles: to ſignifie, that this holy Sacri-

fice dooth reprefent vnto vs , the life of the
Saint of all Saintes , our fole redeemer and
Sauiour Iefus.

Why none of the ould Teſtament is read vpon Sundayes.

Neuer alfo vpon Sundayes , is reade in the
Maſſe , any parte of the ould Teſtament , but
only of the new : to fignifie, that we are now
vnder the law of grace , which after the refurrection of our Lord (myfticallie reprefented
by the Sunday) was publicquelie preached ,
thoroughout the world. As alfo to condemne
heereby , the error of the Iewes , who maintaine, that the law of Moyfes, fhould remaine
for euer.

Why the Epiſtle, is alwayes read on the right hand of the Altar.

The Epiſtle is alwayes read , on the righte
fide of the Altar : to fignifie (as often hath alreadie bin faid) that our Sauiour came firſt to
the people of the Iewes, who were faid to be
on the right hand. According to that of the A-
poſtle, faying. To you it behoued firſt to preach
the gofpel of the kingdom. Actes. 13.46.

Why the Epiſtle is read before the Goſpel.

And it is read before the Gofpel, to declare
that all the predictions of the Prophets, did
only tend to this , to guide and lead men , to
the true light and vnderſtanding, of the gofpel!

pell of Chriſt. As alſo to ſignifie , the office
of S. Iohn Baptiſt , who went before the face
of our Lord , to prepare his wayes, as him
ſelfe teſtifieth,ſaying. I am the voice of a criar
in the wildernes,prepare the way of ourLord.
Mat. 3. And the Apoſtles likewiſe were ſent
before our Sauiour, into euery towne and cittie, where him ſelfe was to goe.

Why the people ſit at the reading
of the Epiſtle.

Al the people are permitted to ſit at the reading of the Epiſtle , to ſignifie the imperfectiõ
of the ould law and the greate difference betwixt it, and the dignitie of the new, And further to declare , that we reſerue our greateſt,
and chiefeſt reuerence , for the reading of the
goſpell.

The different voices, vſed in pronoun-
cing the ould & new teſtament.

But this is much more liuely expreſſed in a
high Maſſe, by the difference of voices which
is vſed in pronouncing the oulde and new
Teſtament : for the one is pronounced , with
a heauie and lowe voice , but the other , with
a cheerefull and highe voice. Which is done ,
to ſignifie the different eſtate of the Church,
vnder the two Teſtaments . For vnder the
oulde, ſhe was in ſeruitude and bondage, vnderſtood by the low and heauie voice : but
F 6   vnder

vnder the new , in freedome and libertie, vnderftood by the cheetefull and high voice.

Why the Subdeacon kiffeth the Priefts hand.

After the Epiftle is read (if it be in a heigh
Maffe) the Subdeacon prefenteth the booke
to the Prieft clofed, who putteth his hande
thereon, and then the Subdeacon kiffeh the
fame: to fignifie, that onely Chrift (according
to S, Iohn) was the Lambe, who could open
the feales of that booke, wherein both Chrift
himfelfe, and his facred myfteries were in-
clofed.

Deo gratias.

Laftlie, the Epiftle being read, anfwere is
made, faying, *Deo gratias,* Thankes be to God.
By which few words. are fullie fignifyed, the
confent, gratitude, and thankefgiuing, of al the
people.

The reading of the Epiftle in the holy Maffe,
hath no leffe antiquitie, then from the Apoftles themfelues , as appeareth out of Clemens, Iuftinus, Tertullianus, and Dionyfius
Areopagita, all whom Durandus l 2. de Rit.
Ecclef. Cath c 18. and Ozorius Inftit. Moral.
l. 10 p, 1636. doe produce for preofe of this
poynt.

Of

C H A P.   XXXI.

Of the Gradual or Responce, and of sun-drie reasons concerning the same.

The 1. Reason.

C Oncerning the Graduall, it is firft to be
noted, that the verie worde it felfe, is
not without fome fpecial myfterie: fignifying,
fteppes, or Degrees, to wit, of perfection, according to the doctrine of our Sauiour, faying,
Be yee perfect, as your Father which is in heauen is perfect.

As alfo to fignifie, that the end of the doctrine of the Apoftles or Prophets, whereunto
wee haue hearkened a little before, is to leade
vs, by little and little to perfection, that wee
afcēding from vertue to vertue, as the Kingly
Prophet faith, Pfal. 38. May fee the God of
gods in Sion.

The 2. Reason.

This Graduall, doeth yet further fignifie,
manie other notable myfteries. As for example, in an heigh Maffe, it is alwaies fong,
with a graue and heauie voice : to fignifie the
great paine and difficultie there is, in afcending from vertue to vertue, and in aduancing
our felues in a fpirituall life, according to the
saying

faying of our B. Sauiour. The fpirit is willing,
but the flefh is weake, Mat. 26.41.

The 3. Reafon.

Myfticallie alfo , the Graduall may be referred to the vocation of the Apoftles: whom
our Sauiour calling , and faying . *Venite poft
me.* Come after me . They forfaking all that
they had, did foorthwith follow, and walke
after their Lord : the difciples after their mafter: the children after their moft louing Father, as faith. Innoc.3.

This Graduall did S. Iohn Baptift firft fing,
when ftanding with two of his difciples, and
feeing Iefus walking he fayed . *Ecce Agnus
Dei, ecce qui tollit peccata mundi.* Iohn. 1. This
Graduall did. S Andrew fing, when finding his
brother Simon, he fayed. *Inuenimus Mefsiam*
&c. Whe haue found the Meffias , which is
interpreted Chrift , and he brought him vnto
Iefus. Ioh. This Gradual did S. Phillip fing,
when he found Nathaniell , and fayed vnto
him. *Quem Moyfes* &c. Whom Moifes wrote
of in the law and the prophets, we haue
found, Iefus the Sonne of Iofeph , of Nazareth, come and fee.

The 4. Reafon.

This Gradual is alfo called by the name of
a Refponce , becaufe that it hath correfpon-
dence to the Epiftle: As for exaple , if the Epiftle contayne matter of ioy , the Refponce or
Gra-

Graduall, doth likewise signify ioy. If matter of sorrowe, it also is conformable, according to that of the Apostle. Rom 12. *Gaudete cum gaudentibus, flete cum flentibus* Reioyce with them that be merrie , and weepe with them that weepe. Rom 12.

The 5. Reason.

Innocentius 3. and some others , doe call the Responce. *Lamentum penitentiæ*, the song of penance, or lamentation . Adding further, that it should be song, with a dolefull and lamentable voice , to signifie the effect of the preaching of S Iohn. For euen as by the Epistle, is represented the preaching & doctrin, of S.Iohn Baptist: euen so this song of lamentation signifieth , that S. Iohn preached no other thinge then pennance, saying. *Penitentiam agite* &c. Doe pennance , for the kingdom of heauen is at hand Mat. 3.

The 6. Reason.

To conclude, this Graduall or Responce, is nothing else, but a briefe spirituall song, composed of two or three verses at the most, commonly taken out of the psalmes of Dauid. As for example , that of the 17. Sunday after Trinitie sunday , is composed of two litle verses, taken out of the 32. psal. *Beata est gens cuius est dominus Deus eorum* &c. Blessed is the people,who haue our Lord for their God: and B. is the people whom our Lord hath chosen
for

for his inheritance. The heauens haue bene eſtabliſhed by the word of our Lord : and all the power of thē, by the breath of his mouth. Pſal 32.

Of the Gradual, Proſe, Tract, &c. Walfridus lib. de reb. Eccleſ cap. 22. Rupertus l. . . de diuin. Offic.cap. 34. Radulphus de Can. Obſer. prop. 2. Rabanus l. 2. de inſtit. Cler. cap 15. Iſidor. l. 6. Ety. c. 29. & l. 1. de eccleſ, Offic. c. 18. and others, doe make both ample and euident teſtimonie.

CHAP. XXXII.

Of the Alleluia, and of ſundrie reaſons concerning the ſame.

The 1. Reaſon.

T He Alleluia is immediatlie ſong after the Gradual, to witte, the ſong of ioye and of mirth, after the ſong of Penance and mourning : to expreſſe thereby, the great conſolation, which is layde vp for thoſe, which lament and mourne in this life: According to the ſaying of our Sauiour. Bleſſed are they that mourne, for they ſhall be comforted. Mat. 5.

The 2. Reaſon.

This worde Alleluia, hath a double ſignification. the one litterall, and common to all: the

other

other myſtical, & proper to diuines. Firſt therfore, to vnderſtand what it ſignifyeth literally,
we muſt know , that Alleluia is compoſed of
two Hebrewe wordes, *Alelu* , which ſignifieth in Latine, *Laudare*, in Engliſh praiſe yee,
and of *iah*, which is one of the ten Hebrewe
names belonging to God, and ſignifyeth in
Latine *Dominum* , Lord. So that the whole
worde, is as much to ſaye as, Prayſe yee our
Lord.

The 3. Reaſon.

The myſticall, or ſpirituall ſence thereof, is
diuers; According to ſome, Alleluia ſoundeth
as much , as ſpirituall or endles ioy: and in
this ſence , is as much, as if the Prieſt ſhould
cry vnto the people, with theſe wordes, Spiritual ioy, ſpirituall ioy. Or if we apply it to the
latter word, to wit, Endles or perpetuall, then
it ſignifyeth as much, as if he ſhould encou-
courage them, with theſe wordes, Endles ioy,
perpetual ioy.

The 4. Reaſon.

According to ſome others, it may be referred, to the ioye of thoſe, which reioyced in
the glorious miracles, of Chriſt our Lord: for
then did all the people, in ioyfull wiſe, ſing
foorth this Alleluia, when ſeeing thoſe miracles, they all gaue glorie to Almightie God,
and reioyced in thoſe thinges, which were
moſt glorioufflie, and moſt miraculouflie done
by

by him, saying. *Quia vidimus mirabilia hodie.*
Luc 5.26. For we haue seene maruelous thinges to day . As also when the seauentie two
returned with ioy saying. Lord the diuels also,
are subiect to vs in thy name. Luc.10.17.

The 5. Reafon.

That this Alleluia , is sometimes twice repeated, is to signifie a double ioy of the bles-
fed Saintes ; one of their spirit , an other of
their flesh : one of their soules, an other of
their bodies. Of the first ioy the royal prophet
Dauid sayth. *Exultabunt sancti* &c. The saints
shall reioyce in glorie, psal. 140. Of the second. *Fulgebunt iusti, tanquam sol in regno Patris.* The iust shal shine like the sunne , in the
kingdome of their Father. Mat.

The 6. Reafon.

The vse , aud custome of this worde , first
came from the Angels, and from certaine holie Prophets. And S. Iohn in his Apocalips,
reciteth, that he hearde the voice , of the heauenlie armie , as the voice of many waters, &
of great thunders, saying *Amen*, and *Alleluia*:
foure times *Alleluia*, and once *Amen*. Wherfore the church hath thought good , to retaine these wordes in earth, & to pronounce
them in the Masse , by the mouth of the
priest, as they are pronounced in heauen , by
the holie Angells.

The

The 7. Reaſon.

And therfore is it left in an vnknowen language, to denote, that we may rather ſignifie obſcurelie, then any way perfectlie expreſſe, the greatnes of the ioyes, which our Lord hath promiſed, to all that loue him.

The 8. Reaſon.

Another reaſon, why the Church retaineth this, and other like woordes, vninterpreted vnto vs, is, becauſe of the greate difficultie that there is, well and truly to tranſlate them, being of ſuch vertu and enegie, that other languages, want proper wordes, ſufficientlie to expreſſe them: & for this cauſe it is much better, to leaue them as they are, then to extenuat their force, by a ſtrange interpretation. And S. Aug. in his booke, *De doctrina chriſtiana.* cap 11. giueth this reaſon ſaying. that in holy writinges, many Hebrue woordes, are lefte without interpretation, becauſe of a certaine ſanctitie that is comprehended, vnder the very wordes them ſelues.

Alleluia, confirmed by miracle.

Finallie, this Alleluia, our Apoſtle S. Aug. vſed, when he firſt entred into our country, to côuert the ſame, as witneſſeth S. Bedel 1. c. 25. whoſe prayer was in this wiſe. We beſeeche thee o Lord for thy great mercie ſake, that thy furie and thine anger, may be taken from this cittie (to wit, Canterbury in Kent) & from

thy

thy holie houfe, becaufe we haue finned, Alleluia.

The fame Alleluia alfo , vfed S. German,
Bifhop of Auxerre in France, who being fent
by the Popes Holineffe, into our countrie, to
confute the error of the Pelagians, gaue commandement vnto certaine fouldiars, whom he
had placed in a valley (thorough which their
enemies refolued to paffe) that fo foone as
they perceiued them comming, het fhould al
foorthwith crie out, as they head him crie.
The bleffed Bifhop, fuddainly iffuing ou before the enemie , cryed out three feuerall
times, Alleluia, and all the reft of the foldiars,
cryed out a loud, the fame with him. Wherewith the enemies were fo affrighted and ama-
zed, that they though, not onely the hilles, but
alfo heauen it felfe, to crie out and fight a-
gainft them. Whereupon they fled with great
feare, and manie of them were drowned in
the riuer, which they were to paffe And fo
the fouldiers that were with the B. Bifhop,
obtained the victorie without any battaile, only by the terrour which God ftrooke vnto the,
by the found and eccho of Alleluia. Bed. lib. 1.
cap. 20.

CHAP.

C H A P. XXXIII.

Of the Prose. And of sundry reasons concerning the same.

The 1. Reason.

THe Prose is commonly tak n, for an ec-
clesiaticall prayer, contayning the pray-
ses of almighty God, of the B Virgin, and of
the glorious Saints and followeth betwixt
the Epistle, and the Gospell.

The 2. Reason.

The first inuention therof, is attributed to
Nocherus, Abbot of S. Gaule in Swisse, afterwards elected bishop of Liege. Durandus
li. 4. cap. 22 de ritibus Ecclesiæ. And Pope
Nicolas the first of that name, greately moued with the deuotion of this holy man, as
also with the rithme, sound, and plesant me-
lodie of the song, permitted the vse thereof.
But amongst many, compoied also by others,
the Church of Rome, hath especially retayned in the holy Masse, four for their excellencie

The 3. Reason.

1. The first is. *Victimæ Paschalis laudis.*
The which is sayed vpon Easter day, in testi-
mony of the ioyfull resurrection of Iesus
Christ, and hankfgiuing for the redemption
of mankind, wrought by his blessed and holy
death.

death. The author is fomewhat vncertaine, but vndoutedly a man endued with notable pietie and deuotion.

The 4. Reafon.

2. The fecond is; *Veni fanƈte Spiritus.* And is fung vpon Withfunday, to craue of the holy Ghoft, to fend from aboue, the beames of his celeftiall brightnes, to illuminate the mindes of thofe, which are couered with darknes. Robert King of France, furnamed. The great Cleark, compofed it: the Church hauing fince approued it, and fung it vniuerfally thoroughout all the partes of chriftendome. As witneffeth Paulus Aemilius, writing of his life

The 5. Reafon.

3. The third is, *Lauda Sion Saluatorem.* Compofed in praife of the moft B Sacrament by S Thomas of Aquin, admirable for his learning to the whole worlde, which was rather diuinly infufed into him, then ether attained vnto by nature, trauaile, or labour of ftudie. Who treated fo fublimely of the holy Euchariſt, as neuer any fince did more fet foorth, & illuftrate the fame: fo that God feemeth purpofely, to haue chofen this great and learned Doƈtor, for a conuenient remedy againſt the heretiques of our times.

The 6. Reafon.

4. The fourth is, *Dies illa, dies iræ.* And this
is

is ſaid in the holie Maſſe, for the ſoules departed. The Canticle is verye lamentable , and
the diſcourſeful of Chriſtian contemplation,
touching the apprehenſion and feare , of the
day of generall iudgment: and was compoſed
by a noble, famous, and religious Cardinall.

CHAP. XXXIV.

Of the Tract . And of ſundrie reaſons concerning the ſame.

The 1. Reaſon.

THe Tract, is ſo called, of this Latin word
Tractus, à trahendo, bycauſe (ſaith Durā-
dus, li.4 cap 41 num.1)it is ſung *tractim*, and
as with a trayling of the voyce: as thoſe may
eaſilie diſcerne , who vnderſtand playneſong.

The 2. Reaſon.

This Tract, is a ſpirituall ſonge compoſed of ſundrie verſes, vſuallie taken out of
the pſalmes of Dauid , and ſometimes out
of certaine other places, of the holy Scripture ; as that vpon the feaſt of Saint Pee-
ters chayre. *Tu es Petrus & ſuper hanc pe-
tram edificabo eccleſiam meam* . Matth. 16.
And ſometimes alſo , compoſed by the
Church , conformable to the holie Scripture , as *Gaude Maria Virgo* , *cunctas he-*
reſes

refes fola interremitt: in vniuerfo mundo. Off B.
Virg.

The 3 Reafon.

Next it is to be noted, that this Tract, is alwayes foung, either after the Alleluia, or fometimes onelie in the fteede thereof. And further, from Septuagefima till Eafter, the Alleluia, which is a fong of iubilation, alltogether ceafeth, both in the Maffe, and alfo in the Canonicall howers; The reafon wherof is, for that by the tyme of Septuagefima, the Church would reprefent vnto vs, the miferable eftate of mans nature liuing, in this wretched world, and therefore ceafeth to fing the fong of ioye, and onelie fingeth the fong of fadneffe and forrow. Alfo to fignifie, the difference betwixt our eftate, and the eftate of the bleffed foules in heauen, whoe fing perpetuallie, without ceafing or intermiffion, this ioyfull fong of Alleluia: whereas we, who liue in this vale of miferie, muft whilft we remayne heere, alwayes intermixe our ioy, with pennance and mourning.

The 4. Reafon.

It likewife fignifieth, the teares and groanes of Chrifts Church, for her finnes, for the prolonging of her felicitie, and for the paynes and afflictions, which fhee endureth, whilft fhee liueth in this world: which caufeth the holie Prophett, in her perfon to fay,

H ij

Hei mihi, quia incolatus meus prolongatus eſt, multum incola fuit anima mea. Pſal. 219. And for this reaſon, ſhee is often compared in holie Scripture , to a Turtle , as Cant. the 2. Wherupon S.Bernard. hom. 59 in Cant. ſayeth , that the Turtle, is a bird. verie ſolitarie, who hauing once loſt her companion , will neuer after take anie other , but euermore abide ſolitarie, and often mourning vpon the toppe of a drye tree.

To applie the ſame to our preſent purpoſe, this Turtle,is the Church of God:her ſolitude, or place of mourning, is in the deſert of this world. Her companion and ſpouſe which he hath loſt, is our bleſſed Lord and Sauiour Ieſus, whome the Iewes haue killed and putt to death: Whoe being riſen againe , is aſcended into heauen , the Church often ſighing and mourning for his departure , and ſtill deſiring to ſee him agayne , and to be there on high in companie with him : And the drye tree, vpon the which ſhee often ſitteth , ſoe mourneſully groning and lamenting , is the holie Croſſe , whereon her dearlie beloued ſpouſe, was put to death.

To conclude, the firſt placing of the Proſe in the holie Maſſe, is attributed, to Teleſphorus, the 9. Pope after S. Peter. As teſtifieth Durandus, lib. 4. cap. 4. num. 1.

G   CHAP.

CHAP. XXXV.

Of the holie Gospell of our Lord Iesus-
Christ. And of sundrie worthie Cere-
monies which are vsed, both before &
after, the reading thereof.

IF I were to explicate vnto you all the mysteries of a solemne Masse, I should make
mention of many most worthie ceremonies,
which here of purpose, I doe omitt. Onlie I
will giue you by the way, a litle tast of some
of them, because they are so exceedinge mysterious, and so contenting and pleasing to
euery deuout and pious person, that loth I
am, wholie to omit them.

The 1. Ceremonie, and its signification.
The Epistle therfore being read, by the
Subdeacon, the Deacon disposing him selfe
to pronounce the Gospell, ascendeth to the
Altar, where the booke remayneth. The
booke remaining alwaies vpō the Altar: signifieth, that the Sacrifice instituted by our B.
Sauiour, is alwayes ioyned with the testament, which is the Gospel, and that the one,
shall neuer be without the other: for so longe
as the Sacrifice shall endure, the Gospell shall
be preached, and when the sacrifice shall be
abo-

aboliſhed, the Goſpel ſhal ceaſe to be announced: as we ſee it is at this day in Turkie, where, as there is no Sacrifice offered , ſo is there
no Goſpel preached.

The 2. Ceremonie, and its ſignification.
And therfore the Deacon being to pronounce the Goſpel. aſcendeth and taketh the
booke from the Altar : to ſignifie , that the
place ordained of God to keepe the holie
ſcripture, is the Catholique Church : as alſo
to ſignifie, that all true and wholſome interpretation of holie ſcripture, ought to be taken
from the warrant and authoritie, of the ſame
Church.

The 3. Ceremonie, and its ſignification.
Hauing taken the booke from the Altar,
before he goe to reade the Goſpell , he reue-
rentlie proſtrateth him ſelfe on his knee before the Prieſt , demanding his benediction:
to ſhew that none ought to intrude him ſelfe,
nor to take vpon him, the office or charge of
preaching, vnles he be firſt lawfullie called,
and ſent therto. Heb. 5. Rom. 10.

The 4. Ceremonie, and its ſignification.
At the taking of the booke, the Deacon kiſſeth the right hand of the Prieſt , and this for
two cauſes. Firſt, to ſignifie , that he preacheth not his owne, but the doctrine of Chriſt
(whom in this place the Prieſt repreſenteth.)
And next, that although he preach the word
neuer

neuer fo trulie, or with neuer fo great zeale, yet that the gift of conuerting foules, dooth wholy proceed from the grace of God.

The 5. Ceremonie, and its fignification.

At the reading of the Gofpell, two Accolytes goe before the Deacon, with two burning lightes : to fignifie, that the affiftants, ought fpeciallie then, to haue their hartes enflamed, in the defire and meditation, of thofe heauenlie thinges, which are conteyned in the gofpell of Chrift. The couftome of lightes, is moft ancient by the teftimonie of S. Hierome aduerf. Vigil: & the caufes are plainelie deduced, out of S. Ifodore cap. Cleros §. acolith, dift. 22.

The 6. Ceremonie, and its fignification.

By this that the two Acolites doe goe before (the Deacon, who is to reade the gofpell carying wax lightes and incenfe:) is fignified, that Chrift fent before him his Difciples, by two and two, into euerie cittie where he was to goe, carying with them, the fhining light of miracles, and the fweete odour of vertues. Luc. 10.

The 7. Ceremonie, and its fignification.

The Deacon lifteth vp his voice on highe, in reading and announcinge the gofpell of Chrift, according to that of the prophet. Afcend thou vpon a high mountaine, who doft euangelife to Sion, lift vpp thy voice in fortitude

tude &c. Eſay cap 40. And our Lord ſayeth in
the goſpell. That which I ſay to you in the
darke, tel yee in the light: and that which you
heare in the eare, preach yee vpon the toppes
of the houſes. Mat. 10

These woorthly pious, and ſacred Ceremonies, are ſeene and performed, when highe
Maſſe is celebrated, but becauſe my purpoſe
is, to treate but brieflie of thoſe ceremonies,
which are vſuallie to bee ſeene in euerie
low and daylie Maſſe, I will therfore returne
to ſpeake of them.

The 8. Ceremonie, and its ſignification.

The Alleluia therfore, or Tract being read,
the Prieſt paſſeth to the midſt of the Altar,
where inclining him ſelfe, and ioyning together his handes, he ſecretly repeateth, the
prayer following. *Munda cor meum & labia
mea omnipotens Deus* &c. Cleanſe my hart and
my lippes, o omnipotent God, who cleanſedſt
the lippes of the prophet Eſay with fire: and
ſo by thy free grace vouchſafe to cleanſe me,
that I may worthely announce thy holie goſpell, thorough Chriſt our Lord, Amen.

The 9. Ceremonie, and its ſignification.

In the meane time, the Clarke or Miniſter,
remoueth the booke, to the left hand of
the Altar; ſignifyng thereby, that the Goſpell, which was firſt preached to the Iewes
(who were on the right hand) was for their
G 3   incre-

incredulitie , transferred from them to the
people of the Gentils: a mysterie sundrie times represented in the holie Masse , as hath
before bene mentioned.

The 10. Ceremonie, and its signification.
This done, the priest tourneth him to the
booke, and all the people rise vp : whereby
two seueral thinges are signified, The one the
corruptnes of our nature , lyinge on the
ground, like vnto bruit beastes , and wallow-
ing in the vncleanes and ordure of our sinnes:
The other , the virtue of the gospell of Iesus
Christ, which raiseth vs vp to newnes of life,
if we receiue the same with fruit,and worthelie expresse it in our liues.

Againe, the rising vpp of the people at the
reading of the Gospell, dooth signifie : that
they shew them selues readie, for the faith of
Christ, and profession of his Gospell , to giue
their liues, and to fight euen vnto the death,
in defence of the same: remembring the wordes which our Lord him selfe spake , saying.
He that hath not a sword, let him sell his
coate and buy it.

The 11. Ceremonie, and its signification.
Before the beginning of the Gospell, he sa-
luteth all the assistants, praying that our Lord
may be with them: which he doth, to render
them more attentiue , to harken to the word
of almightie God. For euen as to the sto-
macho

macho, which receaueth corporall fonde, nothinge is profitable, if it be ill diſpoſed: ſo likewiſe, vnleſſe the heartes of the aſſiſtants be
well diſpoſed and prepared, to receiue the
word of almightie God (which is the foode
of the ſoule) litle will it auayle them, though
it be announced vnto them.

Dominus vobiſcum.

Our Lord be with you. The wordes of this
ſaluation are. Our Lord be with you. As if
he ſhould ſay, I beſeeche our Lord, to ſend his
grace into your hartes, that you may be made
attentiue, and worthie hearers of his ſacred
word, which, as the Apoſtle witneſſeth, is a-
ble to ſaue their ſoules.

Et cum ſpiritu tuo.

And with thy ſpirit. Then the aſiſtãts make
anſwere, praying that our Lord may be with
his ſpirit, that is; that with the ſpirit of man,
the ſpirit of God may be preſent, to direct &
guide him, to the end that he may both faithfullie recite the ſacred goſpell, to the health
and ſaluation, of all that are aſſembled to
heare the ſame: and alſo him ſe'fe expreſſe in
true holines of life, that which he preacheth
vnto others.

Sequentia ſancti Euangelij.

The ſequence of the holie Goſpell. This
done, the prieſt ſayeth. *Sequentia ſancti Euã-
gelij* &c. Thus followeth the holie goſpell, of

G 4   ſuch

fuch or fuch an Euangelift. As touching the
word Euangil, or Gofpell, it is a word which
we retayne of the Greekes, as manie others,
and properlie fignifieth , good and ioyfull
tydings, for what better tidinges can there be
then thefe? Doe penance, for the kingdome
of heauen is at hand. Mat. 3. and, All powre
is giuen me both in heauen and earth. Matt.
18. 14. With diuerfe other thinges, which
are read in the gofpell, of the Diuinitie, and
Natiuitie, of the Sonne of God: of his miracles , preaching, paffion, refurrection, afcen-
tion, and of the faluation and glorification of
his elect.

   Where alfo note, that the name of the E-
uangelift is allwayes expreffed, to the ende,
that the people may giue the more credit, as
vnto the gofpell, penned and written, by one
of the fecretaries of our Sauiour Iefus , and
receaued in the Church , to which appar-
tayneth, the authoritie and prerogatiue, to
difcerne the canonicall Scriptures , and their
fence, if by any aduerfarie, they fhould be called in queftion.

Gloria tibi Domine.

   Glorie be vnto thee o Lord. When he hath
thus taught them, out of what place of fcripture, the gofpell for the day is taken, prefentlie
al the people, hearing the name of the gofpel,
and making reuerence towardes the Altar,
                                        with

with ioyfull acclamation, do anſwere ſaying.
Gloria tibi Domine Glory be vnto thee o Lord.
Giuinge thankes vnto God , who hath made
them worthie partakers of the goſpell of
Chriſt . As it is written in the Actes of the A-
poſtles,that al the peoople glorified our Lord,
for that he had ſent vnto them,the woorde of
ſaiuation,ſaying. God then to the Gentils alſo
hath giuen repentance vnto life. Act. 11. 18.

The 11.*Ceremonie,and its ſignification.*
In pronouncing the wordes aforeſaid , the
Prieſt maketh the ſigne of the Croſſe , vpon
the booke , and vpon him ſelfe. Vpon the
booke, to ſignifie , that it containeth the miſteries of our redemption. Vpon him ſelfe, to
ſignifie, that he is an inſtrument of Chriſt Ieſus, and of him crucified, & that this ſacrifice,
doth repreſent vnto vs , his death and paſſion.

The 12. *Ceremonie, and its ſignification.*
The people likewiſe, do make the ſigne of
the Croſſe , in three places. Vpon their fore-
heades vpon their mouthes, and vpon their
breaſts. Vpon their foreheades (which is the
moſt conſpicuous place of all the bodie:) to
ſhew that they are not aſhamed of the goſpel
of Chriſt. Vpon their lips, to ſhew that they
are allwayes ready, reſolutlie and conſtantlie,
to confeſſe their faithe , if at any time God
ſha'l p'eaſe to call them thereunto . Vpon
their breaſts , to declare that they do ſtedfaſtlie

lie beleeue in hart , that which they confeffe
with their mouthes.

The 13. *Ceremonie, and its fignification.*

The Prieft after the reading of the gofpell,
faith. *Per Euangelica dicta,* &c. By the euã-
gelicall fayinges, let our finnes be forgiuen vs.
And then he kiffeth the booke , not clo'ed,
but open: to fignifie, that the meanes to come
to the vnderftanding of Gods word, is cleerelie manifefted to the Paftors of the Church.
And further to fignifie, that it is the booke of
Chrift crucified, whom the Apoftle affirmeth
to be our reconciliation , and the maker of
our peace and attonement , which is·aptlye
fignified by the kiffe, As alfo to fhew, that he
preacheth the gofpel , of true loue and Charitie for the gayning of foules , and not for
lucre, and temporall profit.

Laus tibi Chrifte.

Praife be to thee ô Chrift. The gofpel ended,
all the people make anfwer faying. Praife be
to thee o Chrift , making the figne of the
Croffe as before, on their forehead , mouth ,
and breaft, to the end , that the wicked fer-
pent, fhould by no meanes, hinder their confidence and confeffion , or dare to breake
open the feale of their hartes , wherein the
word of God is fowne. Alfo , to arme them
felues againft his malice, who would not that
they fhould reape any profit, by the word of
God

God. As is plainly expreſſed in the parable of the ſeede, where it is ſaid, that the foules of the ayre, came and deuoured one part of the ſeede which was ſowne; by which foules are vnderſtood, the foule and vncleane ſpirits.

Miracles wrought by our Catholique Church-bookes.

To conclude, ſuch hath alwayes bene the authoritie of the holy goſpell, that not only the ſacred wordes, but alſo the verie bookes or papers, haue wrought ſundry ſtraunge and notable miracles. Gregorius Turonēſis in vitis patrum cap. 6. declareth, that the cittie of Auerna being on fyer, S. Gallus going into the Church, prayed a long time before the Altar of our Lord, and then riſing vpp, taking the booke of the goſpell, and opening it, offered himſelfe to goe againſt the fier, and ſodainlie the flames were extinguiſhed, in ſuch ſort, that there did not ſo much, as the verie ſparkes remayne.

Saint Macian, when the flames of fier approched neere vnto the Church of S. Anaſtaſius, taking into his handes the holie goſpell, hee gott in through the tiles, and by his prayers and teares, preſerued it from burning.

Zonaras alſo teſtifieth, that the Ruſſians in a great fier, finding the booke of the goſpell ſafe, and preſerued from burning, by the onlie motiue of this miracle, receaued and im-

G 6 bra-

braced the faith of Chrift.

Finallie the reading of the gofpell in the holie Maffe , all Liturgies doe teftifie to be very ancient. Alfo concilium Laodicenum. cap. 16. Carthaginenfe 4. can. 48. Valentinum. cap. 2. Clemens l. 2. conftit. Apoft. cap 16. Anaftafius writing to the bifhops of Germanie and Burgundie, and infinit others , whom here for breuitie fake, I doe omitt.

CHAP.   XXXVI.

Of the Symbole or Creede, and of fundrie myfteries conteined therin.

THe Symbole or Creede , imediatly pronounced after the Gofpell, figniSeth, the fruict which prefentlie enfued, after the preaching of our Lord and his Apoftles. And therfore alfo is it prefentlie pronounced after the gofpell, that by the Gofpell, we may beleeue with the harte vnto righteoufnes, and by the Creede, wee may confeffe with our mouthes vnto faluation, as it is written . *Corde creditur ad iuftitiam, ore autem fit confeffio ad falutem.* With the hart we beleeue vnto iuftice , but with the mouth, confeffion is made to faluation. Rom. 10. cap. 10.

Of the etymologie of the world Symbole.

To vnderftand the Etymologie , and meaning of this word Symbole, we muft note
that

that it is a greeke worde, and ſignifieth diuers
thinges. Sometimes it is taken for a marke or
ſeale wherewith a thing is marked or ſealed.
Sometymes againe, it is taken for a watchword, which a Captayne giueth to his ſol-
diers, whereby they may know one an other,
and the better preſerue them ſelues, from
being ſurpriſed by their enimies, ſoe that if
they ſhold chance to meete any one of whom
they doubted, being asked the Symbole or
watchword, he ſhould be bewrayed whether
he were their friend or foe.

In this preſent place, it is taken for a briefe
forme, or rule of Chriſtian fayth, compoſed
of diuerſe & ſundry ſentences, called Articles,
much like vnto ſoe manie ſinewes or ioyntes,
binding and tying togeather, all the parts of
the bodie; Wherefore verie fittlie may this
ſummarye of the Chriſtian fayth, be called by
this name of Symbole, according to all theſe
ſignifications.

For firſt in verye deede, it is a true marke,
or ſeale, whereby to know and diſtinguiſh, a
Catholike, from an Hereticke: for neuer was
there Hereticke, which did not denye ſome
parte or other of the Creede.

Secondly it may wel be taken for a watchword, giuen to the faithful, whereby to know
one an other, and ſo to keepe them ſelues, frō
the incurſion of their enimies.

And thirdlie, as in this place, for a briefe
forme,

forme, or rule, of our Chriſtian faithe, becauſe
it comprehendeth in ſo ſhort, and compen-
dious a manner, the ſomme of all that, which
were are to beleeue. Durand. l.4.c.25.

Three ſimboles, or Creedes, in the
Catholique Church.

In the Catholike Church, we haue three
Symboles or Creeds. The firſt is, that of the
Apoſtles, which all good Chriſtians ought
to learne by hart, and to ſay it, both morning and euening, for it chaſeth away the diuells, who lye in wayte, both day and night,
to deuoure vs.

The ſecond is, that of the councell of Nice,
which is vſuallie ſayd in the Maſſe, after the
goſpell.

And the third is, that of S. Athanaſius,
which is ſung at Prime vpon all Sundayes.
Both which latter, are no additions to the
former, but expoſitions, or more playne de-
clarations thereof.

The reaſon why the Church admitted theſe
two Creedes, beſides that of the Apoſtles,
was, for that the Heretikes, receiuing the firſt
according to the wordes, or letter, did not
receiue it according to the ſenſe, and meaning of the Cathol ke Church. And for that
alſo the Arrians, and other Heretikes, con-
ſtrued the ſame ſoe confuſedlie, that it was
hard to diſcerne the Catholikes, from the
Here-

Heretikes any waye by the ſame.

In which caſe, the Church was conſtray-ned to putt to her helping hand, adding the two latter as an expoſition, or playner decla-ration of the former, and hath euer ſince, ſer-ued to ſingular good purpoſe, for the conui-ction of ſeuerall hereſies and heretikes, which haue ſprung vp in ſundry times, and vpon ſundrie occaſions.

The Symbole of the concel of Nice, was compoſed vnder Pope Siluester (Plat. in vita Siluestri) in the preſence of the great and moſt religious Emperour Conſtantine, by 318. Biſhops aſſembled frõ all partes of the world, and kept at his expences: whereof many had their right eyes put out, and their right hands cutt off for the defence of the fayth, and Chriſtian religion, in the precedent perſecu-tions, as teſtifieth Nicephorus lib. 8. cap. 1. He honored them with preſents condigne to their eſtates, and royallie feaſted them at his table, cauſing the principall of them, to ſett cloſe vnto him ſelfe, before he would licence them to depart to their Churches: kiſſing alſo their wounds, when he diſmiſſed them. Nau-cler. vol. 2. gener. 11.

This Symbole was made, expreſſelye to condemne the blaſphemie of Arrius, mayn-tayning againſt the doctrine of the Church, the inequalitie of the three diuine perſons of the holy Trinity. Socrat. lib. 4. Eccl. hiſt. c. 31.

By

By the order of Pope Marke fucceffor of S. Syluefter the clergie and people, beganne to fing it with high voyce in the church, for that then the Emperors of the world', affifted and conftantlie defended the Catholicke fayth: It was alfo approued in the firft councell' of Conftantinople but 56. yeares after that of Nice. by 150. Bifhops, affembled vnder the Emperors Gracian, and Theodofius, the elder. See Plat. in vita Marci.

The Symbole of the holie Father Athanafius, was compofed by him againft the aforefaid Arrians, when by their audacious purfuite, they exilled him to Treuers, where he laboured by all meanes, to conferue the faith in his former puritie. Naucler. vol. 2. gener. 13.

The Creed of the Nicene counfell, and which is vfuallie fung in the holie Maffe, conteyneth (like as that of the Apoftles) to the number of 12. Articles: which are thefe that follow.

Credo.

I beleeue. The firft article of this Creede is, to beleeue (to witt) in God : and is to be oppofed againft the ignorance of all Atheifts, & of al fuch, as foolifhlie fay in their hartes, there is no God Pfalm. 13.

In.

In. And heere note, that there is a difference in beleefe. For to beleeue God, is to beleeue

leeue onelie that God is , but to beleeue in
God, is, in beleefe to loue him , to worſhipp
him, and to ſerue him as God: and this is perfectlie to beleeue in God.

Vnum Deum.

One God. For as much as manie heathen
people, doe adore and worſhipp, diuers vayne
things, in ſteede of God, calling them their
Gods, therefore to condemne this error , and
to exclude all pluralitie of Gods , the Creede
of the Maſſe, hath adioyned this word *Vnum.*
One, the more playnelie to explicate the former, which is as much as to ſay . I beleeue in
one onelie God, and not in more.

Patrem omnipotentem.

The Father almighty Which wordes, ought
to be of moſt ſingular comfort vnto vs : for
as he is a Father, he muſt needes wiſh al good
things vnto his children . And in that he is
allmightie , he is likewiſe able to helpe them
in all thinges.

Factorem Cœli.

Maker of heauen, By heauen, which is the
worke of his handes, is vnderſtood , all heauenlie creatures , as Angells , ſunne moone,
ſtarres, and other elemen:es.

Et terra.

And of earth. By earth, is vnderſtood , the
whole globe therof, incrediblie enriched, with
all that is requiſite, for the ornament and vſe
of

of all his earthlie and mortall creatures.

Vifibilium omnium & inuifibilium.

And of all thinges vifible and inuifible. To this firft Article of the Creede, the Church hath alfo adioyned thefe wordes, againft the impietie, and herefie of the Maniches, who peruerflie defended, that God onelie created thinges inuifible, and that the Diuell, pro-created the thinges which are vifible, as wit-neffeth. Niceph.l.6. ecclef. hift. cap. 31. & 32. Wherefore to exclude this error, wee ac-knowledg in the Maffe, that God is the maker of all thinges, both vifible and inuifible.

Et in vnum.

And in one. For as much, as manie tooke vpon them, to be called Chrift, and would needes be foe named of the people, as Anti-chrift likewife fhall when he cometh, there-fore to exclude this error, and to fhew, that there is no trew Chrift but one, the Church hath likewife heere added this word Vnum, One; For as the Scripture foretelleth vs, many fhall fay, Loe heere Chrift, loe there, but ex-preffilie commandeth vs, not to beleeue thē.

Dominum.

Lord. And he therfore is called Lord, to beate downe the impietie of thofe, who doe hold him leffe then his Father, in power, and authoritie, yea and do make him, euen a fer-uant and fubieƈt vnto him, according to his

diui.

diuini:ie as Calluin, l 2. Inst. c. 17. num. 1. and
before him other Heretikes.

Iesum Christum.

Iesus Christ. With the name of Iesus,
which signifieth a Sauior, there is also imposed vpon him, the surname of Christ, which
name is a title of honor, common to diuers
estates and dignities, to wit, to Priests, Prophets, and Kinges. The office of priests, is, to
offer prayers and sacrifices to God, for the
sinnes of the people Of prophets, to foretell
thinges to come,to their singular confort. Of
kings,to raigne in foueranitie, and puissance
of gouernment: All which titles doe wonderfull well agree to our B. Sauiour. For hee was
ordayned a Priest, by God his Father for euer,
after the order of M. Ichisedech; Psalm. 109.
He was also a Prophett, for hee foretold the
secret councells of his Father vnto vs, concerning our saluation . He is also a king, foras-
much as by his prouidence, he doth accom-
plish the wonderfull endeauors and office
of a king , in the behalfe of his Church,
whose king and gouerner he shall be, to the
end of the world.

Filium Dei.

The sonne of God. Which wordes do euidentlie declare, that he is verie God. For as a
man and woman , can begett no child but
man, or woman, of the same substance , euen
ſo

ſo the Sonne of God, muſt needes be God, &
of the ſelfe ſame ſubſtance with God.

Vnigenitum.

Onelie begottē. Where note that although
God hath graunted , vnto thoſe that beleeue
in him , to be his children and ſonnes , yet
this is to be vnderſtood , by grace , and ſpirituall adoption. But Ieſus Chriſt , is his onelie
naturall Sonne , ingendred of his owne ſubſtance, as S. Iohn the Euangeliſt , doth cleerlie teſtifie, Iohn 1.

Ex patre natum.

Borne of the Father. For aſmuch as this holie councel of Nice,was principaꝉlie gathered,
to repreſſe the hereſie of the Arrians, denying
that Chriſt was borne , and begotten of the
ſubſtance of God his Father , and equall vnto
him, as witneſſeth 5. Aug lib 1 de Trinit.c.7.
they were therefore condemned by theſe verie wordes , and the contrarie was there ex-
preſſelie concluded againſt them.

Ante omnia ſacula.

Before all worldes. And for the more manifeſt declaration, that he is coeternal with God
his Father, there is added in this Creed, that he
was borne of him, before all worlds. Tꞧue indeed it is , that the manner is inexplicable, as
S. Cyp. ſaith *in explic. ſimbuli*, and therfore we
ought ſimply to beleeue, and deuoutlie to reuerence , this his ineffable generation . For
who

who will enquire after that which can not be found? Of whom ſhall we learne it? of the earth? It was not ſubſiſting. Of the ſea? It was not liquified. Of heauen? It was not eleuated. Of the ſunne? Of the Moone? Of the ſtarres? They were not as yet created. Of the Angels? He was ingēdred before they had their being. Brieflie therefore, we will conclude with S. Baſill, ſaying, we muſt not enquire after that which hath alwaies bin, of that which hath not allwaies bin.

Deum, de Deo.

God, of God. Alſo, where as theſe Heretikes ſayed, that he was not God of God his Father, but onelie man, of his mother, therefore the holie Fathers, aſſembled in this councell, cō-cluded, that he was God of God, and that he did no whit diminiſh his diuine nature, by reaſon of his incarnation in the B. virgin.

Lumen, de lumine.

Light of light. Theſe holie and venerable Fathers, to make this verisie more apparant, declared the ſame by an apt ſimilitude, to wit, that the Sōne of God, was borne of his Father, euen as the light, produceth and caſteth forth light of it ſelfe, without any manner of dimi-nution of its owne ſubſtance, and can be no more diuided from the Father, then the ſunne and the ſplendor therof, can naturallie be ſe-parated or diuided a ſunder.

Deum

Deum verum, de Deo vero.

Very God, of very God. The same Catholique Church, further to confound , the errour
of the Arrians and Euomians, denying that
he was verie God by naturall propertie , but
onelie by grace, or communication of name,
somtimes giuen vnto them , whom the Psal-
mist calleth Gods, for the rarenes of their vertues (as psalme 81.) declared, that he was verie
God of verie God, that is to say, so verily God,
as God the father was God , and truly sprang
and issued out of him.

Genitum, non factum.

Begotten, not made. And whereas some of
these Heretikes confessed , that Christ was
indeed of the Father, but yet that he was lesse
then the Father, and not of the same , but of
an other substance then the Father was: therfore, to confound this error, there was inser-
ted into this Creede, these wordes , begotten
not made: But with what similitude , may a
mortall man, be able to expresse this diuine
generation ? Or what comparison can be made; betwixt things created, and which haue a
beginning, and things increated , and which
haue no begining ? S. Ireneus , doth hould
them for worse then madde , who enforce
them selues, to conceiue the same by humane
reason, li. 3. aduers. hæres. Valent. cap. 48. And
S. Hilarie , being not able to comprehend it,

comforteth him selfe with this , that the Angells doe not know it. lib.2.de Trinitate.

Consubstantialem Patri.

Consubstantiall to the Father . To prooue
more cleerlie, that the Sonne of God , was
nothing inferior to the Father, this holie con-
cell , deuised againſt thoſe Hereſickes , this
word Consubstantiall, to prooue & confirme,
his coequalitie with the Father . This alſo
was moſt cleerlie pronounced , out of the
mouth of our Sauiour himſelfe vnto the Iewes, aſſuring them , that he who ſaw him,
ſaw the Father alſo. Iohn.10.

Per quem omnia facta sunt.

By whome all things are made. Alſo ſome
enimies there where, who ſayed, that the Father was the maker of all thinges, and not the
Sonne. But contrarie to this , the Church defended, that by the Sonne alſo , all thinges
were made, not that the Father did ayde him,
as an extrinſicall inſtrument to their produ-
ction, but as S. Iohn ſayth Io.1. That without
him nothing was made , noe not the world
nor the heauens them ſelues.

Qui propter nos homines.

Who for vs men. In theſe wordes , the
Church propoſeth vnto vs , the humane nature, which the Sonne of God , tooke vpon
him for our ſaluation : wherof he was ſo de-
ſirous, and ſo carefull , that he expreſlie deſcended

cended from heauen into earth ; to ſeeke out
the ſtrayd and wandering ſheepe Luc: the 19.
and by his bloud , to reconcile him to his Father. What other occaſion had he ſo to doe?
Take away the woundes , ſaith S. Aug. and
what neceſſitie is there of a Surgean.

Et propter noſtram ſalutem.

And for our ſaluation This alſo, was added
by the Church , for aſmuch as ſome there
were,who affirmed,that Chriſt became man,
not onelie to ſaue man , but alſo to ſaue the
Diuell, and all thoſe Angells , who fell from
heauen with him by plaine Apoſtacye . For
remedie and redreſſe of which error , the
Church added theſe wordes , Who for vs
men, and for our ſaluation.

Deſcendit de cælis.

Deſcended from heauen. The better to expres,the beneuolence of our bleſſed Sauiour,
towards mankind, it is ſayed , that he deſcended from heauen: not that he abandoned the
heauens, or that he had neuer bene in earth,
ſeeing that by his deuine eſſence, he filleth &
repleniſheth, both the one and the other, and
is in all places: but for that by taking human
nature,he was there by a new and miraculous
manner of being,to witt, by hypoſtaticall vnion and coniunction, of the diuinitie with the
humanitie, in one perſon, after which maner,
he had neuer bene in earth before.

Et

Et incarnatus est.

And was incarnate. In which wordes, the meanes of his descending is declared, to witt, by his incarnation . Who will not admire, saieth Pope Clement the sixt , that the same person remayned God, as he was from all eternitie, and became man, which he neuer was; he came to be borne in earth , whom the Angells adore in heauen. cap. 6. de pœn. & remis. in extra. communib.

De Spiritu sancto.

Of the holie Ghost. This article, doth confirme vs in the beleefe of the miraculous, and supernaturall operation, of the holie Ghost, by whose vertue , the matter was disposed, wherof the pretious bodie of Iesus Christ was organized and formed, to witt, of the most pure bloud , of the chast and holie Virgin his mother S. Marie. Luc. 1.

Ex Maria.

Of Marye. Some Heretickes there were, who sayed , that Christ brought with him a body from heauen , and that he tooke not his body of our Blessed Ladye: which is refuted by these wordes, saying Of Marye. Octauius (who in his time ruled all the world, and therefore of the Romans was reputed as a God) did consulte with a prophetesse , to knowe if in all the world , there was to be borne a greater then he: and in the same day,

H   wherin

wherin Chriſt was borne of the virgin Marie in Iudea, Sybilla ſaw a golden circle neere the ſunne, in which circle, a fayre virgin did ſitt, hauing a moſt beautifull child in her lap. which ſhe ſhewed to Octauius Cæſar, and did declare vnto him, that at that verie tyme, a more mightie king was borne then he.

Virgine.

A Virgin. Not onelie Mary, but of Mary a Virgin; wherein we acknowledge her perpetuall virginitie, to haue bin no more hurt by his conception, then it was by his natiuitie, her chaſt womb, being miraculouſlie countergarded with fecunditie, in ſuch ſort, that ſhee amongſt all others, obteyneth the title, of mother, and Virgin : which neuer was, nor euer ſhal be graunted, to any woman but to her ſelfe alone.

Et homo factus eſt.

And was made man. Agayne ſome Heretickes mantayned, that Chriſt had no ſoule, but that his Godhead, was vnited to his bodie, in ſteed of a ſoule : and ſo they inferred, that Chriſt was not man, becauſe man is compoſed of a bodie, and ſoule. To refute which error, the Creed of the Maſſe ſayeth, and was made man. For both theſe opinions are of like danger: to beleeue Chriſt to haue bin onlie God, and not man: or to haue beene onlie man, and not God.

Of

Of the genuflexion of the Prieſt, at the reciting thoſe Wordes.

Theſe wordes of the Creede, are in effect the ſame which are reade in that diuine goſpell of S. Iohn. viz. *Et verbum caro factum eſt.* And the word was made fleſh. Wordes trulie full of great maieſtie and reuerence, & therefore both the prieſt and the people , at the pronounciation of them , doe humblie bow downe, and incline to the grounde , in ſigne of thankes giuing for ſoe excellent a benefitt. It is recounted of a certaine perſon, who hearing theſe wordes recited, and making no reuerence thereat , the diuell gaue him a box on the eare, ſaying . If it were reade the worde was made diuell, all we diuels would neuer haue omitted to haue bowed our knees at the pronounciation of theſe wordes. Ludol. cap. 18. part. 1.

Crucifixus etiam.

Crucified alſo. After his miraculous, ſupernaturall, and incomprehenſible incarnation, mention is made of his deathe and paſſion, with the time, maner, and order of the ſame. Wherfore, euen as our firſt parents, did grieuouſlie offende by the wood , in eatinge of the fruit of the forbidden tree: euen ſo would our B. Sauiour, ſatisfie by the Croſſe , vpon the wood whereof, he hath borne our ſinnes in his owne body, and hath reſtored vs life by the fame meanes, by which death entred into all the worlde.

Pro nobis.

For vs. This punishment of the Crosse, was allwayes reputed for a death, the most ignominious and infamous, that could be deuised, as is testified in Deut. 12. And here on was Iesus Christ fastned for our sinnes. O profound wisedome of God, how much more easie is it, to admire such mysteries, then any way to explicate or vtter them with our wordes?

Sub Pontio Pilato.

Vnder Pontius Pilat. This Pilat, beinge gouernour of Iudea, vnder the Emperour Tyberius, and hauinge sundrie times, declared Iesus Christ to be innocent, of the false accusations which were imposed vpon him by the wicked Iewes, yet in the end, did abandon him, for feare to incurre the disgrace of Ceasar. But within a while after, this ambitious officer, hauinge for his owne aduancement, and to the oppression of the innocent partie, peruerted all order of iustice, and let loose the bridle to the popular insolencie, was him selfe ouer-whelmed, with so manie miseries, that in punishment of this wicked fact, he killed him selfe with his owne hands: much after the example of the traitor Iudas, who hanged him selfe, for hauing betrayed his innocent master. Euseb. Eccles.

Eccleſ. hiſt. lib.2.cap.2.

Paſſus.

Suffered. In this his ſufferinge, is comprehended all that, which he endured, to accompliſh the myſterie of our redemption, vnto
his death: whereunto he offered him ſelfe vo-
luntarilie and of his owne accord, to ſatisfie
the diuine iuſtice; and irreuocable decree of
his eternall Father: which could not otherwiſe be accompliſhed, but that the innocent, muſt dye for the nocent, the obedient,
for the diſobedient.

Et ſepultus eſt.

And was buried. Expreſſe mention is heere
made of his buriall, for an infallible argumēt,
and proofe of his paſſion. Which ſome, with
that execrable hereticke Baſilides, did denye,
maintayning that he came into the world in
a phantaſie, and that it was not he that was
crucified, but one named Simion, and that
therefore he was not to be adored. As is teſtified by Tertulian. *ae præſcrip.heret.*

Et reſurrexit.

And he roſe agayne. By this Article, is
declared, the glorious myſterie of our Lords
reſurrection, which poinct is ſo neceſſarie,
that all out fayth were otherwiſe meerelie in
vayne, as teſtifieth the Apoſtle 1.Theſſa. 4.
Neyther is there any one thing, which may
more comfort, and confirme our hope, then
H 3   to

to beleeue; that our head is rifen for our iuftification, as he was dead, for our tranfgreffion. No refurrection of anie perfon whatfoeuer, is to be compared to his, he being rayfed by his owne proper power, without any ayde or affiftance of others. We reade amongft otherexamples of holie Scripture 4 Reg. 13. that the bodie of him who was caft into the Sepulcher of Helias, was rayfed to life, but this came to paffe, by touching the bones of the holie prophet (for whofe fake God reftored life to that dead man) and not by the proper force of him that was deceafed, This therfore was onlie referued to our Lord Iefus Chrift, to returne from death to life, by the onlie power and vertu of him felfe.

Tertia die.

The third day. To the end we may beleeue, that this his death was true and not fayned, he was not refufcitated imediatlie, but remayned truly dead, vntill the third day after, which was a time more then fufficient, to make affured proofe, and to remoue away all dout & ambiguitie, of the truth of his death. Yet was he not in his fepulchre, the fpace of three whole and compleate dayes, but one day onlie entire, part of the day precedent, and part of the day fubfequent, which by the figure Synecdoche, are called three dayes and three nightes.

Secun-

Secundum Scripturas.

According to the Scriptures. This claufe, was neceffarilie annexed by the Fathers of the Church, for as much as at the beginning, it was verie harde, efpeciallie for me of groffe capacitie, and as yet not thoroughly inftru-cted in the Chriftian faith, to comprehend fo great a myfterie, as is the refurrection of the dead, which far furpaffed the lawes of nature: and therefore this was added, as an infallible argument, why we oughte to beleeue the fame.

Et afcendit ad cœlum.

And he afcended to heauen. Where the queftion may be demanded, how he afcended vp to heauen? True it is, that as God, he ne-uer was abfent from thence, but alwayes fil-led it, and all other places, with his diuinitie: but as man, he mounted thither in bodie and foule, leading with him captiuitie captiue, as the Apoftle faith, which he placed and fet in libertie, by his excellent victorie ouer death, the diuell, and hell it felfe. Ephef. 4.

Sedet ad dexteram Patris.

He fiteth at the right hand of the Father. In which wordes the holy fcripture doth acco-modate it felfe to our weake vndeftanding, vfing a metaphoricall fpeech, or locution, to inftruct vs that Iefus Chrift hath receaued of God his Father, all honor and aduancement

of glorie, in his humanitie: euē as we efteeme
here amongft men, the greateeft honor to be
done vnto thofe, to whom we giue the vpper
hand. And it was mofte expedient, that hee
fhould be moft highly exalted, who had foe
greatlie depreffed and humbled him felfe, as
to indure fo manifould diffamations, oppro-
bries, & iniurious intreatments for our fakes.

Et iterum venturus eſt.

And he is to come againe. Hauing made
mention of our Sauiours firft coming into the
world, to repaire the fall and ruine of man,
his fecond coming is next propofed, wherin
he fhall fit in iudgment, and manifeftlie declare to all the worlde, both his powre and
iuftice: rendring to euery one, according to
his deferts. And as his firft cominge was in
great meeknes, fo on the contrarie, fhall his
fecond comming, be in great maieftie and
glorie.

Iudicare viuos & mortuos.

To iudge both the quick and the dead. That
is to fay, the good, & the bad: the one to bliffe:
and perpetuall ioye, the other to woe, and e-
uerlafting paine. Wherein they fhall, both
the one and the other, perpetuallie abide, fo
longe as God, fhall be God, without intermiffion of ioy or paine.

Cuius regni non erit finis.

Of whofe kingdome there fhall be no end.
This

This is the kingdome, which as Daniel declared, to Nabuchodonoſor, and Balthaſar, kinges
of Babilon, ſhould neuer haue end. Dan. 2.7.
This is that kingdome, which the Angell for-
tould to the virgin Marie, ſhould euer endure.
Luc 1. This is that kingdome, prepared for
the bleſſed, from the begining of the worlde,
as teſtifieth. S. Mat. 25. This is that kingdome
into the which the good theefe (acknowledging his miſdeeds) deſired to enter. Luc 23.
This is that kingdome, wherof none can haue
part, vnles he be borne anew, and be without all blemiſhe and ſpot of ſinne Ioh. 3. This
is that kingdome, which is celeſtial, and heauenlie, not terrene and worldlie, as our Sauiour ſhewed vnto Pilat, when he had ſuſ-
pition, that he would make ſome attempt,
againſt the eſtate and Romane Empire. Iohn.
18. Finallie of this kingdome, there ſhall be
no end, for as much as then, al thinges ſhall
be perpetuallie eſtabliſhed, and ſhal neuer be
afterwards chaunged againe.

Et in Spiritum ſanctum.

And I beleeue in the holie Ghoſt. By the name
of holie Ghoſt, is expreſſed the third perſon
of the Ł Trinitie, who is alſo caled by diuers
other names, as Paraclet, Gift of God, liuelie
Fountaine, Fire, Charitie, ſpiritual Vnction, the
finger of the right hand of God, his promiſe
&c. *Ex hymno, Veni creator ſpiritus.* He is caled

Paraclet, which ſignifieth a Defender, an Aduocate, a Patron, an Interceſſor, a Teacher, and
a Comforter. He is caled the Gift of God, for
that he doth communicate, and impart freelie,
to euerie one as he pleaſeth, his gifts & graces. He is called, A liuelie fountaine, for that
he is the ſource and ſpringe, of all diuine and
celeſtial graces, which neuer drieth. He is
called, Fyre; for as much as he doth enkendle
our harts, in the loue of God, and doth warme them like fire. He is called Charitie, for
that he vniteth all the faithfull together, in
one and the ſelfe ſame hart, deſire, and affection. He is called, Spiritual vnction; for that
he ſheadeth forth vpon vs, his diuine graces,
in great aboundance. He is called, The finger
of God, for that God doth deſigne al his graces
by his operations. Laſtly he is called, the promiſe of the Father, for that Ieſus Chriſt, promiſed vnto his diſciples, that his Father would
ſend him vnto them, for their inſtruction and
conſolation, with aboundant infuſion of all
celeſtiall graces. Iohn. 14.

Dominum.

Lord. The third perſon of the Trinitie, is
here caled Lord, to the end that we acknowledge him for God, euery way coequal, with
the Father, and the Sonne: of the ſame might
eternitie, and infinit maieſtie.

Et

Et viuificantem.

And giuing life. Amongſt the effects and operations, which are peculiarlie appropriated vnto the holy Ghoſt, one is, to viuificate or giue life; For if he haue life in him ſelfe, as the Father and the Sonne haue, how ſhall he not giue life vnto others, ſeing it is the propertie of life, to giue life, as it is of light, to illuminat, of that which is hot, to giue and caſt foorth heate? If alſo the humane ſpirit, doth vegitat the bodie? how ſhall not the holie Ghoſt quicken the ſoule?

Qui ex Patre, Filioque procedit.

Who proceedeth from the Father, and the Sonne. By this article we are to beleeue, that the holie Ghoſt proceedeth eternallie, from the Father and the Sonne, as from the ſame beginninge and ſpiration. Which was added, to repreſſe the errors of the Greekes, whereof the heretique Neſtorius was the firſt author, as teſtifieth Theodoſ. lib. 4. eccleſ. hiſt. cap. 8. & 9. Denying that the holie Ghoſt proceeded from the Father and the Sonne. For the which he was condemned by the councell of Epheſus, reuerenced in the Church, as one of the four goſpels. And for the further confuſion of heretiques, and to the greater ioye and conſolation of all Catholiques, the ſaid Simbole was publiquely ſunge, three ſeuerall times of all that were preſent.

H 6 *Qui*

Qui cum Patre & Filio fimul adoratur
& conglorificatur.

Who with the Father and the Sonne.is together worſhiped & glorified. To repreſſe the
impiety of Macedonus the heretique , who
denied the holie Ghoſt to be God, houlding
him for a ſimple creature, and to be alltogether inequall to the Father and the Sonne (as
witneſſeth S. Aug. de Trinit. li. 1. cap 6.) the
Church hath propoſed him vnto vs to be a-
dored and glorified, together with them :
which doth plainlie argue, that he is God, becauſe that ſort and kind of adoration, pertay-
neth onlie to almightie God.

Qui locutus eſt per Prophetas.

Who hath ſpokē by the prophets. To auert
the people, from the falſe opinion of thoſe
which deſpiſed viſions , reuelations, and the
ſacred predictions of the holie prophets, as
lyes, dreames, and fables, the Church aſſu-
reth vs , that the holie Ghoſt hath ſpoken vnto vs by them, according to the teſtimonie of
Saint Peter. 2. 1. Inſtructing and teaching vs,
that prophecie, cometh not by the wil of mã,
but that ſuch men haue ſpoken vnto vs , as
they were inſpired by God him ſelfe.

Et vnam.

And one. There are four ſpeciall notes or
markes of the true church , gathered partlie
out of the Creed of the Apoſtles, and partlie
out

out of that of Conſtantinople. The firſt is, that ſhe is One. The ſecond, that ſhe is Holy. The third, that ſhe is Catholique. The fourth, that ſhe is Apoſtolique The firſt propertie therfore is, that ſhe is One, becauſe hir head is one, to whom ſhe is vnited. Hir ſpirit is one in which, as in one bodie, all are coupled and coapted which do belonge vnto hir. Hir preaching is one. Hir ceremonies are one. Hir end is one. And ſhee alone hath means to cõſerue this vnitie.

Sanctam.

Holie. For hir ſecond marke, ſhe is called holie. 1. By reaſon of hir head, which is Chriſt Ieſus him ſelfe, who is the holie of holies. 2. In reſpect of hir inſtructor, which is the Holie Ghoſt, whom Chriſt promiſed at his departure, to ſend vnto hir. Iohn. 14. 3 3. In reſpect of the holie Saintes which are in hir (according to our Creede) ſanctified by the ſame holie Ghoſt. 4. In reſpect of the vnitie of faith, and abſolute obedience, to one only chiefe & ſupreme paſtor, the biſhop of Rome, 5. In reſpect of the holie lawes and ordonances, wherwith ſhe is gouerned and directed, 6. In reſpect of the holines of the Sacramẽts, which are daylie diſpenced in hir, by the handes of hir paſtors. 7. And laſtlie, becauſe only in hir, and no way out of hir, can any one be ſanctified or made holie.

Catho-

Catholicam.

Catholique. For hir third marke, she is called Catholique, or vniuersall. 1. For the vniuersallitie of faith, which she teacheth al men alike to beleeue. 2. For the vniuersallitie of doctrine, whereby she instructeth, how to auoide vice and follow vertu. 3. For the vniuersallitie of truth, which she defineth in generall Councells. 4. For the vniuersallitie of nations, whom she calleth to the same faith, not excluding any. 5. For the vniuersallitie of times, because from the begining, to the ending, from Christ, to the consumation of the worlde, the Christian religion shall euer continue. So that the Church to be Catholique, is, to haue bene extant, in all places, & in all ages, which neuer heretique could say of his Church. Let them (saith Vinc. Lyr.) shew their errors to haue bene beleeued euerie where, allwayes, and of all, and then let them brag that they are Catholiques.

Et Apostolicam.

And Apostolique. This fourth marke of Apostolique, is also attributed to the Church. for that she is built vpon the immoueable rock, of the Doctrine of the Apostles, and hath had a perpetuall succession of lawfull pastors (without interruption) euer since their dayes, vnto this present. This marke, no heretique whatsoeuer, once dareth to chaleng, it being

being an absolute prerogatiue, only belōging to our Catholique Roman Church.

Ecclesiam.

Church. The worde. *Ecclesia*, is a Greeke word, and signifieth assembly, or cōuocation: and to beleeue the Church, is to beleeue that she is the lawfull assembly of the faithful, vniuersallie dispersed in the same profession of fayth, and diuine worship: hir faith including generallie, that which is requisit to the saluation of the beleeuers : to whom in manie things, it is sufficient simplie to beleeue (especiallie to the vnlearned) that which she beleeueth, without other exact knowledg of all particulars.

Why (In) *is here omitted.*

And note, that the proposition, In, putt in the precedent articles , is here omitted, and it it is simply sayd , I beleeue the Church , and not I beleeue in the Church, to discerne beetwixt the creatures , and the Creator of all things, in whom only we must beleeue , and not in any other.

Confiteor vnum Baptisma.

It is here sayd, I Confesse one Baptisme, for as much as it can not be reiterared , vnder the paines nominated in the holie decrees, *cap. rebaptizare de confec. dist* 4 & to the end that none may thinke him selfe able to amend the worke of the holie Ghost , Which also agreeth

greeth with naturall reaſon it ſelfe, according
whereunto, a man is borne but only once.

In remiſsionem peccatorum.

For the forgiuenes of ſinnes. Here enſueth
the admirable effect of this moſt wholſome
lotion. wherin al ſinne, be it originall , or ac-
tual is pardoned, quite extinct, and aboliſhed,
as if it had neuer at all bene committed, how
enormous and deteſtable ſoeuer it were, together with the paines due to the ſame: & there
is alſo geuen vs (and that in great aboundance) the infuſion of diuine graces , to render vs able, to all endeuors & offices, of Chriſtian pietie.

Et expecto reſurrectionem mortuorum.

And I expect the reſurrectiõ of the dead: For
the more aſſured eſtabliſhmeut of our fayth,
there is here ſet before vs, the reſurrection of
the dead, without the which we were of all
other creatures, the moſt wretched and miſerable, and al our hope planted in Ieſus Chriſt,
were vtterlie fruſtrate. Wherfore, this article
doth teach vs to beleeue , that the bodies of
all, both men and women , which euer haue
bene borne ſince the beginning of the world,
though they be rotten , burnt, eaten of wor-
mes, beaſts, or foules of the ayre, yet ſhall be
rayſed againe at the day of iudgement , and
be truly reunited vnto their ſoules.

                                                    Et

Et vitam venturi seculi.

And the life of the world to come. This is
the marke whereunto all the faithfull ought
to direct their defignes, and to prepofe vnto
them felues, as the hyer and recompence, of
all their labours. Without this, no man can
but iudge him felfe much more vnhappie and
accurfed, then the bruit beafts. Finallie if we
efteeme fo much, and hould fo deere this prefent life, which is fo ficle and fo fhort, that it
may rather be called a death then a life, in
what eftimation ought we to haue the life
that is eternall, voide of all miferie and replenifhed with all beatitude and perpetuall felicitie? Of which ioye our Lord of his mercie
make vs then pertakers, what fonowe foeuer
we fuffer in this world. Amen.

Of the figne of the Croße made at, *Vitam venturi seculi.*

The figne of the holie Croffe, is made at
the wordes, *Et vitam venturi secu i.* Leaft
hauing bene tould of the bliffe of the Saintes,
and of the ioyes of the life euerlafting, we
fhould deceaue our felues, by thinking to obtaine them without any trauel, whereas Chrift
him felte, did not enter into the kingdome of
his glorie, but by the ignominy of his Croffe.
For from the Church militant, vnto the triü-
phant, none can enter but by the Croffe, as
faith Ludolphus, *in vita Chrifti.*

Amen.

Amen.

For confirmation of that, which is contayned in this prefent Simbole, there is added for
conclufion, this woord. *Amen* , that is to fay,
in veritie, trulie, certainlie , or without doubt
we beleeue, that, which is contayned in the
precedent articles.

Of the kiffe of the Altar.

After this, bowing downe him felfe, he kiffeth the altar : teftifying by this ceremonie,
that he willinglie fubmitteth him felfe vnder
the Croffe of Chrift , and that from the bottom of his hart , he imbraceth the fame: con-
feffing with the Apoftle, that the miferies of
this life, are not worthie of the glorie, which
fhall be hereafter reuealed vnto vs.

Dominus vobifcum.

The Creed being ended , the Prieft turneth
to the people, faying. *Dominus vobifcum* Praying that our Lord be with them , that they
may make their profit of that , which was re.
peated and rehearfed, in the aforefayd articles.
And the people anfwere.

Et cum fpiritu tuo.

And with thy fpirit. To the end, that being
vnited together in the fame faith and religion, they may feele the effectes of their faluation . Amalaricus fayeth , that this falutation of the Prieft to the people , denoteth an
entrance, to an other office. And Gabriel Biel
fayth,

ſayth , that the Prieſt now ſaluteth the aſſiſtants, with *Dominus vobiſcum*, that God may be with them to receiue their oblations.

Oremus.

Hauing ſaid *Dominus vobiſcum*, next hē ſaith, Let vs pray. Becauſe, vnles our Lord be with vs, we can not pray to our ſoules health. And then he turneth him to the Altar; admoniſhing hereby , that now eſpecially , euerie one ſhould returne to him ſelfe, and diligentlie ſearch, and diſcuſſe his conſcience , that ſo he may offer vpp him ſelfe , an acceptable ſacrifice to Almightie God.

CHAP. XXXVII.

Of the Offertorie. And of the condicions of the Hoſt that is to be offered.

The 1. Reaſon.

FIrſt the Offertorie taketh its name , *A b offerendo*, Of offering; becauſe in this part of the Maſſe , the people are wont to make their temporal offeringes at the Altar. Which, in a ſolemne Maſſe , is moſt melodiouſlie ſoung , becauſe as the Apoſtle ſaith . Our Lord loueth a cheer full giuer . 2 Cor. 1. Becauſe alſo it is conuenient, that after the goſpel , there ſhould follow faith in hart.
praiſe

praiſe in mouth, and fruit in ,worke , as teſtifieth Innocentius tertius.

The 2. Reaſon.

Secondly,it is called the Offertorie,becauſe
at this time, the prieſt doth take into his handes , and maketh an oblation, of the Hoſtes
that are to be conſecrated . As alſo , becauſe
it is a moſt immediate preparation and diſpo-
ſition, to the holie Canon.

Of the condicions of the Hoſt.

As touchinge the condicions of the Hoſt
that is to be offered, ſundry notable thinges,
are ſignified thereby.

1. This bread is made of wheate : becauſe
Chriſt compared him ſelfe vnto wheate ; ſaying. Vnles the graine of wheate falling on the
ground doe die, it remaineth alone.

2. It is made in the forme or maner of monie: to ſignifie,that it is the ſame peny or reward, promiſed by our Lord in the goſpell,to
the labourers in the vyneard. Mat. 20. 9.

3. It is round: to put vs in minde, that God
is the Creator of all thinges , both in heauen
and earth, Alpha, and Omega, without begining or ending By which alſo it denoteth vnto vs, the diuinity of our B. Sauiour, whereby
he filleth the round worlde.

4. It is white: to repreſent vnto vs ,the moſt
pure fleaſh of our Lord and Sauiour, taken of
the moſt holie, perfect, and moſt pure Virgin.

5. It

5. It is thinne: to ſignifie that both the Prieſt, & the communicants, ought to come faſting to receiue the ſame.

6. It is made without leuain: to ſignifie, that our heartes ought to be made cleane, frō all leuain of enuy and malice.

7. It muſt be whole, not crackt or broken: and that to ſignifie two ſundrie myſteries. The one, that we ought to be allwayes, in loue and charitie with our neighbours. The other, that we ought to liue in the vnity of the Catholique Church, and neuer to be ſundred by ſciſme or hereſie.

8. In this Hoſte is writtē, the name & image of our prince and ſoueraigne: to ſignifie, that we ought to acknowledg our ſelues to be his people, and the ſheepe of his paſture: as alſo, that he hath made, to his image and likenes.

9. Some likewiſe do forme therin, the picture of a Lambe, to ſignifie, that he which is ſacrified, is the true Lambe of God, which taketh away the ſinnes of the world.

Of the Paten wheron the Hoſt is layed. And why the ſame is hid or couered, vnder the Corporall.

The 1. Reaſon.

The Paten is ſo called, a Patendo, that is, of patency, or amplenes: and betokneth a hart large, open, & ample. Vpon this Paten, that is

vpon

vpon this latitude of charitie , the Sacrifice of
iuſtice ought to be offered . This latitude of
harte the Apoſtles had , when Peeter ſaid.
Though I ſhould dye with thee, I will not denie thee: likewiſe alſo ſaid all the Diſciples.
Mat. 26. For which cauſe our Lord ſaid vnto
them. The ſpirit indeed is prompt , but the
fleſh is weake. Mat. 29. 41.

The 2. Reaſon.

And becauſe this latitude of hart, fled from
them and lay hid, when they all forſooke and
abandoned their maſter , therefore after the
oblation is made , the Prieſt hideth the paten
vnder the Corporall (or the Deacon remoued from the Altar , houldeth it couered:)
whereby the flight of the Diſciples is ſignified: who whilſt the true Sacrifice was offered,
fled and forſooke Chriſt, as he him ſelfe fore-
tould them ſaying. Al you ſhall be ſcandaliſed
in me in this night. Mat. 26. 31.

Of the two Palles or Corporals.

And here it is alſo further to be noted, that
there are two Palles , called Corporalls : the
one layd vpon the Altar , vnder the Hoſt and
Chalice, extended : the other layed vpon the
Chalice, foulded . That extended, ſignifieth
Faith. That foulded . betokeneth vnderſtanding : for here the myſterie ought to be beleeued, but can not be comprehended , that
faith

faith may haue merit , where humane reason can make no demonstrance.

CHAP. XXXVIII.

Of the preparation of the bread and wine for the oblation: and how therin is most liuely represented, the action of our B. Sauiour , in the institution of this Sacrament .

The 1. Ceremonie, and its signification.

FIrst,by seeing the priest prepare the bread and wine for the oblation , we may be put in minde , how the disciples went before our Lord , to prepare his passouer , as the E-uangelist witnesseth, saying. The first day of Azimes the disciples came to Iesus, saying. Where wilt thou, that we prepare for thee to eate the pasche? Mat. 26. 17.

The 2. Ceremonie, and its signification.

His offerring vpp the Host vpon the Paten before confecration : signifieth, the great affection , where with our Lord and Sauiour, offered vp him selfe to his heauenly Father, to suffer his death and passion for vs . As also the great desire which he had to ordayne this ho-lie Sacrament, saying . With a desire haue I
desie-

defiered, to eate this paffouer with you before
I fuffer. Luc. 22. 15.

The 3. Ceremonie, and its fignification.
The prieft preparing him felfe to performe the Offertorie, remoueth away the Chalice a litle from him, and then houlding vpp
the Paten with the hofte in both his handes,
he fayeth this prayer following . *Sufcipe fan-
Ete pater* &c. The remouing away the Chalice
a litle from him: doth fignifie, how our Sauiour in the garden, went a litle a fide from
his Difciples, as the fcripture faith, about a
ftones caft. The laying of the Hoft downe
vpon the Paten, reprefenteth the very maner
of his prayer, to wit, *procidit in faciem fuam,
orans* as S. Mat. fayeth, cap. 26. He fel vpon
his face, praying.

The 4. Ceremonie, and its fignification.
The prayer alfo it felfe , is imediatlie dire-
Eted to God the Father, as likewife that of
our Sauiours was, faying. *Sufcipe fancte pater.*
For euen fo our Sauiour immediatlie directed
that of his, faying. *Pater* &c My Father if it
be poffible, let this chalice paffe from me. ibid.

Of the mingling of the wine and water, and of fundrie notable circumftances concerning the fame.

Hauing ended the former prayer, he maketh the figne of the Croffe with the Paten,
then

then layeth the hoſt vpon the Corporall , and afterwardes poureth wine and water into the Chalice : of the which (as likewiſe before of the Bread) many notable circumſtances , are to be conſidered.

The 1. Ceremonie, and its ſignification.

Firſt , as the Bread which is prepared for the conſecration, ought to be of pure wheat, ſo likewiſe the wine, for the ſelfe ſame reaſon, ought to be of the naturall grape. Becauſe; as our Sauiour compared him ſelfe to bread, ſaying. I am the bread which came downe frō heauen. Iohn. 6. ſo likewiſe he compared him ſelfe to a Vine, ſaying. I am the true Vine, and my Father is the husband man. Iohn. 15. 1.

The 2. Ceremonie, and its ſignification.

The wine is firſt poured into the Chalice, without the water: and this is done according to the example of Ieſus Chriſt him ſelfe, as S. Ciprian teſtifieth lib. 2. epiſt. 3. to ſignifie the blood which he poured foorth at the time of his agonie in the garden of Gethſemanie.

The 3. Ceremonie, and its ſignification.

Th water is firſt bleſſed , before it be mingled, but not ſo the wine . The reaſon wherof is, for that the wine , in this place , ſignifieth Chriſt , who needeth no benediction: & water the people , who in this life, can not be without ſinne, & therfore haue very great neede of benediction.

I   The

The 4.Ceremonie, and its ſignification.

Next is to be noted , that in this mixtion, there is more wine put into the chalice, then water : and this in ſignification , that the Church ought to be incorporated into Chriſt, and not Chriſt into the Church . And Pope Honorius affirmeth , that it ſhould be a pernicious abuſe , to doe the contrarie. cap. perniciosus de celeb. Miſſ.

The 5.Ceremonie, and its ſignification.

In the Chalice of our Lord , wine is not alone without water, nor water alone without wine: becauſe both flowed foorth together out of his ſide at the time of his paſſion , as ſaith S. Alexander Pope and martyr , the fifte from S. Peter. Which S. Cyprian very notablie confirmeth, ſaying. *Si vinum tantum quis offerat* &c. If any man offer wine alone , the blood of Chriſt beginneth to be without vs: and if the water be alone , we beginne to be without Chriſt: but when both are mingled, then is a ſpirituall and celeſtiall ſacrament accompliſhed epiſt. 65. And Theophilus vpon the 19 of S. Iohn , ſaith, that the Armenians are hereby confounded , becauſe they doe not mingle in the myſteries, water with the wine, for that they beleeue not, as it ſeemeth, that water iſſued out of our Lordes ſide.

The 6. Ceremonie, and its ſignification.

Againe water is mingled with wine: to ſignifie

gnifie the effect of this diuine sacrament, to wit, Christ vnited to the people beleeuing, and the people beleeuing, vnited to Christ in whom they beleeue. For by water, is vnderstood the people, as Apocalips. 17. 15. *Aquæ multæ, populi multi.* Manie waters, are manie people.

The 7. Ceremonie, and its signification.

He which assisteth or serueth the priest, nether layeth the host vpon the Altar, nether poureth the wine, nor water, into the Chalice, but both are done by the priest him selfe: insinuating, that Christ him selfe, first instituted this sacrament, and after recommended the same to his Apostles. For as the Euangelist saith. He tooke the bread and blessed it : and after, he tooke the chalice and consecrated it: and said to his Apostles, doe this in remembrance of me.

Offerimus tibi Domine.

We offer vnto thee o Lord. Hauing mingled the water with the wine, as aforsaid, he taketh the Chalice and offereth it vp, saying, We offer vnto thee o Lord. Signifying by this ceremonie, how our blessed Sauiour most willinglie offered vp him selfe vnto his Father, to be the oblation and sacrifice, for our redemption. And here offer your selfe to his grace, by true and vnfeyned contrition of hart, for all your offences.

I 2   Then

Then he makethe the figne of the Croffe
with the Chalice , fetteth the fame vpon the
Corporall, couereth it with the palle, and next
ioyning his handes together vpon the Altar,
a litle inclined, he fayeth.

In fpiritu humilitatis, & animo contrito,
fufcipiamur à te Domine.

To witt , in the fpirit of humilitie, and in
a contrit hart: for the fpirit of humilitie, ack-
nowledgeth the want of vertues : aud a contrit hart, the number of vices.

Veni Sanctificator, omnipotens æterne
Deus .

Come o fanctifier, omnipotent eternal God.
Eleuating his eies to heauen, and contemplating the greatnes and fublimitie of this myfterie , which he prepareth him felfe to offer,
he humblie requireth the affiftance of the
Holie Ghoft, to fanctifie his oblation , (from
whom alfo it is, that all good defiers and holie infpirations doe proceede) that by his fu-
pernaturall and miraculous operation , that
which he defiereth , may be effected, faying.
Come therfore o fanctifier, come by thy mercie, come by thy grace , come by thy goodnes, come by thy fweetnes, come by thy loue,
come by thy benignitie , come by thy pietie,
and infinit bountie.

Et

Et benedic hoc ſacrificium, tuo ſanƈto
nomini preparatum.

And bleſſe this ſacrifice, prepared to thy holy
name. At which wordes, he bleſſeth the offeringes, calling vpon the Holie Ghoſt : who
albeit he is named alone, yet he can not be a-
lone, but is euen both from, and with, the Father, and the Sonne.

To conclude, of the Offertorie, mention is
made by Walfridus de reb. ec. cap. 21. Rab.
lib. 1. de diuin offic. cap. 2. Amal. lib. 3. de eccl.
offic. cap. 19. Microlog. de ecclef. obſer. cap.
10. Iſid. l. Etymo. 6. cap. 19. Innoc. lib. 2. de
myſt. Myſſæ cap. 53. and others.

CHAP. XXXIX.

Of the Prieſts waſhing his handes.

The 1. Reaſon.

HE that looketh diligentlie, and narrow-
lie, to the firſt inſtitution of this ceremonie, ſhall finde it expreſſie to be taken,
from the modell and example of our Sauiour
him ſelfe, when he firſt ordayned this holie Sacrament. For before he conſecrated his
bodie and blood, or communicated the ſame
to his Apoſtles, he firſt prepared them, by
waſhinge their feete. Iohn. 13. 5.

I 3   The

The 2. *Reason.*

This verie custome, the Church obserued somtime, after his example.

Tertullian witnesseth, that this custome of the priest, to wash his handes at the Altar, was obserued amongst the Christians in his time, Tertul ad vxorem lib. 2. And S. Ambrose also, and diuers others, make mention thereof. Amb. li. 5. de sacr.

The 3. *Reason.*

Misticallie, this ceremonie admonisheth, that euerie one ought with strict examination to cleanse his conscience presenting him selfe at this holie table, if he desire trulie to feele the effects therof, to the health of his soule.

The 4. *Reason.*

In particular the priest washeth his handes at this present, notwithstanding he had washed them before, that if perhaps by humane frailtie, he hath admitted vnto his minde, any vaine phantasie or imagination, he may now at the least, cast it from him, and take as it were vnto him, another new cleannesse. For he ought to procure so much the more puritie, by how much he approacheth the neerer, to the woorke of this most pure, and most immaculat mysterie, that so he may touche with the more cleannesse, the most immaculate and pretious bodie of our Sauiour Iesus.

The

The 5. Reaſon.

He waſheth not his whole handes , but onlie the tippes or endes of his fingars : to ſignifie, that our greater faultes , and groſſer offences, ought firſt to be cleanſed elſe where (to wit, in Confeſſion) ſo that at the Aultar, we ſhould not neede to waſhe , but the tippes of our fingars onlie, that is to ſay , ſome light affections, which may ſometimes diſtract or diſturbe our ſpirit.

Then enclining a litle before the middeſt of the Altar , his handes ioyned theron , he ſayeth the prayer following.

Suſcipe ſancta Trinitas , hanc oblatio-
nem quam tibi offerimus &c.

Receiue, o holie Trinitie ,this oblation which we offer vnto thee . Hauing now placed the bread and wine in a readines to be conſecra-ted, he requireth the holie Trinitie, to accept his oblation, and that in the memorie, of the moſt ſublime and high myſteries , of the Paſ-ſion, Reſurrection, and Aſcenſion of our Sa-uiour Ieſus: which pointes are here propoſed, as the moſt principall articles , of the beleefe and health of all the faithfull.

I 4   **CHAP.**

CHAP. XL.

Of orate fratres &c. And of the reafon
of the prieftes turning vnto the
people vpon the left hand.

THis done the prieft kiffeth the Altar, and
then maketh one whole turne thorough
out, from the left hand to the right, faying.
Pray brethren, that myne, and your facrifice,
may be made acceptable in the prefence of
God the Father almightie.

The 1. Reafon.

Touching the reafon of the prieftes tour-
ning to the people vpon the right hand, we
haue alreadie fpoken before, fhewing that by
the right hand, the prieft reprefenteth the
perfon of our Sauiour, as now by the left
hand, he reprefenteth his owne perfon: for
by the right hand, is vnderftood vertu and
perfection: and by the left hand, frailtie and
imperfection. The prieft therfore reprefenting our Sauiour, paffeth not to the left hand:
to fignifie, that in our Sauiour, there was no
finne nor imperfection. But when he reprefenteth him felfe, to acknowledge that he is a
finner, frayle, and imperfect, he paffeth to the
left hand, faying. Pray for me bretheren.

The

The 2. Reason.

Againe by the right hand, is signified mirth, and ioy: and by the left, hand, sorrowe, and sadnes. Wherfore, the priest turning him to the Altar on his left hand, beginneth to represent the mysteries of the death and passion of our Sauiour Iesus, a matter full of great sorrowe and sadnes, and signified by the left hand, as ioy by the right hand. For of the Angell which declared the ioyfull resurrection of our Sauiour Iesus, the scripture saith, that he sat on the right hand of the sepulcher Marc. 16. 5.

The 3. Reason.

The good Hester (as we reade in hir booke cap. 4.) before that she would speake to kinge Assuerus, in the behalfe of all hir nation, was not content to betake hir alone to hir prayers, but also recommended hir selfe to the prayers of all the people. The priest therfore doth here the verie like, considering that at this time he presenteth him selfe before the kinge of all kinges, to speake in the behalfe of all his nation, that is to say, in the behalfe of all the Church of God.

The 4. Reason.

Againe, it may be said, that therfore the priest requireth to be assisted with the prayers of the people, for that he iudgeth him selfe insufficient to consecrate so great a sacra-

I 5   ment,

ment, vnles he be also holpen, and seconded with the prayers and supplications of all the assistants.

Sufcipiat Dominus hoc facrificium &c.

The people immediatlie make answere, & pray for him, saying. Our Lord receiue this sacrifice of thy handes, to the praise and glorie of his name, also to our vtilitie, and of all his holie Church. Wherin they imitate the counsell of the holie Scripture, which sayeth. *Orate pro inuicem vt faluemini.* Pray one for an other, that yee may be saued: Iames 5.

2. Secondlie, because also it is requisite, that both the people pray for the priest, and the priest for the people, for both the priest and the people are all sacrificers, though in a far different maner, the priest sacrificeth by him selfe, and the people by the priest, which is his speciall commission in this behalfe.

3. And rightlie say they, Our Lord receiue this sacrifice of thy handes &c. to witt, at the handes of the priest, because it is the selfe same sacrifice which before the celestiall Father him selfe, vouchsafed to receiue at the handes of his Sonne. Wherfore with this oblation, the deuout soule may likewise offer her selfe to almightie God.

CHAP.

C H A P. XLI.

Of the Secret of the Maße, and of sun-
drie reaſons concerning the ſame.

The 1. Reaſon.

First, to declare why it is called by the name of Secret: All agree, that it is ſo called, becauſe it is pronounced in a ſecret, and
ſilent maner: there being nothing more be-
ſeeming this high and ineffable myſterie, then
ſilence, as witneſſeth Fortunatus lib. 3. de
eccleſ. offic. cap. 21.

The 2. Reaſon.

To declare what this ſecret is: it is no other
thinge, then certaine petitions, which the
prieſt maketh vnto almightie God, that it may
pleaſe him, to accept the prayers and ſacrifices, which there are preſented vnto him in the
name of the church vniueſſall.

The 3. Reaſon.

And here let it be noted, that theſe Secret
prayers, muſt alwayes agree with the Collects
in number, order, and matter. As for example, if the Prieſt doe take three Collects. The
firſt of the Sonday. The ſecond for the peace
of the Church. The third, that which is common for the liuing and the dead. Then muſt

I 6   the

the firft Secret alfo be of the Sonday . The
fecond for the peace of the Church. And the
third for the liuing and the departed: not
that ether the number or order , maketh fo
much in this matter, but becaufe the Church
herein followeth the doctrine of S. Paul, faying. *Omnia honeſte & fecundum ordinem fiant
in vobis.* Let euerie thing be done decentlie,
and according to order amongſt you.

The 4. Reaſon.

The prieſt reciteth thefe prayers in fecrett,
and that efpeciallie for fiue caufes. Firſt , to
ſhew, that the vertu of the facrifice , which
our Lord was to make for the redemption of
man, was conceaſed and hid from the world,
vntill the time, that he offered him felfe vpon
the Croſſe.

The 5. Reaſon.

Secondlie, to ſhew, that the Iewes, prefentlie after the raiſing of Lazarus, confpired a-
mongſt them felues to kill our Lord ; for
which caufe , he did not walke openlie a-
mongſt them (as the fcripture faith) but re-
tired him felfe in fecret , into the citie of
Ephrem. Iohn. 11. 53.

The 6. Reaſon.

Thirdlie, to put vs in minde what our Sauiour did, during the time he was thus rety-
zed . Whereof Rupertus li. 2. de diuinis offi-
cijs, rendreth the reafon, fayinge . The prieſt
therfore,

therfore, standing in silence, and secretly praying vpon the offeringes, prepareth the holie sacrifice: because our Lord, euen when he hid him selfe, and walked not openlie amongst the Iewes, prepared for vs, the wholsome Sacrament of his passion. Thus he. Neyther can the priest more conuenientlie represent vnto vs, the mysteries of the death and passion of our Sauiour Iesus, and the order of them, then by beginning at the conspiration of the wicked Iewes, from which he withdrew him selfe in secret, because as the Euangelist saith, his time was not yet come.

The 7. Reason.

Fourthly, to represent the great taciturnitie and silence, which our Sauiour vsed, at the time of his examination before the Iudge: which (as the gospel witnesseth) was so great, that the Iudge him selfe did wonder thereat.

The 8. Reason.

Fiftlie to put vs in minde, of the silence which he vsed at the time of his passion, when he was led as a meeke and innocent lambe vnto the slaughter. Which example the holie Martyrs doe therfore imitate, of whom the Church singeth. *Non murmur resonat, non querimonia*. There is nether murmur, nor complayning heard.

of

CHAP. XLII.

Of the Preface; And of fundrie reafons concerning the fame.

The 1. Reafon.

T Ouching the name, interpretation , and
etymologie of the worde , the worde
Preface, is a word, which we retaine of the
Latins, as that of Trinitie , Sacrament , and
the like : and fignifieth no other thinge then
a certaine preparation,preamble , or prolocu-
tion , which is vfed before we come to the
principall narration , or matter entended,the
better to prepare and difpofe the auditors :
like vnto the Proemes and Exordiums,which
Orators vfe before they enter into their nar-
rations. And for this reafon, this exhortation
and Preface, ferueth to prepare and difpofe
the Chriftians to deuotion , whilft the prieft
addreffeth him felfe to recite the holy Canon:
which contayneth the moft ineffable and in-
comprehenfible myfterie , of the confecration of the bodie and blood of our Sauiour
Iefus.

The 2. Reafon.

According to the interpretation aforefaid,
this Preface, may be referred to that action
of

of our Lord , Luke 22. Where he ſent two
of his diſciples to wit Peter and Iohn ſaying.
Goe and prepare vs the Paſche that we may
eate. Who as our Lord willed them, went &
prepared the ſame.

Per omnia ſecula ſeculorum.

World without end . The prieſt (being
come to the end of the Secret, lifteth vpp his
voice, pronouncing his wordes on high to be
heard and vnderſtood of all the aſſiſtants : to
ſignifie , that our Sauiour hauing abſented
him ſelfe from Hieruſalem , returned thither
againe fiue dayes before his paſſion , ſhewing
him ſelfe openlie to his enimies , and making
his entrance into the cirie, with a great multitude of people following him.

Amen.

Amen. The reply of the people anſwering
Amen, doth ſignifie the ioyfull acclamations
of the people , who to honour our Sauiour,
ſome of them cut downe branches from the
trees, others caſt their garments in the way
where he was to paſſe, and others cried out on
high, ſaying . *Benedictus qui venit in nomine
Domini*. Bleſſed is he that cometh in the name
of our Lord.

Dominus vobiſcum.

Our Lord be with you Then the prieſt to
diſpoſe the aſſiſtants to be the more attentiue to that, which he goeth about to doe ſaluteth

luteth them a new, requiring, that our Lord
be with them. And that not without neede:
for greate were the miferie of man, not to be
with him, without whom he can not be.

Et cum spiritu tuo.

And with thy spirit. The people hauing receaued this fo wholfome a falutation of the
prieft, doe likewife refalute him againe;
praying, that euen as he hath wifhed, that
God may be with thē, fo alfo he may be with
his fpirit, to the end that he may fpiritually ac-
complifh his office, with al decencie.

Iohannes Diaconus, in the life of S. Gregorie, recounteth. That Saint Gregorie in the
time of Maffe faying, *Dominus vobifcū*, & his
chaplins which attended him, being negli-
gent to make him anfwere, an Angell from
heauen fupplied their default faying. *Et cum
fpiritu tuo.* Ioh. Diac. in vita Greg. lib. 4.

Surfum corda.

Our hartes on high. This is another falutation of the prieft to the people, to the end, that
they fhould againe with new feruour, lift vpp
their hartes on highe to heauen, to confider
the maruelous greatnes of the myftery which
is there vndertaken. Yea we may trulie fay,
that in this falutation, he further exciteth the
Angels them felues, and all the celeftiall hierarchies, to laude the maieftie of almightie
God.

Habe-

Habemus ad Dominum.

We haue them to our Lord. Of this *Surſum corda* S. Aug fer. 44. de tempore. sayeth. The hartes of the faithfull are a heauen, becauſe they are daylie directed vpp to heauen, the prieſt ſaying, *Surſum corda*, and the aſſiſtants anſwering him. *Habemus ad Dominum*. Yea this the verie woorke of nature it ſelfe: and the proportion of our hart wherewith we pray, doth likewiſe preache, and proclaime vnto vs; wherof, that part which is turned downwards towardes the earth, is verie litle and picked, and that which is directed vpwardes to heauen, is large and extended. Which being conſidered, let thoſe that are preſent at this dreadfull myſterie, well and dulie remember, what they haue proteſted to the Prieſt at *Surſum corda,* anſwering him, *habemus ad Dominum.*

Gratias agamus.

Let vs giue thankes. As in the former exhortation, it was needeful to craue of the diuine goodnes eleuation of minde, wherewith to pray well : ſo it is next expedient, that hauing receiued this eleuation of minde, we render hartie thākes to our Lord God for the ſame: & for this cauſe the Prieſt admoniſheth the people ſaying. Let vs giue thankes.

Domino Deo noſtro.

To our Lord God. For he is God, which of nothing

nothing created vs. He is Lord, who with his blood hath redeemed vs. He is Ours, who liberallie communicateth him felfe vnto vs. Againe, he is God, who in creating, gaue vs nature. Lord, who in redeeming, gaue vs grace. Ours, who in fauing vs, will giue vs glory.

Dignum & iuftum eft.

It is meete, and iuft. The people make anfwere, acknowledging that it is meete and iuft. Meete in refpect of him, becaufe he is our Lord. Iuft, in refpect of vs, becaufe we are his people, and the fheepe of his pafture. Againe. Meete, in refpect of his manifould benefits. Iuft, in refpect of our gratitude and obligation.

Verè dignum & iuftum eft, equum & falutare.

It is verilie meete, and iuft, right, and wholfome. Which wordes the prieft repeating after the people, addreffeth vnto almighty God; contayning fo manie feuerall myfteries, as there be fundrie woordes repeated. For I finde, that the learned and holie Doctors of Chrifts Church, haue taken great delight and pleafure, to explicate vnto vs thefe fiue wordes of the Preface.

Firft Albertus Magnus, referreth them to fiue dignities or excellencies, contayned in this holie facrament, faying that this facrament is a facrament of vndouted veritie : of a

meft

moſt excellent dignitie: of exceeding liberallitie: of weighed equitie: and of moſt wonderful efficacie. For to the veritie thereof,
anſwereth this worde, *verè* : to the dignitie
thereof, anſwereth this worde, *dignum*: to the
liberallitie thereof, anſwereth this worde,
iuſtum: to the equitie thereof, anſwereth this
worde, *equum* : and to the efficacie thereof,
anſwereth this worde, *ſalutare.*

Others referre theſe wordes, to foner principall benefits which we receiue of allmightie God, to wit, our Creation, Redemptiõ,
Iuſtification, and Glorification. And amongſt
others Innocentius the 3. thus expoundeth
them. Trulie Meete, becauſe thou of thy
meere Goodnes haſt created vs. Iuſt, becauſe
of thy pure mercie thou haſt redeemed vs.
Right, becauſe gratis thou iuſtifieſt vs.
Healthfull, becauſe thou doſt perpetuallie
glorifie vs.

Nos tibi ſemper, & vbique gratias agere.

That we alwayes, and euerie where, giue
thankes vnto thee. By which wordes, *ſemper*
& vbique, alwayes, and euerie where : is vnderſtood, the greatnes and immenſitie of allmightie God, who is preſent euerie where, &
in all places. Or alwayes, that therfore we
ought to render him thankes, in all times and
in all ſeaſons. And euerie where, becauſe
where ſoeuer we be, in him we liue, moue,
and

and haue our being.

Domine fanƈe, pater omnipotens æterne Deus.

Holy Lord, Father omnipotēt, eternal God.
Which other wordes, expreffe diuers moſt
high attributes of his moſt excellent maieſtie.
As by the word *Domine*, that he is a Lord,
& therfore to be ſerued. By the world *Sanƈe*,
that he is holie, and therfore that his ſeruants
ought alſo to be holie. By the worde *Pater*,
that he is our Father and we his children. By
the worde *omnipotens*, that he is almightie, &
able to defend vs from the power of ſathan,
and of all our enimies. By the worde *æterne*,
that he is euerlaſting, and can glorifie vs eter-
nailie. By the word *Deus*, that he is ſole and
abſolute God, our onlie maker, redeemer,
and preſeruer.

Per Chriſtum Dominum noſtrum.

Thorough Chriſt our Lord. Which wordes doe giue vs to vnderſtand, that we miſerable creatures which haue offended a God of
ſuch goodnes and excellencie, a Lorde, a holie Lorde, a Father, an omnipotent Father, a
God, an eternall God, being of our ſelues
nothing elſe but duſt and aſhes, and moſt
vnworthie to preſent our ſelues before his
maieſtie, doe therfore not onlie giue humble thankes for all his benefits, but alſo doe
ſeeke to appeaſe him for our offences, and
that

that, *Per Chriſtum &c.* Thorough Chriſt our Lord.

Per quem maieſtatem tuam laudant Angeli.

Firſt this name of Angell is a name of office, and not of nature: wherfore when they are ſent, they are called Angells or meſſengers, for as much they reueale the minde of God vnto men: which name is common to all the celeſtiall ſpirits, though in this place, it is perhaps vnderſtood particularlie, of thoſe which are of the loweſt order, wherof euerie man hath one for his keeper (vnles he driue him away by his euil life.) For ſo S. Aug. ſaith of thē, that they loue, what God loueth: keepe, what God keepeth: and forſake what God forſaketh Soliloq. cap. 7. Of theſe mention is made in the 1. of S. Marc. 18. of S. Mat. and Heb. 1.

Adorant Dominationes.

The Dominations adore. Dominations are thoſe, by whome the other Angells receiue the ordinances of God, and who do ſee them executed: of which preheminence and predomination ouer other Angells, they are called Dominations. Now then if theſe ſo noble ſpirits to whom, by reaſon of their office, adoration doth ſeeme to be due, doe them ſelues with moſt profound reuerence, adore almightie God, how much more ought we, who are but duſt & aſhes, to humble our ſelues

felues vnder his almightie hand. Of Princi-
pallities, Powers, Vertues, and Dominations,
S. Paul maketh mention, all in one epiftle.
Ephef. cap. 1.

Tremunt poteftates.

The powers doe tremble. The powers are
fuch, to whom the wicked powers are fubiect:
and hereof thy receaue their name, becaufe
the malignant fpirits by their power, are
bridled and reftrained, that they can not doe
fo much hurt as they defire. Of thefe it is faid,
that they tremble, not for timerous feare,
being perfectlie bleffed, but (faieth Gabriell
Biell) for obedience, reuerence, and admiration of fo ineffable a maieftie, acknowledging
their power to be nothing, in refpect of the
diuine and immenfe powre of him, who is
contayned in this dreadfull Sacrifice.

Cæli cælorumque virtutes.

And the powers of the heauens. In this
place thefe wordes doe fignifie all the companie of the celeftiall fpirits which are the
intellectuall heauens. But fome vnderftand
them of the materiall heauens, in that fenfe
of the 19. Pf. *Cæli enarrant gloriam Dei.* The
heauens declare the glorie of God. For as Eu-
thymius in Pfal. 148. and S. Chrifoftome fay;
The heauens, and alfo the ftarres, although
they want a voice, and haue nether life nor
foule, yet doe they laude & praife the maieftie
of

of God by their greatnes , beautie , ſituation, nature, vtilitie, miniſterie, perſeuerance, and by other like meanes: wherby alſo they doe draw the mindes of their beholders, into the admiration and praiſe of their Creator.

Et beata Seraphim ſocia , exultatione
concelebrant.

And the bleſſed Seraphim , with mutuall ioy doe ioyntly celebrat. Seraphim in Hebrue, is interpreted *irdente* , burning , or inflaming, for that they are enkindled and inflamed in charitie aboue all others; betwixt whom and God , there are no other Angells: being ſo inflamed with the brightnes of the diuine light, that as the Prophet Eſay ſaith. (cap.6.) They couer the face and feete of him that ſitteth in the throane.

Cum quibus & noſtras voces vt admitti
iubeas deprecamur, ſupplici confeſ-
ſione dicentes.

With whom we beſeech , that thou wouldeſt commãd our voices to be admitted, with humble confeſſion ſaying, For as much as all the celeſtiall orders of Angells aforenamed, are chieflie employed in continuall praiſes & thãkſgiuinges before the preſence of almightie God rtherfore the prieſt maketh his humble petition to our Lord in the name of them all , that he would vouchſafe to receiue our laudes and praiſes, amongſt the praiſes of the holie

holie Angells: that fo men affociated with
the celeftiall fpirits, as the lower ftringes of
an harpe, with the higher, they may ioyntlie found foorth the heauenlie hymne of
Sanctus following.

Of the facred hymne of Sanctus, and of fundry reafons concerning the fame.

The 1. Reafon.

FIrft, Gabriell Biel in his expofition of the
Maffe, faith, that *Sanctus* is fo called of
Sancio, which is to confecrat, dedicate, efta-
blifh, ratifie, or confirme: and thus lawes,
cuftomes, and men alfo, are called holie.

The 2. Reafon.

The fame author faith, that *Sanctus* may be
fo called, *à fanguine hoftiæ*, of the blood of
the hoft, for amongft the people of the ould
law, that was called holie, which was confecrated or fprinkeled with the blood of the
hoft; and fo *Sanctus* may be as much, as *fanguine unctus*.

The 3. Reafon.

Cyrillus, or rather Origines faith, that the
word *Sanctus*, with the Greekes is called Ha-
gios, which is, faith he, *extra terram iffe*, to
be, out of the earth: lib. 11. in Leuit. which
thing doth in verie deed, moft perfectlie and
excel-

excellentlie agree with that moſt diuine , and pure nature of almightie God.

The 4. Reaſon.

S. Deniſe in his 7. cap. of his heauenlie Hierarchie, ſaith, that this ſanctus , is a voice of exceeding praiſe , ful of much dread and reuerence . And S. Ambroſe ſaith , that we finde nothing more pretious , wherin we may ſet foorth and extoll almightie God, then in that we call him holy li. 3. de Spir. Sancto cap. 12. Adde, that holy , is one of the names of almightie God. Luc. 2.

The hymne of Sanctus , confirmed by miracle.

Gabriel Biell in his learned expoſition vpon the Maſſe ſaith , that when Conſtantinople was ſhaken with an earthquake,& the people for feare prayed in the fieldes , in the ſight of all, a litle child was taken vpp into the ayre, for the ſpace of an hower, and afterwards deſcending againe, ſaid, that from heauen this Angelicall hymne , reſounded in his eares, as from a great multitude , or quyre of celeſtiall ſingers; and that he was commanded to declare that ſong of praiſe to all the people; which as ſoone as they began to ſing, God deliuered them from that iminent danger.

Sanctus Sanctus Sanctus.

Holie, Holie, Holie. Theſe ſacred wordes thrice repeated , may putt vs in minde of the

K   three

three perſons of the moſt B. Trinitie (the
Father, the Sonne, and the holie Ghoſt (euery
one of which are infinitlie holie, with the
ſame ſanctitie. Which ſanctitie in theſe three
perſons, doth far ſurpaſſe the ſanctitie of all
other creatures by manie degrees. For firſt,
the ſanctitie of God is infinit, without bound
or meaſure. Secondlie, it is independent, and
nether ſpringing nor flowing from any other
fountaine. Thirdlie, it is to God eſſentiall, and
not participated.

Dominus Deus.

Lord God. The Church in this deuout Canticle, doth moſt liuelie declare and ſet foorth
vnto vs hir faith, in the doctrine of the B. Trinitie. For the word *ſanctus*, thrice repeated,
plainlye ſignifieth the Trinitie of perſons : &
the word *Dominus*, once repeated, truly declareth the vnitie of eſſence.

Sabaoth.

Of hoſtes. The woorde *Sabaoth*, ſignifieth
as much as *militiarũ*, of hoſtes or armies: for
ſo manie armies hath God in earth, as there
are ſeueral orders in the Church: and ſo many
armies hath he in heauen as there are ſundrie
orders of holie Angells. And rightlie doe we
call the Angelicall ſpirits an armie: becauſe
they fight againſt the ſpirituall powers, to
wit, the Diuels.

Pleni

Pleni ſunt cœli & terra gloria tua.

Heauen and earth are full of the maieſtie of thy glorie. To wit Angells and men , repleniſhed with diuine grace. Or heauen and earth are full of his diuine glorie, becauſe his dietie is euerie where: aboue all thinges not elated: vnder all thinges , not proſtrated: with in all thinges , not included: without all thinges, not excluded.

Againe, heauen and earth are full of his glorie: becauſe the ſelfe ſame glorie, which is in heauen with the Angells , is likewiſe with vs in earth : the ſelfe ſame glorie , which is ſitting vpon the throane and right hand of the Father , the ſelfe ſame glorie is vpon the Altar: and therfore both heauen and earth at one and the ſelfe ſame time, is filled & repleniſhed, with the ſelfe ſame glorie.

Hoſanna.

Hoſanna, in Hebrue, is compoſed of Hoſiach, ſaue. and anna , which is an Interiection of beſeeching, and being put together, ſoundeth as much as , ſaue we beſeeche thee. Which Pope Simachus interpreteth more manifeſtly, ſayng Saue me o Lord I beſeech thee.

In excelſis.

In the higheſt. Theſe other wordes , *in excelſis*, ioyned to *hoſanna*, doe cleerelie ſhew what this ſauing is , which is before vnderſtood in the word *Hoſanna*, to wit, *in excelſis*

K 2   in the

in the higheſt, that is in heauen, becauſe Chriſt came to giue, not earthlie, but heauenlie, not temporal, but eternall ſaluation.

Benedictus qui venit in nomine Domini.

Bleſſed is he that cometh in the name of our Lord. Bleſſed is he which cometh, once to offer him ſelfe for vs in a cruentall oblation vppon the Croſſe: & bleſſed is he which cometh daylie to be offered incruentallie for vs, vpon the Altar: and bleſſed is he which commeth to repleniſh vs, with aboundance of all ſpirituall graces and benedictions.

Hoſanna in excelſis.

Hoſanna in the higheſt. This *Hoſanna* is twice repeated, for the two parts of glorie, the one of the body, and the other of the ſoule: or for the ſaluation of two people, the Iewes and the Gentils.

Of the ſigne of the Croſſe, made at the end of the aforſaid hymne.

The wordes *Benedictus* &c. were (as before was ſaid) the prayſes and acclamations of the people, when our Sauiour returned to Hieruſalem, at the pronounciation whereof, the Prieſt maketh the ſigne of the Croſſe before his face: to ſignifie, that this honorable entrie of Chriſt, with all thoſe high acclamations of the people, was not to receiue the pompe of a worldly kingdome, but by his paſſion and death, to purchaſe our redemption.

The

The vſe of ſinging of ſundry Prefaces in the holy Maſſe, is very ancient, as appeareth out of Clemens Romanus, Cyprianus, Chriſoſtomus, Baſilius, Ambroſius, and ſundrye others, cited by Durant. in li. de rit. Eccleſ. Cath. lib. 2. cap. 30.

CHAP. XLIII.

Of the holy Canon of the Maſſe, and of ſundrie notable myſteries contained in the ſame.

FIrſt Canon, is a Greeke woord, which ſignifieth a rule, or a thing regularly cōpoſed: and this part of the Maſſe is ſo called, becauſe it containeth, certaine preſcriptions and ordonances, for the conſecration of ſo high a ſacrament. As alſo, becauſe it hath by the authoritie of the Church of Rome, obtaitained the force of a preſcript or law.

Of the holie Canon doe make mention moſt authors which euer tooke vpon them to write of the Maſſe, euen from the Apoſtles vnto this preſent: and therfore it ſhall not be needful in this place or in the diſcourſe enſuinge, to fill vp paper with the particular names of anie ether ancient or moderne.

Why the holy Canon of the Maſſe, is ſaid in ſecret.

The holy Canon of the Maſſe is ſaid in ſe-

crets

cret:becaufe that which is performed therein, if fo hiden and fecret, that no human reafon, is able fully to comprehend it.

Durandus faith, that the holy Canon of the Maffe is faid in fecret, leaft otherwife thofe facred words fhould be made ouer common, or wax contemtible amongft the fimple people, who by daylie vfe of hearinge thē, might carelefly recite and fing them in the open ftretes, and other places not conuenient.

For as the fame author recounteth, when in former times the holie Canon of the Maffe was pronounced publiquelie, almoft all maner of perfons learned it by rote, and would finge it in the fieldes & open ftreetes. Whervpon it happened, that certaine fhepheardes finging it for recreation, and laying bread vpon a ftone, at the prolation of the facred wordes, the bread was turned into flefh, but they by Gods iuftice, were ftriken with fyre fent downe from heauen. For which caufe the holie Fathers of Gods Church haue euer fince ordayned, that thefe facred wordes, fhould alwayes be faid in filence.

The like alfo happened to three litle boyes, who to make them felues fport, would feeme to take vpon them to fing Maffe. Who firft placeing a ftone infteed of an Altar, and then laying their bread theron, infteed of an Hoft, and after putting water into a wodden difhe, infteed of a Chalice, were foddainlie ftroken to the earth-, and their bread and water, confumed with fyre which fel from heauen:& for the ſpace of three dayes (to the great amazement of their parents) remayned ſpeechles: but after three dayes,coming againe vnto thē ſelues,recounted openly, all that, which had befell thē:al which is teſtified,more at lardge, by Ioannes Moſcus , and by manie others.

The premiſſes therfore conſidered , I am here to pray the gentle Reader to pardon me, if I doe not turne the wordes of the ſacred Canon, immediatlie enſuing , into our vulgar tongue,as I hau done the former,which I proteſt in regard of their dreadfull venerablenes, I dare not to doe. Hoping neuertheles, ſufficientlie to explicate , their ſence & meaning, by the enſuing method . Now then, according to S. Hierom. let vs ſprinkle our booke, and the poſtes of our houſes,with blood. And with Zara let vs binde a red thrid vpon our fingar, that we may ſet foorth the paſſion and death of our redeemer, and ſorrowfullie conſider , the vnſpeakeable paines , which he vouchſafed to ſuffer for vs.

CHAP. XLIV.

Of the ſacred Canon of the Maſſe.

T E.

FOr as much as in the holie Canon of the Maſſe,ſpecial memory is made of the paſ-

K 4 ſion

ſion and death of our redeemer, therfore perhaps it was ordained by deuine prouidence, and not by humane induſtrie, that the ſacred Canon, ſhould take its beginning from that letter, which by his proper forme, doth liuelie expreſſe the ſigne of the Croſſe in the figure of Thau. As the Prophet Ezechiel ſaith cap. 9. The ſigne of Thau in the fore-heades of the men, which ſorrow and mourne.

Igitur.

Which word *Igitur*, is a particle Illatiue, connecting the ſacred Canon, vnto the Preface before rehearced. As if he ſhould ſay; After ſuch preamble of prayers, and celebration of prayſes, at the lenght we enterpriſe that, which hitherto for reuerēce we haue deferred.

Clementiſsime.

Clemencie, by S. Thomas, is defined to be, A lenitie, or gentlenes, of a ſuperior, to an inferior, and which out of a certaine ſweetnes and tendernes of affection, doth moderate paines. Seneca in like maner, defineth it to be. An inclination of the minde, to lenitie or pittie; in the execution of puniſhments. Rightlie therfore in this place, our Lord is ſaid to be moſt clement, becauſe, as for our ſinnes, he doth not in this life, exact of vs to the vttermoſt fartbing, ſo nether in his diuine ſeruice, doth he rigorouſlie require, at our handes, that which is due to ſo highe a maieſtie:

iestie nay, he doth rather greatlie tollerate, the suppliants infirmity; supplying his defects, with the aboundance of his pietie.

Pater.

As touching the name and title of a Father, it belongeth to a Father, 1. To produce a childe like vnto him selfe. 2. To loue it being produced 3 To prouide it of necessaries. 4. And to teache and instruct it. All which, almightie God hath most mercifullie performed vnto vs: for he is a Father in creating vs. A Father in tendernes of affection towards vs. A Father in prouiding for vs. And a Father in instructing vs, by his diuine and most holie spirit.

Per Iesum Christum Filium tuum.

In which wordes, is clearlie alleadged, the virtu of the Mediator: the which, of what maruelous operation and efficace it is, plainlie appeareth, by the great propinquitie which he hath with both parties, betweene whom, he is in the midst as Mediator. For first with God he hath propinquitie, becaufe he is the Sonne of God: also with vs he hath propinquitie, becaufe he is the Sonne of man. Whence it followeth, that he first praying to his heauenlie Father for vs, doth set open his eares to our petitions, and in a sort, addicteth them to heare our suplications.

Dominum nostrum.

And worthelie is he said in all these to be

ours, to wit, our Iefus, our Chrift, and our Lord: giuen, for a preferuatiue of our health: in foode for our refection : in facrifice for our reconciliation : in facrament for our fan-ctification: and in price for our redemption.

Supplices rogamus ac petimus.

Which two wordes, doe fomewhat differ in fignification : for to aske, is fimply to de-maund: but asking ioyned with befeeching, is an obfecration which is made with earneft entreatie and perfwafion. And therfore aptlie by two diuers wordes the demaund is dou-bled, that fo the prayer which is made may be of greater moment.

Why the Prieſt here kiſſeth the Altar.

This deuout ceremonie may fignifie vnto vs, that Chrift not onlie of his humilitie, o-bedience, and loue to his Father, gaue him felfe to death for vs, but alfo of his exce-eding loue and charitie towardes vs. For as God fo loued the world, that he gaue his on-lie begotten Sonne for it : fo alfo his Sonne loued the fame, that he would likewife wil-linglie dye to redeeme it; not compelled by anie neceffitie, as him felfe fignified faying. I haue power to lay downe my life, and to re-fume, or take the fame againe.

Vti accepta habeas, & benedicas.

God is faid to accept our offeringes, not that they are, ether profitable, or delectable to
him,

him, but that according to the accuſtomed and
wonted maner of acceptance , we doe beſeeche him , that vpon thoſe thinges which we
offer vnto the glorie of his name , he would
poure downe the increaſe of his heauenlie benediction . And therfore there is ſubioyned.
Et benedicas.

Hæc + dona, hæc + munera, hæc + ſan--
cta ſacrificia illibata.

Which three wordes, *Dona, munera, ſacri-*
ficia, may be thus diſtinguiſhed . Firſt, thoſe
thinges are called *Dona*, which are giuen vs
of God for our ſuſtentation , as teſtifieth the
Apoſtle ſaying . Euerie beſt guift and euerie
perfect guift, is from aboue . Iames. 1. Furthermore *Donum* , according to S. Iſidor, is
that which the ſuperior, giueth or beſtoweth
vpon the inferior . Or as Cyrillus ſayeth, a
thinge which is giuen to ſuch as are in neede.
Cyril. in Collect. 2. They are called *Munera*,
in as much as they are receiued of vs with a
gratefull minde. Or rather in as much as we,
who are poore and inferior , preſent them to
God as to our ſuperior , expecting in lieu of
them, to receiue ſome better thinge from his
bleſſed handes. 3. They are called ſacrifices, in
as much as we offer them vp to God, to pleaſe
and pacifie him for our ſinnes . Or as they are
offered vnto him , to honor him with the
higheſt latrial honor . So that they are to be
K 6   conſi-

confidered. 1. As they refpeȼt the giuer, and fo they are called Guiftes. 2. As they refpeȼt the receiuer, and fo they are called Rewardes. 3. As they refpeȼt the offerer, and fo they are called Sacrifices.

Againe fome of our holie Doȼtors there be, who accommodate thefe three wordes, (*Doná, Munera, Sacrifícia*) marueloufly well, to the moft pretious bodie and blood of our Sauiour Iefus : as for example. 1. It is a Guift (fay they) becaufe God hath giuen it vs of his meere liberallitie: and it is of fuch exceȼlent greatnes,that he could not poffiblie giue or beftowe a greater vpon vs. 2. It is a Reward or prefent, becaufe of all the oblations that we can prefent vnto him, we haue nothinge of price, but his moft pretious bodie and blood which he hath giuen vnto vs, that we may giue or render againe vnto him. 3. It is alfo a Sacrifice, for that it is the verie lambe of God, which trulie was facrificed for the finnes of the world. And laftlie, this fo worthie a Sacrifice is faid to be, *Illibata*, for as much as it ought to be offered vpp, without any fpot of foule or bodie.

Of the 3. Croffes, which are made at the prolation of three wordes aforfaid.

Concerninge the 3. Croffes, which the Prieft maketh at the prolation of the three
wordes

wordes aforefaid. Stephanus Eduenfis faith,
that the bread and wine , are figned with a
triple Croffe, to declare the whole myfterie
to be wrought by the maruelous might of all
the Trinitie,

According to Albertus magnus, and Innocentius tertius, by thefe three Croffes, may
be vnderftood,three derifions, or illufions of
our B. Sauiour. The 1. before the high Prieft.
The 2 before king Herod. And the 3. before
Pontius Pilat.

Imprimis qua tibi offerimus pro Ecclefia.

Euerie Sacrifice ought to be offered vp for
all, that is to fay , for the Church vniuerfall,
for it is great reafon , that euerie Prieft pray
for all , becaufe Chrift , the proper Hoft of
this Sacrifice, was offered vp for all: as writeth S.Cyprian. epift.63.

Tua.

This word is added to the former, by way
of obfecratiou, wherin we craue , that he
would be good and mercifull vnto his Church
not for hir owne merits , but for his owne
guifts and many moft fingular graces, which
he hath vouchfafed to beftowe vpon hir , and
wherwith he hath maruelouflie adorned and
enriched hir. And Gabriel Biel faith , that the
Church vfeth this word *Tua* , calling hir
felfe *bis*, the rather to infinuat hir felf into his
grace and protection. For as S. Ambrofe noteth,

teth euerie one doth willinglie keepe and proteƈt his owne, lib. 2. de pœnit. cap. 8.

Sanƈta.

This Church is called holie for fundrie reaſons. Holie, for hir holie religion. Holie, for hir holie lawes. Holie, for hir holie Sacramēts. Holie, becauſe hir head is the holie of holies. Holie, becauſe the Holie Ghoſt, hir ruler and direƈtor, is holie. Laſtlie holie, becauſe ſhe is vowed and confecrated vnto-almightie God, and fanƈtified and waſhed, in the moſt pretious blood of our Sauiour Ieſus, as writeth the Apoſtle. Epheſ. 5.

Catholica.

Next this Church is called Catholíque, that is to ſay vniuerſall, for as much as ſhe hath bene diffuſed by the ſplendor of faith, euen to the vttermoſt endes of all the world. In which name S. Aug. doth admirablie reioyce, becauſe he was contayned with in the lap of that Church, vnder the facred name of Catholique. *Epiſt. Quam vocant fundamenti. cap. 4.*

Quam pacificare.

Rightlie in the firſt place, doe we pray, for the pacification and peace of the Church, this peace being the bond of all concord, and the redreſſe of all difcord: and which Chriſt our Sauiour, departing from his Diſciples, laſt of all bequeathed vnto thē. Iohn. 14. And
after

after his refurrection, firſt of all preached vnto them. Luc. 24. Secondlie, aptlie is peace here asked of almightie God, becaufe God is the God of peace, and not of diffention. Thirdlie, verie well is peace required, in the time of facrificing, becaufe this Sacrifice is a Sacrifice of peace. Fourthlie, becaufe as no communitie can confiſt without peace, fo neather the Church.

Cuſtodire.

In the next place, we pray that our Lord would keepe his Church, efpeciallie from the deceitfull allurements, of the world, the fleſh and the diuell. From the dangerous incurfions of all rauening wolues, as from Infidels, Turkes, Heretikes, wicked Paſtors, and from all falfe brethren. Which prayer, Chriſt him felfe, before his departure, made for his Church and chofen, faying. That thou keepe them from euill. Iohn. 17. Againe three fundrie wayes, God preferueth his from euil. 1. By a bleſſed and happie death, that they liue not to fee them, as we reade of king Iofua. 2. That they efcape them by flight, as did S.Paul from Damafco. 3. By giuing them fortitude, conſtantlie to ouercome them, as diuers holie Martyrs, and Confeſſors haue done.

Adunare.

And for as much as Chriſt himfelfe faith, that he hath other ſheepe, which are not as

yet

yet of the fame fheepe fould Iohn. 10. therfore for thefe alfo doe we pray, that they may be brought to the vnitie of the fame Church. In which worde, according to S. Aug. we pray for that, which allwayes ought to be praied for, in the Church of Chrift: to wit, that faith may be giuen to Infidels: vnitie to Schifmatikes: and refociation to fuch, as by the cenfure of the fame Church, are for a time, feuered to doe penance for their offences. Cont. Iulianum cap. 3.

Et regere digneris, toto orbe terrarum.

Which wordes, together with the other before recited, may be more brieflie thus expounded. To pacifie, from enimies, that fhe be not oppreffed. To keepe, in peace, that fhe be not difturbed. To vnite, from fcifmes, that fhe be not diuided. To gouerne, in the difpofition of hir councells, that fhe be not deceaued.

Vna cum famulo tuo Papa noftro N.

Where note, that *Papa*, is faid of the Interiection *Pape*, which is an Interiection of admiration, as admirable for fanctitie. And right worthelie is this name attributed to the bifhop of Rome, for where as in many other feates, faith and religion hath fayled, to this chayre and feate of Rome, neuer could perfidioufnes haue acceffe.

Et.

Et Antistite nostro N.

A Bishop in this place , is tearmed by the name of *Antistes*, so called of these two latin wordes, *An.e*, and *stes*, becauſe he standeth and is placed, before other Priestes. Touching this our Bishopp , we ought alſo to haue remembrance of him, for ſo S. Paul willeth vs ſaying. Remember your Prelates which haue ſpoken the word of God to you. Heb. 13. 7. And. Obey your, Prelates, and be ſubiect vnto them , for they watch ouer you , as being to rendar an account for your ſoules. verſ. 17. Seeing therfore , that they ſtand anſwerable and accountable for our ſoules , ſhould it not be verie great ingratitude in vs, to forget them in our prayers?

Et omnibus orthodoxis.

Doxa in Greeke, ſignifieth ſentence or opinion, and Orrhodoxos, as much as right beleeuers. By which word it is moſt plaine, that all Infidells, Heretikes, and Sciſmatikes, ſeperated from the myſticall bodie of our Sauiour Chriſt, are excluded from the fruite and benefit of this ſacrifice.

Atque Catholica & Apostolica fidei cultoribus.

Where it is to be noted, that to worſhipp the Catholique faith, is not onlie for a man to beleeue it in him ſelfe , but alſo to declare and expreſſe it in his deedes : as namelie , to
ſuſtaine

ſuſtaine and defend the ſame , againſt all ſuch
as ſhall impugne it : all which are trulie termed , defenders and aduancers , protectors
and worſhipers of the Catholique faith.

Of the firſt memento.

C H A P.   XLV.

Memento Domine.

HItherto the Prieſt , hath prayed for the
Church vniuerſall , and for hir rulers.
And now in this place he doth recommend
vnto the diuine clemencie, his owne particular frindes , for whom he intendeth to offer
vp Sacrifice : as , his parents, bretheren,ſiſters,
kinsfolkes, and others benefactors, or ſuch as
he hath taken in charge vnto him, as ſpeaketh
S. Aug. Epiſt. 59. quæſt. 5. ſaying. *Memento
Domine*. In which wordes , he deſiereth that
our Lord would be mindfull of thoſe, whom
in his preſent prayers , he offereth vpp vnto
him: becauſe, to be had in minde of God, is to
be holpen of God . And Gabriel Biell addeth,
that when he asketh that our Lord would remember them , he demandeth that he would
haue mercie on them.

Famulorum, famularumque tuarum.

Firſt, as the ſame author ſaith, men are ſet
before women, for the dignitie of their ſex,
becauſe

becaufe as the Apoftle S. Paul faith, the man is the head of the woman. 1. Cor. 11. & Tim. 2. Next he calleth all thofe for whom he prayeth vnto almightie God, not fimplie men, but his feruants : therby acknowledging him for their good Lord and maifter, full of al mercie, clemencie, and fweetnes.

Why the Prieſt ioyneth his hādes together, and meditateth a while in prayer.

In this place, the Prieft meditateth a while, and calleth to minde all thofe aforefaid, for whom he is obliged and bound to pray: as his owne parents, friendes, and benefactors. And this trulie greatlie moued diuers of our holie anceftors, to induce fome one or other of their children, to the office of Prieft hood, becaufe they knew verie wel, that the Prieftes were bound, to pray and offer Sacrifice particularlie for their parents, friendes, and benefactors. For how fhould the Prieft at this prefent, ftanding in the prefence of Chrift and his Angels, not remember his faithfull & louing frindes, their benefits beftowed vpon him, their particular neceffities, and their pious, holie, and deuout intenfions? This therfore the Church dulie obferueth, as being grounded vpon the law, both of God and nature.

Et omnium circumſtantium.

The fame holie Maffe, is further particularlie applied, to all thofe which in feruent
faith

faith and attentiue deuotion, doe afift at the
fame, that they efpeciallie, may participat of
the fruit, of the death and paffion of our Sa-
niour Iefus, who by particular deuotion, haue
adioyned them felues to afift at the Sacrifice.
And well doth he pray for all thofe that ftand
about, that is, who ftand firme in quietnes,
inward recollection, and eleuation of minde
in almightie God: & not for thofe who walke
or ftare about them, for all fuch, doe rather
ftir, then ftand ftill.

Quorum tibi fides cognita eft, & nota deuotio.

Faith according to S. Paul, is defined to
be, an argument of thinges not appearing;
To the end therfore, that all thofe which are
prefent at the Sacrifice of the Maffe, may
reape the fruit which they defire, there is here
required in them, thefe two thinges principallie. 1. A firme, and vnmoueable faith, to
beleeue without ftaggering, that the bodie &
blood of Iefus Chrift, together with his fou'e
and diuinitie, are trulie, reallie, and fub-
ftantiallie prefent, vnder the fpecies of bread
and wine, after the prolation of the facramentall wordes. 2. Deuotion; which is defined to
be, a fpirituall acte of the will, readilie obey-
ing vnto almightie God. For it is not enough
that the vnderftanding be vnited to God by
faith, vnles the affection likewife, be con-
ioyned

ioyned vnto him by pure deuotion.

Pro quibus tibi offerimus, vel qui
tibi offerunt.

The Prieft doth pray and offer Sacrifice,
not onlie for thofe that are prefent, but for
others alfo which are abfent. Becaufe fome
there are, who nether in bodie are prefent at
Maffe, nor yet in intention: fuch are the foules in Purgatorie, litle infants, and alfo many wicked and euil Chriftians, for whom not-
withftanding the Prieft doth offer, and that
in particu'ar. Others there be who are prefent at maffe, ether in intention onlie, and
not in bodie, or both in bodie and intention:
and thefe both offer them felues, and the
Prieft alfo doth offer for them, although in a
far diftinct and different maner; for the people offer fpirituallie, the Prieft properlie: the
people in affection, the Prieft in function:
the people offer in hart, holie defire, faithfull
afiftance, vniforme confent, and humble prayer, the Prieft by actuall, externall, and vifible
miniftrie, with abfolute power to confecrate
and facrifice.

Hoc facrificium laudis.

This oblation is here called a Sacrifice, of
the effect; *quia facros no effcis*, becaufe it maketh vs holy. And of praife, 1. Becaufe Chrift,
with praife and thankfgiuing, firft inftituted the fame. 2. Becaufe he him felfe, offered

red it vp to the honor and praiſe of his eternall Father. 3. Becauſe there is nothing in
this Sacrifice, which is not abounding and
full of praiſe. For if reſpect be had to Chriſtes diuinitie, it is here. If his ſacred humanitie be ſought for, here is his ſoule, here is his
bodie, here is his blood, all moſt worthie of
praiſe and honor.

Pro ſe, ſuiſque omnibus.

In theſe wordes, the Prieſt who maketh
this oblation, ought firſt (according to the
well ordered rule of charitie) to remember
him ſelfe, and the care and ſafetie of his owne
ſoule. Next that all ſuch as haue any charge
committed vnto them, to rule or gouerne, that
they doe not onlie commend them ſelues vnto God, but alſo all thoſe that are committed
to their charge and ouerſight: as, the Paſtor,
for his flock, the Prince, for his ſubiects, the
Captaine, for his ſoldiears, the Father of a
houſe, for his familie, the Maſter, for his ſcho-
lars, and ſo of others.

Pro redemptione animarum.

Which wordes doe ſhew, that the Prieſt
ought not to pray, nether for any earthlie ap-
petite, nor temporall gayne, but purelie and
ſincerelie for the ſaluation of their ſoules: for
to doe otherwiſe, were with Simon Magus, to
buy and ſell the guiftes of God for monie.

Pro

Pro ſpe ſalutis incolumitatis ſuæ.

That is to ſay , for hope of health , as touching the ſick: for hope of ſafetie as touching
the healthie,for frindes,if they be fallē at eni-
mitie; for their ſafe returne , if they be in iorney; and for their amendement, if they liue
viciouſlie.

Tibique reddunt vota ſua.

Where note, that a vowe in this place , is
not properlie taken for a promiſe of ſome
ſpirituall thinge made vnto God , but for
pious intentions holie deſires,and other good
workes , which the Prieſt requireth to be accompliſhed with a moſt inward affection, by
the aſſiſtants , according to the ſaying of the
Prophet Dauid.Offer vp to God the ſacrifice of
prayſe,& render thy vowes vnto the higheſt.

Eterno Deo, viuo, & vero.

In which three wordes , are plainlie excluded three ſortes of creatures , which falſlie
haue bene taken and reputed for Gods , to
wit, Diuels, Men,and Idols . For the Diuels,
they are liuing, but not eternall : firſt becauſe
they had a begining ; and next becauſe they
haue loſt the life eternall . The ſecond alſo
are liuing, but nether eternall, nor true ; not
eternall, becauſe they ſhall haue an end ; not
true, becauſe as the Apoſtle ſaith. Euerie man
is a lyar. The third are nether true , nor
liuing, nor yet eternall , as being without all
maner

maner of fenfibilitie or motion.

To conclude, concerning the firft part of
the holie Canon, four thinges are chieflie to
be noted; to wit, to whom; for whom; how,
and wherfore we ought to offer vp this facrifice of praife. To whom? Onlie to God, that
is to the moft B. and vndeuided Trinitie. For
whom? For the holie Catholique Church,
that is for all true and faithfull beleeuers.
How? In the vnitie of faith, that is to fay, in
the communion of Saintes. Wherfore? To
wit, for all benefits, temporall, fpirituall, and
eternall.

CHAP. XLVI.

Of the Comemoration which is made
of the B. Saintes.

Communicantes.

IN four thinges doe we communicat with
the B. Saintes. 1. In faith; beleeuing what
foeuer they beleeued, concerning the veritie
of this B. Sacrament. 2. In Hope; becaufe the
Saintes did hope, and we doe hope, for we
ftill hope, and expect in patience, that which
they alreadie pofeffe in full affurance. 3. In
Charitie; for fuch is the prerogatiue of Charitie, that though Faith doe ceafe, when bea-
tificall vifion is prefent; though Hope doe
       defift

defiſt when pleaſant fruition is poſeſſed, yet in heauen, Charitie neuer faileth, but is more increaſed and perfected. 4. We doe cōmunicat with them, in the vſe and oblation of this B. Sacrament, whoſe former viaticum this hath beene, to bring thē to that moſt bleſſed life, wherunto they are ſo happelie arriued: Becauſe alſo it is ſaid of the Saintes, that they were perſeuering in the doctrine of the Apoſtles, and in the communion of breaking bread.

Et *memoriam venerantes.*

The 1. reaſon why before the conſecration of the bodie of Chriſt, the Church hath ordained the commemoration of the Saints to be made, is, becauſe ſhe hath bene taught & learned this out of the figures of the ould teſtament. For as the legal prieſt and Biſhop, entering into the holie of holies, brought in with him the names of the twelue tribes, written vpon his Rationall: euen ſo the euangelicall prieſt, entring into the holie of holies, bringeth in with him, the name of the B. twelue Apoſtles.

But beſides this, there are ſundrie other reaſons, for the commemoration, and veneration of the B. Saints. 1. Becauſe the odor and fame of their vertues, is euerie where diſperſed thoroughout the world. 2. Becauſe their holie bodies and reliques, are had in

L   high

high veneration , and viſited and frequented
with many pious pilgrimages. 3. Becauſe both
Churches and Altars , of vnſpeakable riches,
are dedicated vnto God , in their names and
memories. 4. Becauſe vpon the tōbes of Martyrs, reliques, & bodies of the bleſſed Saints,
the ſacrifice of the Maſſe, is daylie celebrated.
5. Becauſe at the ſepulchres, and memories of
the B. Saintes , God doth worke manie maruelous miracles. 6. Becauſe in this the Chu ch
doth that , which all antiquities was accuſtomed to doe: for it hath euer beene the
practiſe of the Church , to make commemoration of the B. Saints , in all hir prayers
and ſupplications . As Exod. 32. Gen. 38.
and Dan. 3.

Imprimis.

Firſt. Where being to ſpeake of our bleſſed
Ladie, he well ſayth ,firſt,to wit,before al Angells before all men, and before all creatures.
For to which of the Angels was it at any time,
ſaid. The holie Ghoſt ſhall come vpon thee?
Or to what man was it euer ſaid. The power
of the moſt high ſhall ouerſhadow thee? Luc.
1 35 . Or to what creature was it euer ſaid,
that which of thee ſhall be borne holy , ſhall
be called the Sonne of God?

Glorioſæ.

Where note , that to this moſt excellent
queene , four moſt ſingular and renowned
titles,

titles, are attributed and giuen 1. She is ſaid to be glorious , becauſe ſhe is moſt gloriouſ- lie aſſumpted both in ſoule and bodie. 2. Glo- rious for the great glorie which ſhe enioyeth in the kingdome of heauen. wherein ſhe far ſurpaſſeth all Cherubins, and Seraphins , yea all the Angelicall Spirits and orders of Sain- tes being put together. 3. Glorious , for the high honor which the Church militant doth giue vnto hir: for wheras other Saintes , are ſerued with the honor which is called *Dulia*, ſhe is worſhiped with that honor which is termed *Hyperdulia* , which Hyperdulia is an eſpeciall honor, due vnto hir, for the affini- tie and heroicall vertu , euen contracted with almightie God.

Semper Virginis.

In the ſecond place , that moſt excellent and ſupernaturall gift, to haue beene alwayes a virgin. For ſhe was a virgin in bodie , a vir- gin in minde, and a virgin in profeſſion. A virgin before hir childbirth, in hir childbirth, and after hir childbirth ; without any corrup- tion of hir virginall chaſtitie.

Mariæ.

The name of Marie, hath three interpreta- tions. Starre of the ſea. Illuminated . And Empreſſe or Ladie. Firſt ſhe is Marie (that is ſtarre of the ſea:) for as much as all that are labouring in the bitter ſea of pennance , and

ſorrow

forrow for their finnes, she fafelie bringeth to
the fecure harbour of health and faluation. She
is Marie, (that is illuminated) : becaufe thofe
thar walke in the darknes of finne and of error, are conuerted by the meanes of hir fingular merits . She is Marie (that is empreffe or
Ladie): for she sheweth her felfe to be Empreffe and Ladie of abfolute power, ouer all
the diuells and infernall fpirits, in defending
vs againft them, both in our life, and at the
dreadfull and fearfull hower of our departure.

Genetricis.

In the third place, she which before was called a mayde, is called a mother . A maruelous
fecunditie is expreffed, when mother is mentioned: for maruelous trulie was the holie virgins fecunditie, whereat the prophet admit-
ring, faieth. A woman shall compaffe about a
man. Ierem. 31. to wit, Marie, Chrift: a may-
den, God.

Dei, & Domini noſtri Ieſu Chriſti.

In the fourth place, she is adorned with the
fupereminent title, not onlie of a mother, but
of the mother of God, and of our Lord Iefus
Chrift . For the holie virgin did not beare or
bring foorth onlie a meere man, but true
God : nether was she onlie Chriftipara, mother of Chrift, but alfo Deipara, mother of
God .

Sed

Sed & beatorum Apostolorum.

After the glorious virgin Marie, mention is made of the blessed Apostles, and that not without iust cause. For first they were the only witnesses of this diuine Sacrament, who were present, when our Lord first instituted the same. Secondlie they were those who receiued first authoritie and commandement to celebrate the same. Thirdlie they were those who first put in practise the celebration of this diuine Sacrament. And fourthlie, they were those, who set downe the chiefe orders and prescriptions, to all Christian nations, for the administration of the same.

Ac Martyrum tuorum.

After the Apostles, the holie Martyrs are also named, because of their great constancie which they shewed in the hoat persecutions, and sheading their bloodes in the defence of their faithes: who therfore were truelie martyrs, that is to say, witnesses of the veritie of the Christian faith: for martyr, properlie signifieth a witnes, and martyrs are trulie witnesses, yea euen vnto death. For great is the worke of martyrdome, and manifould the praises belonging therto. The first praise is, that it is an act of most noble Fortitude. The second, that it is an act of most perfect Patience. The third, that it is an act of most firme Faith. The fourth,

L 3   that

that it is an act of moſt feruent Charitie. For as our Sauiour ſaith, Greater charitie then this no man hath, that a man yeald his life for his frindes. Iohn. 15. 13.

And here in this place may occurre a queſtion : why in the Maſſe, no commemoration is made of the holie Confeſſors, ſeeing the Church, amongſt the Saints, doth ſo highlie worſhip their memories. The cauſe wherof ſeemeth to be this; for that in the ſacrifice of the Maſſe, (in which is repreſented the paſſion of our Lord) the memorie of none was to be made, bnt onlie of martyrs, who ſheding their blood for the loue of Chriſt, are made thereby perfect imitators of his paſſion: which the Confeſſors, though otherwiſe holie, haue not done.

Petri.

Amongſt the Apoſtles, the name of Peter is firſt expreſſed, as being the chiefe and head of the Apoſtles. He was in great reputation at Rome, the Emperour Nero being angrie therwith, cauſed him to be crucified, with his head towards the earth, and his feet vpward; the which he him ſelfe requeſted, not thinking him ſelfe worthie to be crucified in that maner, as his Lord and maſter was . The people of Rome vppon this occaſion , embraced the faith & Chriſtian religion with great feruour. He was buried on the ſide of Ne-

roes

roes garden at the Vatican. He held the ſeat
of Antioche in the time of the Emperor Ti-
berius, the ſpace of 7. yeares. And 25. yeares,
that of Rome.

Et Pauli.

S. Paule a veſſell of election, & indued with
ſingular diuine graces, was called from heauē,
to beare witnes of the name of Ieſus, before
kinges and Potentates. Of whom a religious
father ſaith, He would haue no other vniuer-
ſitie but Hieruſalem, no other ſchoole but
mount Caluarie, no other pulpit but the
Croſſe, no other reader but the Crucifix, no
other letters but his woundes, no other com-
maes but his laſhes, no other full points but
his nayles, no other booke but his open ſide,
and no other leſſon, but to know Ieſus Chriſt
and him crucified. He ſuffered innumerable
trauels in the promulgation of the goſpell.
He was the ſame day, that S. Peter ſuffered at
Rome, beheadded, in the yeare 17. from the
paſſion of Ieſus-Chriſt, & the 14. Yeare of the
Emperor Nero. He was buryed in the way of
Oſtia, where ſince is built a moſt ſumptuous
Church & monaſterie vnder his inuocatiō, not
far from whence are to be ſeene yet at this
preſent, three fountaines of ſpringing water, which did breake foorth of the places,
vpon which his head leaped thrice after his
decollation.

L 4   *Andrea.*

Andrea.

Who at the voice of one onlie calling, followed our Sauiour Chrift. Who brought his brother Peter to be inftructed of our Sauiour. Who difputed with the Proconfull Egæus of the veritie of this B. Sacrament. Which Proconfull caufed him to be crucified after the example of Iefus Chrift, but in a maner different, for that he had not his handes and feete peirced with nayles , but ftreightly bound with cordes , to the end to put him to a more flowe death.

Iacobi.

S. Iames the greater, was a Gallilean by nation, the fonne of Zebede , and brother of S. Iohn. Both which agreed to follow our Lord with fuch affection , that they forfooke at an inftant their carnall father , and companie of fifhers. They were fo greatlie beloued of our Lord, that their mother douted not to require feates for them on ether fide of him , in his kingdome. He tooke them with him for witneffes of his glorious transfiguration . Alfo at the rayfing of the daughter of the prince of the Sinagogue Iairus, for proofe of the inward loue which he bore vnto them, He was put to the death of the fworde by Herod, in the time of the Emperor Claudius . He was the firft of the Apoftles, who expofed his life for the loue and faith of his mafter Chrift.
Our

Our Lady, and all the Apoſtles, were preſent at his martyrdome.

Ioannis.

S. Iohn, Ieſus Chriſt did moſt dearlie loue, and for this reſpect he was called his Euangeliſt. He was ſent with S. Peter to prepare the Paſſouer. He onlie leaned vpon the breaſt of our Sauiour at his laſt ſupper, from whence he ſucked thoſe diuine miſteries, which he hath left written vnto vs. At the point of the death of Ieſus Chriſt, he recommended vnto him his mother, for an aſſured argument of his confidence and amitie. After his reſurrection he ran the firſt of the Apoſtles, to enioy the ſight of him. His martyrdome was to be put into a veſſell of hoat oyle, but by the prouidence of God, it could not hurt him. Hauing religiouſly preached the goſpell in the leſſer Aſia, he entred at the age of 99. yeares into a ſepulcher, which he was accuſtomed to frequent, and was neuer ſince ſeene in earth.

Thomæ.

This Thomas was alſo called *Dydimus*, which is interpreted, doutfull, becauſe he douted of our Lords reſurrection, vntill he firſt had touched his woundes, and therby hath taken from vs all woundes and dourfulnes of infidellitie; in ſuch ſort, that ſince then, the groundes of the Reſurrection were layd in him. He preached to the Parthians, Meedes,

L 5   Perſes,

Perfes, Hircans, Brachmans, and Indes . After he had well deferued of Chriftendom, he was thruft thorough the fide. His memorie is yet very much reuerenced in the Indes, not onlie of the Chriftians which dwel there, but of the Iewes, Mahumetans, and Paynimes, as is declared in the hiftorie of the conqueft of the eaft Indes, written by the Bifhop of Sylues. lib. 3.

Iacobi.

To wit, the Leffe, who was called the brother of our Lord. He was held for iuft from his mothers wombe, becaufe of his excellent vertue. He did neuer eate flefh, drinke wine, nor euer clothed him felfe with cloth dreft, or fhorne. Moreouer he was fo affiduous in prayer, that he had his knees as hard as a Camels. He afifted at the firft Councell held by the Apoftles. The Iewes, angry at his innocent life, for hatred caft him downe from the top of the Temple. He had his head cleft with a Fullers hooke . The citie of Ierufalem being fackt by Titus Vefpafian, this heauy difaftre was imputed by fome, to the cruell and inhuman maffacre committed vpon the perfon of this bleffed Apoftle.

Phillippi.

S. Phillipe, receaued expreffe commandement from Iefus Chrift to follow him, wherin the bleffed Apoftle promptlie obeyed . He

alfo

also brought Nathaniel with him to see our Lord, of whom he was presentlie acknowledged for the Sonne of God, & kinge of Israell. He instantlie besought him to shew him his Father . Of him our Sauiour asked the fiue loaues, wherwith he miraculously fed so manie thousandes of people in the desert. He preached in Samaria , and after in Hieropolis of Phrigia , which he cleansed and purged from the worship of Idols: yea of the impure and venemous viper there referued . In the end the vulgar people rose vp against him, & hunge him on a piller: but after acknowledging him , honnored him with a goodlie sepulcher , and embraced with vnspeakeable feruour , the faith and religion which he had preached.

Bartholomai.

Who onlie amongst the Apostles is said to haue bin of noble birth , and a philosopher. He preached to the Indians the Gospell of Christ , which he tourned into the vulgar tongue, as it was written by SaintMathew.He passed vnto the great Armenia , and there conuerted the king, his wife, and twelue cities . to the true worship of almightie God. Where vpon the brother of the kinge, being enraged against him, caufed him cruelly to be fleane a liue in contept of Christianitie, at the instigation of thofe, which adored the Idols.

L 6   *Ma-*

S. Mathew, called to follow Ieſus Chriſt, was a rich man. Of a common publican, he was made an Apoſtle. And of a receiuer of cuſtome, a diſtributer of ſpirituall treaſures. The Indians and Ethiopians, were by him, and by his prayers conuerted, with their kinge and his wife vnto the faith, by reaſon of the miraculous raiſing of their daughter from death to life. Hirtacus diſpleaſed, that by the Apoſtles aduiſe ſhe had vowed vnto God perpetuall virginitie, made him paſſe by the point of the ſworde, as he was celebrating at the Aultar. He wrote the Goſpell preached by him, in the Hebrew tongue : wherof the text (written by the hand of S. Barnabe) was found vpon his breſt, at the inuention of his body, buried in Cypres.

Simonis.

S. Simon was the brother of S. Iames the Leſſe. The zeale of this Saint, was verie great, by which hauing carefullie planted the word of God in Egipt, Cyrene, Afrique, Maritaine, and all Libia, he was put to death in the raigne of the Emperor Traian, at the age of fourſcore yeares, vnder pretence that he was a Chriſtian, and of the yſſue of the royall lyne of Dauid. Euery one maruelled, to ſee a ſpirit ſo ſtoute, reſolute, and couragious, in a body ſo craſie, feeble, and decrpid by age.

Et

Et Thadæi.

S. Thadeus, called Iudas, was the third brother of Iames the Lesse, and of Simon. Thadeus, is interpreted houlding: and this Thadeus most firmlie and constantlie held the faith of Christ. He wrote most sharplie against the corrupters of the truth, as his Catholique epistle doth very well testifie He animated the faithfull, to constancie in the faith once receaued, by fearfull examples of the relapsed Angells, and commemoration of the future iudgment. He announced to Mesopotamia, and the adiacent contries the worde of God by the sweetnes wherof he mollified and made tractable the mindes and spirits of the people, otherwise fearfullie barbarous, feirce, and wilde.

Lini.

To these twelue Apostles are added, the number of twelue glorious Martyrs, who in the begining of the Church, offered them selues to God liuing hostes, and shed their bloodes, for the Confession of the name, and faith of Iesus.

In the first place is named S. Linus, who was the first Pope after S. Peter in the gouerment of the Church of God In which seate, he sate vntill his passion. Hauing indured sundry kindes of torments for the loue of Christ, he rendred vp his holie soule vnto his Sauiour.

Cleti

Cleti.

S. Cletus fucceeded Linus in the popedom.
And albeit the defire to be a Bifhop is a thing
right laudable, not withftanding S. Cletus
could not be wonne to accept of the bifhop-
pricke of Rome, but by the perfwafion of S.
Clement, deputed by S. Peter for his fucceffor. Hauing religiouflie ordered the affaires
of the Church, the fpace of twelue yeares, he
was martyred vnder the Emperor Domitian.
The feate by occafion of his death, was va-
cant 20. dayes, with the vnfpeakable griefe of
the people, deftituted of their incomparable
good paftor: hauing neuer bene touched in
his actions, but with the zeale of pietie, holie,
and religious deuotion.

Clementis.

Saint Clement was the difciple of S. Peter,
and the fourth pope after him. He chofe him
amongft others, to be his immediat fucceffor in the Apoftolat: but he would not of humilitie accept the charge, but deferred it to
S. Linus, and S. Cletus, by whofe deceafe it
was committed vnto him. The Emperor
Traian offended that by his exemplar life, the
Romans were daylie conuerted to Chriftia-
nitie, confined him within an iland, in the
which two thoufand Chriftians were condemned to fawe marbles for the ornament
of Rome. The people of the iland, in great
distreffe

diſtreſſe for want of freſh water, were by him refreſhed, hauing found a ſpringing fountaine vnder the feete of a Lambe. Wherupon the Emperor more offended then before, cauſed an anchor to be faſtned about his neck, and his bodie to be caſt into the ſea.

Sixti.

S. Sixtus was the eight Pope after Saint Peter. He ordayned in the ſolemnities of the Maſſe, the holie hymne of Sanctus to be ſunge, and of Agnus Dei. He was greatlie giuen to diuine thinges, as his holie decrees doe ſufficientlie teſtifie. He alſo receaued the glorious crowne of martyrdome in the time of the Emperor Valerian.

Cornelij.

S. Cornelius was the twentith Pope in the time of the Emperor Decius. He tranſported, by the ayde and aſſiſtance of S. Lucina, an honorable matrone of Rome, the bodies of S. Peter and S. Paul, from the place of their buriall to put them in ſauegard. Whereof the Emperor being aduertiſed, and that he conuerted manie of the people to the faith of Chriſt, ſent him into banniſhment, where S. Cyprian often comforted him by letters, exciting him to conſtancie. The which, was imputed vnto him for treaſon to the ſtate, for the participation and intelligence which he was ſaid to haue with the publique enimies.

For

For this he was beheaded, & for not yealding
to adore the Idol of Mars. His martyrdome is
confirmed by the teftimonies of S. Ambrofe
and S. Auguftine.

Cypriani.

S. Cyprian Bifhop of Carthage, fuffered
alfo vnder the Emperors Valerian and Galian,
in the eight perfecution raifed againft the
Chriftians: the fame day that S. Cornelius, but
not the fame yeare. The actions and deport-
ments of this good Father were fuch, that
there is none who in reading his writinges,
can choofe but thinke to heare fpeake a true
Chriftian Bifhop, and one defigned to martyrdome, for the honor of God. His life and paffion, are written by Pontius his Deacon. He
had at his death fuch firme conftancie, that at
the pronounciation of the iudgment againft
him, vnderftandinge that he was to fuffer by
the fwoord, he cryed out aloud in the confi-
ftorie of the Tyrant, faying. *Deo gratias.* After his execution there was found in his hart,
the figure of the Croffe made in gould, in witnes of his his inuincible faith.

Laurentÿ.

S. Laurence was difciple of S. Sixtus, and
Archdeacon of the Church of Rome; He re-
ceued of him (being prifoner for the caufe of
religion, in the eight Valerian perfecution
after Nero) expres commandement to diftri-
bute

bute vnto the poore , the treafures of the Church , which he had in his keeping: the which he performed, with no leſſe care, then fidelitie. Vpon this occaſion , he was committed priſoner vnder the cuſtody of the gayler Hippolitus , whom he conuerted to the faith, with nineteene more of his familie. In the end he was cruellie roſted vpon a gridiron, with a ſlacke and prolonging fire , in the preſence of the Emperor Valerian.

Chryſogoni.

S Chriſogonus , hauing refuſed the digniⁱ ties and offices , which the Emperor Diocleⁱ ſian offered vnto him , to renounce Chriſtiaⁱ nitie , and to adore the falſe and counterfet Gods , was by his commandement beheaded at Aquila. Nicephorus inferteth in his eccleⁱ ſiaſticall hiſtorie , ſome epiſtles written vnto him by S. Anaſtaſia , and of him to hir. This deuout Ladie did liberallie ſuccour and aſiſt him with meanes, during the time of his impriſonment.

Ioannis & Pauli.

S. Iohn and Paul were bretheren , no leſſe zealous of Chriſtian pietie , then noble and rich , who had bin brought vp in the court, vnder the ſeruice of the daughter of the great Emperor Conſtantin , and greatlie fauoured of hir. After his diſeaſe , Iulian the Apoſtata being come to the Empire , placed them in the

the eftate of his houfhold feruants, knowing that they would refufe this condition by reafon of their religion. Which they hauing done, he commanded that they fhould be beheaded: fo that the felfe fame death and paffion made them true bretheren, albeit they were fo already by nature In honor of their holie and inuincible refolution, the Church calleth them Oliues and Candlefticks fhining before God, in the Epiftle of the Maffe vpon their feaft, taken out of the 11. cap. of the Apocalips.

Cofma & Damiana.

S. Cofme and Damian were alfo bretheren, and Arabians of nation. They were famous in the arte of Phifick, and Chirugerie, which arte they exercifed freelie and purelie for the loue of God, and were imployed by the true phifition more to cure the difeafes of foules, then of the bodies. For this caufe, Dioclefian and Maximian forced them to paffe by water, fire, and fword, in the maner defcribed in their Legend: but God who neuer forfaketh thofe that are his; refrefhed them, and gaue them happie repofe, according to the confolation promifed to the afflicted by the Royall prophet.

Et omnium fanctorum tuorum.

Whofe number and multitude is fo great and maruelous, that Conftantin the Emperor paffing ouer the feas, and finding Eufebius,
Bifhop

Biſſiop of Ceſaria , deſired him to aske ſom-
what of him to enrich his Church . Who answered the Emperor, ſaying. Sir my Church a-
boundeth ſufficiently in riches, but I beſeeche
you , to ſend out into all partes of the world,
to knowe and vnderſtand the names of the
Saints: the times of their paſſiõs: vnder whom:
how: and in what places they ſuffered martyrdome . Which being done , there was found
for euery feaſt in the yeare , more then fiue
thouſand Saints : excepting on the day of the
kalendes of Ianuarie , in which the Gentils
gaue them ſelues to their banquettinges and
ſolemnities , and not to the martyring of the
bleſſed Saints.

Quorum meritis percibuſque concedas.

And here leaſt any ſhould thinke it in vaine
to craue the interceſſion of the moſt B. Saintes, or dout that thoſe holy Saints whom ſpeciallie we pray vnto , doe not againe employ
their eſpeciall protection towards vs , S. Gregorie, in his hom. 35, telleth of a certaine ma-
tron , who often frequenting the Church of
the bleſſed martyrs, Proceſſus, and Martinian,
vpon a day was met with all by the two holie
Martyrs them ſelues , who ſpake vnto hir,
ſaying. Thou doeſt viſit vs now, we will therfore demaund thee in the day of iudgment,
and all that we are able , we will performe,
and doe for thee.

Vt

Vt in omnibus.

To wit, which ether in the behalfe of the
glorie of thy moſt bleſſed name, or of the ſaluation of our owne ſoules, is on our part to be
beleeued, deſired, or to be accompliſhed.

Protectionis tuæ muniamur auxilio.

In faithfullie beleeuing, clearelie vnderſtanding, hartelie deſireing, and readilie accompli-
ſhing in all thinges, thy good will and holie
pleaſure: and thereby may be protected againſt
the machinations of all our enimies, viſible
and inuiſible.

Per eundem Chriſtum Dominum
noſtrum, Amen.

The aforſaid prayer concludeth, like as
all others, thorough Ieſus Chriſt our Lord.
Which concluſion plainlie declareth, that in
the veneration of the bleſſed Saints, we doe
not ſo much worſhip the Saints, as our Lord
in the Saints: For whilſt in them, we praiſe
and magnifie the wonderfull giftes and goodnes of God, what elſe doe we, but magnifie
God him ſelfe? who as the Apoſtle ſaith, wor-
keth all thinges in all.

To conclude, this part of the holie Canon,
as ſome graue authors affirme, was vndoutedly compoſed by the inſtinct and ordonance
of God him ſelfe. In confirmation wherof
they report, that ſome Fathers, out of a ſingular deuotion which they boare to ſome other
Saints,

Saints, added their names to the holy Canon, and remoued the names of ſome of theſe, alreadie added. But, the day being paſſed,on the morrowe,they found thoſe blotted out,& the former written againe in letters of gould.

Of the prieſts ſpreading his handes ouer the Chalice.

At this part of the Canon, next enſuing,the prieſt lifteth vp both his handes from the Aultar, and ſpreadeth, or extendeth them ouer the Chalice: to ſignifie, that now at this preſent, he ought to lay away from him all temporall cares, and to haue his minde wholie fixt, and attent to his ſacrifice. All the people therfore behoulding this ceremonie, ought ſpirituallie to imitate his example.

C H A P. XLVII.

Hanc igitur oblationem.

FIRST he ſaith. Therfore, to demonſtrate that this part of the Canon, is the concluſion of that which went before, as if he ſhould ſay. Therfore, becauſe there is no place to offer the ſacrifice of vnitie, out of the vnitie of the Catholique Church, we communicating with the memorie of the Saints, and in communion with them, offering vp this ſacrifice vnto thee, doe beſeeche thee,

thee, that by their interceffion, thou wouldeft accept and receiue this facrifice at our handes.

Seruitutis noſtræ.

Out of which wordes it is manifeſtlie to be gathered, that neuer in the law of the gofpel, was it permitted to al men a like to offer facrifice, but onlie to fuch as were prieſts, ordayned and confecrated by the impoſition of the handes of an Apoſtolicall Biſhop. Thefe wordes therfore, are to be vnderſtood of the cleargie, which in all humble feruice, obedience, and fubiection, haue this peculiar charge committed vnto them.

Sed & cuncta familia tua.

But becaufe the prieſt is the publibue officer, and that all the prayers and oblations which he offereth, are for the Church vniuerfall whereof he is an officer, therfore he adioyneth, as alfo of all thy familie. Wherfore as the former wordes concerne the cleargie, fo thefe latter comprehend all the layte, which are alfo a part of the great familie of almightie God.

Quæſumus Domine, vt placatus accipias.

Here the prieſt requireth, that God, appeafed by the prayers of the Saints, would accept this oblation: not of the part of the Sacrifice it felfe, (which, can no way difpleafe God, becaufe it contayneth his onlie Sonne, of whom himfelfe hath teſtified faying. This is
my

my beloued Sonne in whom I am wellplea-
fed:) but of the part of the Sacrificer. In which
respect somtimes it is reiected, by reason of his
indeuotion or prophanation: lik; as the facrifices of the ancient law, vnduelie offered.

Diesque nostros in tua pace disponas.

In which wordes may be vnderstood, three
fortes of peace which we demaund of almightie God. Peace in our soules. Peace in our bodies. And peace in our worldlie goodes or
substance. The peace of our soules, is disturbed
by euil thoughtes, desires, and disordinate appetites. The peace of our bodies, by sundry sortes of diseases, and corporal indispositions. The
peace of our goodes, by warres, famins steri-
litie, drinesse, and such like calamities : who
then may giue vs these three sortes of peace,
but onlie he who hath command and power,
ouer our soules: ouer our bodies: and ouer our
goodes: and can deliuer vs from all euills of
minde: from all diseases of bodie: and from all
misfortune of our temporall substance.

And aptlie in this place is added the woord
Tua, Thy. For as Odo saith, there are two sortes of peace. There is the peace of the world,
and there is the peace of God. The peace of the
world is vnprofitable ; but the peace of God,
is both wholsome, and delectable.

Atque ab æterna damnatione nos eripi.

He which prayeth to be deliuered from
euer-

uerlafting damnation , without dout prayeth
alfo, to be preferued from the finne which deferueth damnation. For in vaine doth he praie
to be deliuered from eternall deathe, who
choofeth to abide in deadly finne.

Et in electorum tuorum iubeas grege numerari.

The flock of the elect is double . The one,
the good Paftor hath , vpon his proper fhoulders, brought already into the fould . The o-
ther, is as yet preferued & kept in the paftures.
Thofe in the fould, are the fecure triumphant.
Thofe in the paftures , are the doutfull mili-
tent . We therfore now pray , that thorough
the grace of the Holie Ghoft, we may be
made of the number of the elect , and be placed in heauen , in the focietie and companie
of the bleffed.

Thefe three petitions before recited , were
added by S. Gregorie , which are verie fhort,
but verie fweet, For what can be more fhort,
or what can be more fweet , then that which
is contained in thefe three petitions ? For to
difpofe our dayes in peace. For deliuerie from
euerlafting damnation. And for the obtaining
of euerlaftinge faluation. Out of thefe wordes
therfore , many notable thinges may be col-
lected. Firft, that God is foueraigne Lord of all
thinges, both temporall and eternall: both of
earth, hell, and heauen. Of the earth, faying.
Dife-

Diſpoſe our dayes in peace. Of hell ſaying Deliuer vs from euerlaſting damnation . Of heauen, ſaying And place vs among the number
of thyne elect.For if God were not ſoueraigne
Lord of the earth,how could he giue vs peace
in our dayes , and in all our temporall goodes
and ſubſtance ? And if he had not all power
ouer hell, how could he deliuer vs from euerlaſting damnation ? And if he were not Lord
of heauen, how could he place vs amongſt his
elect, in perpetuall felicitie and ſaluation?

Againe theſe wordes may be expounded in
another ſenſe. Diſpoſe our dayes in peace. To
wit, thorough him, which for vs was betrayd
into the handes of thoſe that hated peace.De-
liuer vs from euerlaſting damnation . To wit,
through him , who for vs was condemned to
a temporall death. And place vs amongſt the
number of thyne elect , or bleſſed . To witt,
thorough him, who for our ſakes, was num-
bred amongſt the wicked.

Per Chriſtum Dominum noſtrum,
Amen.

This prayer is concluded , thorough Chriſt
our Lord: to the which, ſaith Albertus, none
doe anſwere *Amen* , but only the Prieſt him
ſelfe, and the bleſſed Angells , who are pre
ſent in this miniſterie.

M   *CHAP.*

CHAP. XLVIII.

Of the begining of the principall part of the Canon.

Quam oblationem tu Deus.

HEre begineth the principall part of al the holie Canon, which is the Conſecration, where the prieſt inſiſteth, and beſeecheth almightie God, that the creatures of bread and wine, requiſite to the confection of the holie Euchariſt, may be ſanctified and bleſſed, yea changed and conuerted into the pretious body and blood of our Sauiour Ieſus. This part of the Canon, is cited by S. Ambroſe aboue 1200. yeares agone. l. 4. de Sacram. cap. 5.

In omnibus, quæſumus.

Which wordes, *in omnibus*, in all, may be diuerſlie vnderſtood: and firſt thus. In all, to wit, thou ô God, being in all creatures and natures, without definition: in al places, without circumſcription: and in all times, without alteration, bleſſe we beſeeche thee, this oblation. Or, In all, to wit (make this oblation bleſſed) in all wayes, in all maners, and in all circumſtances. Or, In all, that is to ſay (vouchſafe to make it bleſſed) aboue al hoſtes,

by

by transferring it into that Hoft, which is bleſſed aboue all Hoftes. Or, In all, to wit, (bleſſed) in all degrees, both cleargie and laitie,
both in the prieſt, and the people. Or, In all,
to wit, in all our vnderſtandinges, in all our
powers, in all our thoughtes, and in all our
intentions.

Bene+dictam.

The prieſt in this word prayeth, that the
oblation made in the begining, of giftes not
bleſſed, God would make bleſſed, to wit, by
that mifticall benediction, wher with of bread,
it may be changed into the bodie of Chriſt
(the cauſe of all benediction) Or bleſſed, to
wit, with glorie, that it may be made glorious.
Bleſſed with imortallitie, that it may be made
immortall. Bleſſed with incorruption, that it
may be made incorruptible. Bleſſed with diuinitie, that it may be deified.

Adſrip+tam.

Not finite. And in this ſence he craueth, that
his oblation, which before Conſecration, is
circumſcriptible and finite, God would make
incircumſcriptible and infinit. For as much as
in this moſt holie Sacrament; Chriſt is incircumſcriptible, as deuines doe teache, and as
the Catholique Church doth hould.

Ra+tam.

We call that ratified, which we account
for certaine, fix, and firme. Let it therfore be

made

made firme or ratified, that is, let it not remayne instable, and subiect to be altered, or
changed by corruption.

Ratio † nabilem.

The blood of Bullocks & of Calues(being
vnreasonable creatures) was not sufficient to
purge man from sinne,they being much inferior,and lesser then man. For a reasonable
man therfore, a reasonable host is requisit, to
wit Christ, that we may offer a true man, for
men, and that so for mans sake, God may be
propitious and mercifull vnto men.

Accepta † bilemque facere digneris.

That can not be but acceptable, which
hath receiued the three former species of all
sortes of benediction. God can not hate
God: but because God is charitie, God loueth
God, and the host which is God, is acceptable to God. Why then pray we, that to be
made acceptable, which no way cã displease?
Because though it be acceptable for it selfe,
yet we may displease in respect of our selues.

Others againe haue interpreted these wordes in another sence, as thus.That God would
vouchsafe to make our oblation. *Benedictam*
blessed, whereby allthat participat thereof ar
made blessed. *Adscriptam*, Written, by the
which we are written in the booke of eternall life. *Ra am*, Ratified, by the which we
are incorporated in the bowells of Christ.

Ratio-

Rationabilem reaſonable (not vnreaſonable)by
the which we are made cleane from all vncleane and beaſtlie deſires . *Acceptabilemque,*
and acceptable,wherby we,who haue diſpleaſed him . may be made acceptable vnto him
in his onlie Sonne.

Vt nobis.

That to vs. That is to our health and profit.
Or,to vs, for whom he deliuered his bodie to
death, that he m ght giue vs the ſame body in
foode to euerlaſting life. Againe aptlie ſayeth
he. To vs, that is to vs worſhippers of the Catholike faith, to vs communicating , to vs
worſhiping the memorie of the Saints To vs,
excludeth Pagans, Iewes, Heretiques, and all
ſorts of Infidels.

Corpus & ſanguis.

The wordes aforegoing were darke,obſcure,
and hard to vnderſtand, but now the gate is
opened, all is made manifeſt, to wit, that
there be made to vs, the bodie & blood of Ieſus Chriſt ; which onlie is an hoſt, in all, and
aboue a'l, bleſſed, adſcript, ratified, reaſonable, and acceptable.

Fiat.

And worthelie in this place is the word
Fiat , added, becauſe now there is required
the ſame almightie power in this conuerſion,
which was in the incarnation of the almighty
word , and in the creation of all the world.

For God said whē he was to create the world, *Fiat lux* . And our Ladie said to the Angell, when Christ our Lord was to be incarnat, *Fiat mihi* . And the priest therfore in this place, *Fiat corpus*

Againe he saith *Fiat*, by way of deprecation: to denote, that the priest by his owne naturall abilitie , cannot worke that supernaturall conuersion . And therfore he saith not in his owne person. *Facio*, I make: but *Fiat*, let it be made, to wit, by the omnipotent power of almightie God.

Dilectissimi Filij tui Domini nostri Iesu Christi.

That of the substance of bread and wine which are offered vnto thee, may be made by diuine and miraculous transubstantiation, the body and blood of thy best beloued Sonne: The substance of bread, to be conuerted into his blessed body: and the substance of wine, into his pretious blood.

Of the fiues Crosses which are made at the prolation of the fiue wordes aforesaid: and what the same doe signifie.

The 1. *Reason.*

You are here to vnderstand , that there is no ceremonie in all the Catholique Church, more proper to represent the mysteries of the death and passion of our Lord , then is the
                                    signe

figne of the Holie Croffe. Where it is further
to be noted, that commonlie the order and
number of Croffes, which are made vpon
the Sacrifice, doe reprefent the order and
number of the myfteries of his bleffed paffion.
Wherfore if you confider how our Lord and
Sauiour was fould for monie, you fhall fee in
this fale, fundrie perfons, and fundrie practifes.
You haue the Prieftes, Scribes, and Pharifes,
who were the buyers: You haue Iudas, who
onlie was the feller. And you haue our Lord,
who onlie was fould. The three firft Croffes
therfore, fignifie the Prieftes, Scribes, and Pharifes, who brought him. The fourth, Iudas
who fould him. And the fift, our Lord who
was fould by him.

The 2. *Reafon.*

Againe, fome of our Doctors, haue marked
the very maner of making thefe Croffes, and
fay, that the firft three are made together vpon
the whole oblation: to fignifie, that the Prieftes, Scribes, and Pharifes, confpired altogether with one intention, againft our Lord and
Sauiour Iefus. But the other two are made a
funder, the one vpon the bread, the other vpon
the wine; to fignifie, the different intention
betwixt our Sauiour; and the traytor Iudas: for
the intention of our Sauiour, was loue and
charitie: but that of Iudas, auarice, and trea-
cherie.

The 3. Reaſon.

Againe by theſe fiue Croſſes, may be conſidered fiue principall places, wherein our
Lord ſuffered ſundrie torments and abuſes.
In the garden of Getſmanie, where he did
ſweat blood and water, for the great feare and
apprehenſion which he had of death. In the
houſe of Annas, where he receiued a blowe
on the face by a wicked varlet. In the houſe of
Caiphas, where he receiued many outrages,
reüylinges, hidinge of his eies, ſpittinges in
his face, and ſtrikinges. In the houſe of Pilat,
where he was bound to a Pillar, lamentablie
ſcourged, crowned with thornes, and clothed
in mocquerie. And vpon the mount Caluarie,
where he was ignominiouſly crucified, betwixt two theeues.

The 4. Reaſon.

Againe, theſe fiue Croſſes may be referred
to the fiue principall partes of our Lordes
body, wherein he receiued his holy woundes,
to wit, in both his hands, both his feet, and
his bleſſed ſide. And the two laſt Croſſes
which are made a part (the one vpō the bread,
the other vpon the wine) ſignifie vnto vs, that
our Lord trulie died for our redemption: for
the blood ſeperated from the bodie, is a moſte
true and certaine ſigne of death.

The 5. Reaſon.

Againe, the three firſt Croſſes which are
made

made vpon the oblation, may signifie three
speciall thinges, which our Lord did in his last
supper, concerning the bread and the wine:
to wit, he tooke, blessed, and gaue to his Disciples. Afterwards one Crosse is made vpon
the bread, because he said. *Comedite, hoc est
corpus meum.* Eate, this is my body. Another
vpon the Chalice, because he said. *Bibite ex
hoc omnes, hic est sanguis meus* Drinke yee all
of this, this is my blood. And according her-
unto rightly is subioyned that which followeth. *Qui pridie quam pateretur.* Who the
day before he suffered.

CHAP. XLIX.

Qui pridie quam pateretur.

THe time of the institution of the holie
Eucharist is here declared, by the ordonance of Pope Alexander the first. The day
before, that is to say, the fift feria, which was
next vnto the holie feast of the passouer,
vpon which day this blessed Sacrament was
first instituted. Wherfore the priest celebrating this holie mysterie, ought to direct
his intention, to that end which our Sauiour him selfe then did, sitting in the
middest of his Disciples. For this verie
day Iesus Christ, hauing eaten the paschall

M 5   lambe

lambe with his Difciples, for the finall accomplifhment of the law of Moyfes, prepared for
them a new fort of meate , giuing him felfe
vnto them in fpirituall foode , vnder the formes of bread and wine.

Accepit panem.

After the obferuation of the time of this in-
ftitutiõ, is expreffed the matter which he vfed,
to wit, bread (trulie) not yet flefh. And therfore bread, becaufe as the material bread comforteth the hart of man aboue all other naturall meates: fo this holy Euchariſt, ſerueth him
to the nourifhment and fuftentation of his
foule, aboue all other fpirituall meates.

In fanctas ac venerabiles manus fuas.

By verie good right , the Church doth call
the handes of hir fpoufe Iefus Chriſt, wherewith he touched the bleffed Euchariſt, holy &
venerable, for as much as the deuine and human nature, are both in him cõioyned. Thefe
are thofe facred handes, by whom the admirable worke of the world was formed , without any patterne, or example. Man made after
his deuine image. Bread fo many times multi-
plied to his vfe . The pofeffed , deliuered of
malignant fpirits . The leprous and fick, healed. The dead raifed. And we daily repleniſhed
with deuine benedictions.

Et eleuatis in cœlum oculis.

None of the Euangeliſts , doe teſtifie, that
                                        Chriſt

Chriſt in his laſt ſupper , lifted vp his eyes to heauen , but Apoſtolicall tradition hath deliuered this to the Church ; For this hath the Maſſe of S. Iames the Apoſtle . The Liturgie of S. Baſil. And alſo S. Ambroſe in his 4. booke *de Sacramentis* Where S. Iames and S. Baſil , doe not content them ſelues to ſay that he lifted vp his eies to God his Father almigh-ie,but furthermore that he ſhewed vnto him the bread which he held betwixt his handes. Whereby they would ſignify vnto vs,that our Lord intended to worke ſome ſuch great and maruelous thinge, as required there vnto, the whole omnipotencie and power of almightie God.

Ad te Deum Patrem ſuum.

Our bleſſed Sauiour , about to conſecrate his pretious body and blood, lifted vp the eies of his humanitie vnto God his Father , not thoſe of his diuinitie , becauſe he was in nothing vnlike or inferior to his Father : who as he is coequall to him in dignity, ſo likewiſe in his euerlaſting viſion and comprehenſion.

Omnipotentem.

Where ſpeciall commemoration is made of the almightie & diuine omnipotencie, to ſetle and confirme our faith, that we feare not the conſecration to be a thinge impoſſible, nor dout of the truth or veritie therof.

M 6   *Tibi*

Tibi gratias agens.

And hereof it is that this facrifice is called, a facrifice of prayfe or thankfgiuing, becaufe the beft procurer of benefits, is the minde-fullnes of benefits, ioyned with continuall giuing of thankes. Or therefore our Lord gaue thankes, being fo neere his paffion: to teache vs to beare all thinges, which we fuffer, with thankfgiuing. Or, he gaue thankes to his omnipotent Father, for fo excellent a grace, for fo effectuall a foode, for fo woorthie a facrament, and for fo profound a myfterie; yet not for him felfe, but for vs, that is for our redemption and reparation, which was to be brought to paffe by his death and paffion, wherof this fhould for euermore, re-maine a perpetuall commemoration.

Benedixit.

After the giuing of thankes, he imparted the vertu of his holie benediction vpon the bread, and conuerted the fubftance thereof in to that of his pretious bodie. The fame like-wife he d d at the creation of the world, when he ordayned the increafe & multiplication of his creatures, euerie one accordinge to his kind. Neuer doe we reade that he bleffed the bread, but that there infued fome notable mi-racle, as in the multiplication of the fiue loaues and the two fifhes, whereof the frag-ments, were twelue baskets, after the refec-tion

tion of fiue thousand soules.

In pronouncing this word, the Priest maketh the signe of the Crosse, because as Saint Aug. saith, from the same all Sacraments doe receaue their efficacie, and that nothing without it, is decently accomplished. Adde, that the Crosse, is the onlie carecter of all benediction, euer since it touched the blessed body of our Sauiour Iesus.

Fregit.

Which is not so to be vnderstood, that Christ did first breake, before he did confecrate, but after: like as in the genealogie of Christ, S. Mathew nameth Dauid before Abraham, who yet was not before, but after Abraham.

Deditque.

To wit, his B. body vnto his Disciples, who then were present in body, and now also he giueth the same to all the faithfull: to the end, that to those for whom he was to giue him selfe in price of redemption, he woulde likewise giue him selfe in foode and refectiõ. For Christ two manner of wayes gaue him selfe for vs: once vpon the Crosse, for the sinnes of all the world, which needed not to be renued: the other, being miraculouslie instituted, and diuinelie ordayned, to preserue the daylie memorie of his death, may wholsomelie be againe renewed, the latter being a
true

true commemoration and remembrance of the former.

Difcipulis fuis, dicens.

Where it is faid, to his difciples, to teach vs, that none can worthelie receiue this Sacrament, vnles he be his true Difciple, that is to fay, doe faithfullie beleeue what is to beleeued, of this moft high and diuine Sacrament. For this caufe, the Caphernaits were not his true difciples, who hearing the doctrin of Chrift, touching this diuine myfterie, went back, faying. How can this man giue vs his flefh to eate? This is a hard fpeeche, & the like.

Accipite.

By which word the adminiftration of this B. Sacrament is expreffed, fuch being the office of the Prieft in the Church, that it is not lawful for any other whofoeuer, were he Kinge or Emperor of al the world, to difpence the holie Eucharift vnto the people: Chrift hauing refigned this charge onlie to Prieftes, and not to any other, ether man or Angell.

Et manducate.

Here is expreffed the principall caufe of the inftitution of this moft holie and bleffed Sacrament: which is not onlie to be confecrated, and honorablie referued. but to the end that the faithfull Chriftians may receiue, eate, and employ the fame to their neceffities, with firme faith, ardent deuotion, and exact
proofe

proofe and examination of their conſcience, and by this meanes, to be vnited and dwell in Ieſus Chriſt, and he in them.

Ex hoc omnes.

Firſt Florus Magiſter ſaith, that theſe wordes commend vnitie and peace vnto vs: that by this miſterie participating of Chriſt, we may be all one in Chriſt. Next, theſe wordes (eate you all of this) are not ſo to be vnderſtoode, as that diuers might eate diuers partes of the ſame, and not eache one Chriſt entirelie, who although in reſpect of the diuers ſpecies, he may ſeeme to receiue one particle, and he another, yet according to the veritie, it is all one and the ſame, the whole and entire ſubſtance, of our Lordes body, which all doe eate, nether doe a thouſand receiue more then one, nor one leſſe then a thouſand, becauſe all receiue the whole body of our Lord, which now can no more be deuided into parts.

Hoc eſt enim corpus meum.

As theſe wordes of God (Encreaſe, multiplie, and repleniſh the earth) ſpoken once in the conſtitution of the world, haue ſtil as yet their effect vnto this preſent, ſo that nature, obeing his Creator, engendreth, produceth, and multiplieth in conuenient ſeaſon, all thinges according to their kinde, ſpecies, propertie, and condition: euen ſo, euer ſince that

Ieſus

Iefus-Chrift in his laft fupper , pronounced thefe words,faying (This is my body)he gaue them fuch benediction , force and vertu, that they are not only fignificatiue , but further-more effectiue, and as inftruments of his holy wil, to change that which was before comon bread,into his true, reall, and bleffed body.

Of the worship and adoration of the bleffed Sacrament.

The wordes of the holy Sacrament being pronounced, the Prieft houlding in both his handes, the bleffed bodye of Iefus Chrifts in the forme of bread, doth prefetly kneele him downe and adore the fame: fhewing herein, that by the vertu of the diuine word , our Lord, our God, and our Redeemer, is there reallie prefent. And then rifing vp,he doth ele-uate the fame on high,to the end that the af-fiftants alfo behoulding the fame , may adore their Lord and maker, and craue of him,that which may profit them to their faluation.

By which eleuation, we alfo are admonif-hed to haften vs, and foorth with, with trem-bling and feare , to proftrate our felues vnto the ground, and humblie to befeeche of him (who fomtimes being reallie lifted vp vpon the Croffe,and now trulie lifted vp vnder the forme of bread) that he, whofe glorie and magnificence is lifted vp aboue the heauens, would vouchfafe to drawe vs vpp thither to

him,

him, who ſayd, I; when I ſhall be exalted, wil
drawe all vnto me.

Simili modo.

Where he ſaith, in the llke maner, becauſe
the ſame ought to be vnderſtood and done,
touching the bleſſed blood of our Sauiour Ieſus, which was done before concerning his
bleſſed body, ſeing they are both one and the
ſame Chriſt: not the one more, and the other
leſſe, not his bodie in the Hoſt, without the
blood, nor his blood in the Chalice without
the bodie, but his whole bodie and blood in
the one, and his whole bodie and blood in
the other: all in heauen, and all vpon the Aultar: ſitting at the ſame time vpon the right
hand of his Father, and remayning likewiſe
preſent, vnder the ſpecies of the Sacrament.

Accipiens & hunc.

Where it is ſaid, that Chriſt tooke this
Chalice: if we ſhould referre the word (this)
to the veſſel, it is not the ſame, as touching the
matter and ſubſtance of the mettall, but if
we referre it to that which is contayned in
the veſſell, then that, and this, is all one. Againe, it is called (this) becauſe it is daylie bleſſed
with the ſame intention, that it may be made
now, that which it was made then. Againe
(this) becauſe this faith is one thoroughout
the whole Church, and he alſo one, to whom
both then and now, the ſame is offred.

Præcla-

Præclarum.

The Chalice, as yet but wine, is called noble, becaufe prefentlie it is made noble, by being conuerted into blood. As it is written; My chalice inebriating, how nóble is it? Or noble, by comparifon with that which Melchifedec, in the law of nature, and others of the ould Teftament offered. Or becaufe of the great and noble maieftie of him to whom it is offer'd. Wherupon in that which prefentlie followeth he faith. We offer to thy noble maieftie.

Calicem.

Chalice, is taken in three fundrie fenfes. 1. For fufferance, or paffion, as Mat. 20. Can you drinke the Chalice which I ám to drinke? 2. For the drinke contayned in the Chalice. 3. For the cup or veffell which contayneth the liquor, and fo Chrift tooke the Chalice into his handes. Which veffell, according to Albertus, is called. *Calix, à calore,* that is to fay, of heate or calor; becaufe it enkindleth in vs the fire of Chari:ie.

In fanctas ac venerabiles manus fuas.

Pe fectlie holie, becaufe of the Holy Ghoft, and the plenitude of graces, infufed into him. Venerable, becaufe of the fundrie ftupendious miracles which he wrought with them. Perfectlie holie, becaufe neuer was there found in them any kinde of iniquitie. Venerable. becaufe

caufe they were of power to fanctifie.

Item tibi gratias agens.

To wit , for the redemption of mankind, which was to be purchafed and wrought , by the fhedding of his blood . Againe , giuing thankes to thee , to wit , for his infirme and weake feruants, who were daylie to be refie-fhed and comforted , with this moft pretious and celeftiall nourifhment.

Benedixit.

The prieft taking into his handes the ho-lie Chalice, giueth thankes , as aforefaid, and with the wordes of Iefus Chrift , doth like-wife bleffe the fame, making the figne of the Croffe theron, as before vpon the bread. And vpon the Chalice, (as before vpon the bread) the figne of the Croffe is but once made: be-caufe our Lord was but once crucified·. And therfore once vpon the bread, when it is con-fecrated, and once againe vpon the wine when it is confecrated : becaufe our Lord was cru-cified for the faluation of two people.

Deditque Difcipulis fuis, dicens.

He gaue , and neyther fould , nor rendred what he had borrowed of others, but as a free gift, he gaue it freelie: that after his example, we fhould not giue the fame , nether for fa-uour, nor any price of mony , to vnworthie dogges , or obftinat finners , but hauing re-ceued freelie, we fhould giue it freelie, to the worthy

worthy receiuers.

Accipite & bibite ex eo omnes.

Where Iefus Chrift comanded all to drinke of the faid Chalice : but this commandement was made onlie to his Apoftles, ordayning them Prieftes in his laft fupper : which is fufficiently demoſtrat d by the nuber of twelue, curiouflie noted by the bleffed Euangelifts, and namely by S. Mark witneffinge that they all (to wit the Apoftles) drank, without expreffing, that any other drank thereof, befides them felues.

Hic eſt enim calix fanguinis mei.

In this place is expreffed the forme which Iefus Chrift vfed in the confecration of the Wine, together with the order and maner thereof. Where it is called the Chalice by a metaphor, for that which is contayned in the Chalice: as in the promife of the reward of him, who fhall giue for, and in, the name of Iefus Chrift, a cup of cold watter. Where the gift is not vnderftoode of the cup, but of the water in the cup.

Noui & æterni.

Firft according to Innocentius 3. it is called *nouum, id eſt vltimum,* new, that is, laft : as the laft day is called, *dies nouiſsima,* a new day. And next eternall, not for want of a beginning, but for deniall of the fucceffion of any other, for neuer fhall any other follow it: for

no-

nothing can succede that which is eternall, o-
therwise it should not be eternall. Againe, it is
called new, and eternal, for the old testament,
promised onlie thinges transitorie, and temporall, not permanent and eternall, as doth
the new.

Testamenti.

Firft. Testament, is not here taken onlie
for a writing, but for a promise. Next, a
Testament, is the finall diftribution of goodes, ratified by the death of the teftator. And
Chrift in this his laft Teftament, diftributed,
ordayned, and promifd euerlafting inheritance to his beloued children, that is, to all
faithfull people. Againe, the fore is it called a Teftament, becaufe he confirmed, all the
promifes teftified, in his blood. In figure
whereof, Abraham hauing made a league,
with Abimelech and Phicol, offeredvp fheepe
and oxen, and with their blood confirmed
the league. And Iacob, flying into Galaad,
hauing made an oath to his ouncle Laban,
offered facrifice, that by the blood of the facrifice, the oath of the conuenant might be
confirmed. And Moyfes, that he might confirme the Teftament, which he receaued in
Syna, fprinkled all the people with the blood
of the offeringes.

Myfterium fidei.

This word is borrowed of the Greekes, fignifying

nifying a secret, which we must vndoutedlie beleeue by faith, albeit we can not see it sensiblie to the eie, nor apprehend it by humane reason. The misterie of faith, because it belongeth to Catholique faith, to beleeue after cõsecration, that it is true blood, so that now he is an Infidell, which beleeueth not the same. The misterie of faith, because one thinge is seene, and another thinge is beleeued. *Nam verus sanguis creditur, quod vinum visu sentitur & gustu.* For that is beleeued to be true blood, which both to sight and tast, seemeth wine: it tasteth wine, & is not; it appeareth not blood, and yet it is blood.

Qui pro vobis & pro multis.

For you, to wit, for you that are present. For many, to wit, for all Pagans, Iewes, and false Christians. And the wordes for many, seeme purposelie to be added, to the end that this speeche should not onlie be referred to the persons of the Apostles, but generallie to all faithfull. For although one onlie drop of the blood Christ, is in it selfe sufficient to purge the sinnes of all, and to giue life and saluation to the whole world, yet it is not simply or absolutelie shed *pro omnibu*, for all, but onlie, *pro multis*, for many. The reason wherof is, because all doe not receaue benefit therby, but onlie such, who by faith and good workes, doe labour and endeuour to make
them

them ſelues gratefull in the ſight of God . Durandus ſaith, that it is ſhed for the predeſtinate
onlie, as touching the efficacie , but for all,
as touching the ſufficiencie: for the iuſt, ſaith
he , the blood of the iuſt: yet ſuch is the riches of this treaſure, that if all vniuerſallie beleeued, all vniuerſallie ſhould be ſaued.

Effundetur.

Where he ſpeaketh not according to ſome
part thereof, but according to the whole:
For liquour which is ſhed foorth of a veſſell,
according to ſome part thereof , is trulie ſaid
to be ſhed , but not to be ſhed out , becauſe
ſome remayneth within: but of the blood of
Ieſus Chriſt, it is here ſaid, not, *fundetur*, ſhed:
but *effundetur*, that is, ſhed out: to wit, wholie and entirelie ſhed out of his bleſſed bodie.
And euen as the louing Pellican douteth not,
to ſhed hir owne blood, to reuiue hir younge
ones which are dead: euen ſo Chriſt our Lord
feared not for vs that were dead by ſinne , to
power out his pretious blood , to reſtore vs
to life.

In remiſsionem peccatorum.

The cauſe for the which the aforſaid effu-
ſion was made, is the remiſſion of ſinnes.
Which is done by two maner of wayes : The
firſt is, by way of lauer and waſhing . The ſecond, by way of payement and ſatisfaction.
Touching the firſt; as he that entereth moſt
foule

foule into a bathe of wholfome waters, commeth foorth moft cleane by the lauar of the
fame: euen fo the foule which is foule by the
fpottes of finne, entering into the bath of
Chriftes moft pretious blood, is purelie wafhed by the ver u therof. Touching the fecond; as he that payeth another mans det, fets
the partie as free as if he had payed with his
owne monie: euen fo Chrift thorough hi- bitter death, hauing fhed his blood hath thereby
paid our det, and fatisfied the iuftice of his Father on our behalfe; and that much better,
then if we our felues had payed with our proper blood.

Hæc quotiefcunque feceritis, in mei me-moriam faciatis.

Firft thefe wordes are to be referred to
both partes of the Sacrifice, as well to the
bread, as to the wine: and to the confecration,
as well of the one, as of the other. Next they
may alfo be vnderftood two maner of wayes.
Firft thus; So often as you fhal eate this bread,
and drinke this Chalice, doe it in the remembrance of my death and paffion: and this belongeth more generallie to all. Secondlie as
thus; So often as you fhal confecrate this bread
and this wine, according to this my inftitution, due it in the remembrance of me: and
this appertayneth particularly to prieftes. And
well is it faid, in the remembrance of me. For
this

this trulie was one cauſe of the inſtitution of this moſt holie Sacrifice, in the Church mili. tant, that it ſhould be a ſigne, repreſentation, and remembrance, of that high and excellent Sacrifice which Chriſt offered vp vpon the Croſſe. Againe, In remembrance of me. For this laſt remembrance of him ſelfe, our Lord left and recommended vnto vs. Euen as ſome one going into a far countrie, ſhould leaue ſome ſinguler pledge or token of his loue to him whom he loued, that as often as he ſhould ſee the ſame, he ſhould remember his frendſhip and kindnes; becauſe if he loued him perfectlie, he can not behould it, without verie great motion or affection of mind.

Vnde & memores Domine.

Mindfull, as if he ſaid, this we doe according to thy commandement. After the example of Elias, who praying that God would approue his ſacrifice. Heare me, ſaith he, ô Lord, becauſe I haue done all theſe thinges according to thy commandement. Mindfull; becauſe our Lord him ſelfe commanded that we ſhould doe this in memorie of him, therfore three thinges the Church propoſeth in the wordes following to be remembred: his bleſſed Paſſion: his Reſurrection: and his Aſcenſion.

N   *Nos*

Nos ferui tui.

To wit, we prieftes, who according to the degrees receaued of cleargie, doe ferue thee in the oblation of this facrifice: and doe celebrate the fame, after thy example, and in the memorie of thee. For the people performe that onlie in minde, which the Prieft both performeth in minde, and alfo inexternall and peculiar maner.

Sed & plebs tua fanĉta.

The people alfo are faid to be mindfull, beeaufe Chrift died, not onlie for the Prieftes, but alfo for the people: and ordayned this Sacrament for the comfort, as well of the one, as of the other: and therfore as well the one ought to be mindfull of him, as the other. And this people is faid to be holie, becaufe hauing receaued baptifme and Gods holie grace, they are therby truly fanĉtified, how far foeuer they be difperfed, being firmelie lincked together in the vnitie of the fame Church.

Eiufdem Chrifti filij tui Domini noftri tam beatæ pafsionis.

And very rightlie is the paffion of our Lord and redeemer Iefus, called bleffed: becaufe by it we are deliuered from all curfe and malediĉtion, and by it we receiue all bliffe and benediĉtion.

Nec

Nec non & ab inferis Resurrectionem.

Ianſonius in his expoſition vpon this place, hath very well noted, that becauſe in the wordes aforegoing, mention is made of our Sa>uiours paſſion, therfore ſaith he. Chriſt wil not haue the hinder part of his mortall life to be ſeene, but paſſing, like as God ſhewed himſelf to Moyſes: that is he will not haue his death to be commemorated, vnles we alſo beleeue in his reſurrection.

Sed & in cælos glorioſa Aſcenſionis.

The holie Doctors who haue expounded the Miſteries of the Maſſe, doe bring ſundrie reaſons, why in making remembrance of our Lord, we principallie doe mention his Paſſion, his Reſurrection, and his Aſcenſion. And ſome ſay, that this is done, becauſe by theſe three meanes principallie, he hath wrought and accompliſhed our Redemption. For, he died, ſay they, to deliuer vs from death. He roſe againe, to raiſe vs to life. And he aſcended into heauen, to glorifie vs euerlaſtinglie. His paſſion, exciteth our Charity: his Reſurrectiõ ſtrengtheneth our Faith: and his Aſcenſion, reioyceth our Hope. By his Paſſion he hath blotted out our ſinnes: by his Reſurrection he hath ſpoyled hell. And by his Aſcenſion he hath ſhewed vnto vs, the way to heauen.

Offerrimus præclaræ maieſtati tuæ.

That is to God the Father: for often in the

N 2   Scrip-

Scripture, by the titles of omnipotency, glory, maieftie, and the like, the perfon of the Father is vnderftood ; as Heb. 1. and in fundrie other places .

De tuis donis ac datis.

The bodie and blood of Chrift, are off-rin- ges prepared by God for vs : yea true offerin- ges , but placed in heauen . Offeringes, when they are made to God : guiftes, when they are giuen in earthe to men . Yet both here and there, trulie the fame.

Hoſtiam.

Firft fome explicating this word (Hoft) fay, that it is deriued *ab Oſtio* . in Englifh , a doore : becaufe in the ould law , the Hoftes were immolated in the porch, or entrie of the temple . The Chriftians doe giue it the fame denomination , becaufe that Iefus Chrift (Sa- cramentallie immolated at the Aultar) hath opened vnto them the gates of heauen , fhut thorough the preuarication of Adam. When- ce the Chutch at the Eleuation of the Hoft fingeth this verſe . *O ſaluaris Hoſtia qui cęli pandis oſtium, bella premunt hoſtilia, da robur fer auxilium.*

The Paynims and Gentils haue deriued this terme *ab Hoſte.* in Englifh, an Enimie, becaufe being to make warre againft their enimies, they did firft facrifice , to the end that they might ouercome. And after happie fucceffe, they

they ordayned other facrifices which they called victimes, leading their enemies boūd euen
to the Aultar. Wherupon Ouid compofed the
difticque following.

Hoſtia quæ cecidit dextra victricevocatur,
hoſtibus a victis, victima nomen habet.

And Chriſt Iefus, being to fight againſt
the enimie of mankind, offered vp his body
and blood in an Hoſt, wherby he hath deliuered vs out of the bondage and feruitude of
the diuel.

† *Puram.*

Next this hoſt is called (Pure) becaufe it
is the fountaine of all puritie, cleanfing vs
from al pollution by the force of its vertu: cō-
trarie to thofe of the old Teftament, which
did not cleanfe, but onlie bodilie foulenes.

Hoſtiam † *fanctam.*

It is alfo called (Holie) becaufe it contayneth Iefus Chrift, the holie of holies, and
the onlie fountaine of all holynes, from
whom the graces of the holie Ghoft poure
downe vpon the faithfull, in vnfpeakable a-
boundance,

Hoſtiam † *immaculatam.*

Conceiued and borne without all finne,
and liued in this world without all finne, and
therfore immaculat. Conceiued of a virgin,
without the helpe of a man, and therfore immaculate.

maculate. Onlie by power diuine, and therfore immaculate.

Panem † *fanctum.*

Where this holie Hoſt is named Bread, not
that the ſubſtance of bread now any more remayneth after Conſecration, but becauſe it is
inſtituted or ordayned vnder the ſame ſpecies.
Adde, that in holie Scripture, the creatures are
called, earth, and aſhes, becauſe they are formed of ſuch matter. Simon was ſurnamed le-
prouſe, of that which he had bin, and was
no more &c.

And this bread is rightlie called *fanctum* holy; becauſe it trulie ſanctifieth the receauers.

Vitæ eterna.

And of eternall life, becauſe, as the goſpell
faith, he that eateth of this bread, ſhall liue
for euer, Againe of eternall life, becauſe it is no
more common as it was before conſecration,
but ſpirituall, celeſtiall, diuine, Angelicall;
ſurpaſſing all corruptible meate, an incorruptible aliment, a foode giuing life to our ſoules; and by vertue of which, in the generall
reſurrection, our bodies alſo ſhalbe made immortall.

Et Calicem † *falutis perpetua.*

The prieſt, beſides the Euchariſtical bread,
offereth to God the holie Chalice, to wit, the
blood of Ieſus Chriſt, contayned vnder the
ſpecies of wine. The conſecration of both
which,

which, is made separatlie, and yet neuertheles is but one Sacrament: euen as the materiall foode of the bodie, is but one meale or banket, although it consist, both in meate and in drinke.

Of the fiue Croßes made at the rehearsall of the fiue wordes aforsaid.

Becaufe the Church hath faid before, that shee was mindfull of our Lordes bleſſed paſsion, therfore prefentlie after the Eleuation of the pretious-bodie and blood of Iefus Chrift, the prieft maketh fiue Croſſes, in the remembrance of his fiue moft pretious and principall woundes, to wit, two in his handes, two in his feet, and one in his fide. The firſt three that are made vpon the Hoft and the Chalice together, may fignifie, that Chriſt trulie fuffered, trulie died, and was trulie buried. And the two laſt which are made, one vpon the Hoft, and the other, vpon the Chalice a funder, doe infinuate the confequence of thofe his bitter paines, to wit, the feperation and difiunct on of his holie foule, from his bleſſed bodie.

Supra quæ propitio, ac fereno vultu, refpicere digneris.

Vpon the which (to witt, Bread of eternall life, and Chalice of perpetuall health) vouchfafe to looke with a mercifull and gratious countenance. Which is to be vnderftood in

N 4   refpect

reſpect of vs , leaſt we put any impediment, which may hinder the benefits and graces, that otherwiſe we ſhould receiue of almightie God.

Et accepta habere.

Not of his part who is offered , who no way is , nor no way can be vnacceptable vnto thee, but of his part who is the offerer. For it can not be, that the onlie Sonne of God , in whom he is well pleaſed , and who reſteth in the boſom of his Father , ſhould not be moſt acceptable to him.

Sicuti accepta habere dignatus es munera.

Where it is to be noted , that we doe no wayes meane by theſe wordes, to equalize the ſacrifice of thoſe (who are immediatlie to be named) with this of ours, which is infinitlie more worthie and acceptable, then all other ſacrifices that euer were , or euer ſhall be (for they offered ſheepe and lambes , but we the Lambe of God : they creatures , and we the Creator: they the figure, we the veritie:) but the ſence is, that God would receiue as acceptable, this Sacrifice at our hands, like as he did the ſacrifices of thoſe holie Fathers , who for the ſincere deuotion of their hartes , were acceptable vnto him .

Pueri tui iuſti Abell.

Two titles are here giuen to Abell, the one be a childe ; the other to be iuſt . 1. To be a child,

child, in holie Scripture is often taken to be
harmeles, and to liue in simplicitie and innocencie Wherupon our Sauiour said in the gospell, Vnles you become like litle children you
can not enter into the kingdome of heauen.
Mat 19.2. This title of Iust, is giuen vnto Abel
by our Sauiour him selfe, saying. That all the
blood of the iust which is shed vpon the earth
may come vpon you, euen from the blood of
Abell the iust. Mat 23. Adde, that Abell was
a figure of our B. Sauiour: for the blood of
Abell was shed by his brother Cain: and the
blood of Iesus Christ, by his bretheren the
Iewes. Abell was a Priest, a Martyr, a Virgin,
and the first Shepheard: & Christ was a Priest,
a Martyr, a Virgin; and the chiefe shepheard
or Pastor of our soules.

Et Sacrificium Patriarchæ nostri Abrahæ

In the second place is proposed the example of the sacrifice of Abraham, who thorough
singular faith and obedience, offered to God
his onlie sonne. For the patriarch Abraham,
was of such singular faith and obedience, that
at the commandement of almightie God,
without any maner of dout or hesitation, he
had presentlie sacrificed his onlie Sonne, if the
voice of an Angell from heauen, had not spee-
dilie preuented the execution.

*Et quod tibi obtulit summus sacerdos
tuus Melchisedech.*

Melchisedech is placed in the third place,
who is here called the high priest of God, for
two respects: The one, because his priesthood was preferred before that of Aaron, and
for that he gaue his benediction also to Abraham. The other, because he was the first that
euer we reade, to haue offered sacrifice in
bread and wine, the true figure of this blessed
Sacrament.

In the sacrifices of these three holie men
aforementioned, is trulie represented vnto
ys, the conditions requisite for all such persons, as will offer vp sacrifice agreeable vnto
God: 1. Innocencie of life, signified by Abel.
2. Faith and obedience signified by Abraham.
3. Sanctitie and religion, signified by Melchisedech.

Sanctum sacrificium.

The sacrifice of Melchisedech is called
holie, not absolutelie, nor as touching it selfe,
but in respect of that of the new testament,
the which it represented more expreslie, then
did all the other oblations. And it was fore-
tould in the law of nature, that Iesus Christ
should be established a priest for euer, after
the order of Melchisedech.

Immaculatam hostiam.

The same sacrifice, is also for the selfe same
reason

reaſon called, immaculat, for the which before it was called holie; to wit, becauſe it was
the figure of the veritie of the ſame that
was to be offered in the Church, without any
maner of ſpot or blemiſh: and it may be very
well, that theſe two laſt clauſes, are rather
meant of the preſent ſacrifice, then of that
of Melchiſedech.

Of the prieſts inclination : ioyning his handes : and laying them vpon the Aultar.

The 1. Ceremonie, and its ſignification.

Firſt the Prieſt here lowlie boweth, or en-
clineth him ſelfe towardes the Aultar: to ſignifie, how our bleſſed Lord and Sauiour giuing vp the ghoſt, enclined his head vpon his
breaſt ſaying. O Father into thy handes I
commend my ſpirit.

The 2. Ceremonie, and its ſignification.

Next he ioyneth his handes before his
breaſt: to ſignifie, that humble prayers (de-
noted by his foiſaid inclination) are then eſpeciallie heard, when they proceed by faith
from the bottom of our harte.

The 3. Ceremonie, and its ſignification.

And he layeth them vpon the Aultar: to ſignifie, that not euerie faith, but onlie that
which woiketh by loue, is acceptable to God
which worke is wel vnderſtood by the hādes.

Sup-

Supplices te rogamus omnipotens Deus.

Together with the performance of the a-
forfaid ceremonies, he ioynltie pronounceth
the wordes of the holie Canon, faying. *Sup-*
plices &c. We humble befeeche thee, ô omnipotent God, we hartilie pray thee, we proftrate our felues before thee, we meekelie in-
treat thee &c. For prayer is an act of fubiection
and fubmiffion, as noteth Caietan vpon S.
Thomas.

Iube hæc præferri.

But what is all this which is defired with fo
great inftance? Verelie this, that God by the
minifterie of his Angells which at end both
vpon vs, and vpon the holie myfteries, would
command the bodie of his Sonne our Lord to
be carried vp before him: not according to
changing of place, or locall mutation of the
facrament, but according to his gratious accep-
tation of our feruice

Per manus fancti Angeli tui.

This place Hugo de S. Victore, expoundeth
to be of the Angell keeper of the prieft. And
Thomas Waldenfis (who wrote fo learnedly
againft Wicliffe)calleth this Angell. *Angelum*
vernaculum facerdotis. The proper or peculiar
Angell of the prieft: fignifying hereby, that
euery prieft, as he is a prieft, hath an Angel deputed to him by almightie God, to ayde and
afift him in the difcharge of his function.

In

Iu sublime altare tuum.

As the Church hath a visible Aultar belowe in earth , so hath she an inuisible Aultar
aboue in heauen. And because the Angells are
said to be ministring spirits, therfore we pray
that by the handes of the holie Angells , the
Hostes which we haue here vpon the Aultar in
earth, may be presented aboue vpon the Aultar in heauen. For as S. Chrisostom sayth , at
the time of Consecration , there are present
many thousand, of Angells, who enuiron the
Aultar , and do honor and homage vnto our
Sauiour Iesus.

In conspectu diuina maiestatis tua.

To wit , the same first entring and going
before, we also by meanes thereof may be admitted to follow after, and to enter in, before
the sight of the same maiestie.

*Vt quotquot ex hoc Altaris parti-
cipatione.*

The Church , as we said before, hath a visible Aultar here in earth , and an inuisible
Aultar aboue in heauen. And because we doe
participate of Christes body and blood two
maner of wayes, Sacramentallie and reallie,
or by faith and spirituallie, therfore all good
Christians haue often recourse to these two
Altars, sometimes to the one, and somtimes
to the other : and so we participate of the same bodie and blood, both vpon the Aultar in
earth,

earth, and vpon the Aultar in heauen . When we receiue our Lord from the one , we goe vp by faith vnto him ; and when we receiue him from the other , he defcendeth and cometh downe vnto vs.

Of the kiſſe of the Aultar.

The prieſt at the prolation of theſe wordes doth kiſſe the Aultar : by which ceremonie is repreſented vnto vs , our reconciliation with God, made in the death of Ieſus Chriſt,by the commemoration of this Sacrifice: for a kiſſe (as before we haue ſaid) is a true repreſentation and ſigne of peace.

Sacro ſanctum Filij tui corᵗpus & ſanᵗguinem ſumpſerimus.

To expreſſe the excellencie of the holie Communion , the body and blood of Ieſus-Chriſt therein conᵗayned, is called, ſacroſanct, or moſt holie. Which prayer doth not only concerne the prieſt who doth celebrate , but the people alſo who doe cõmunicat by faith, and deuout aſiſtance in time Maſſe , with intention to communicat often, and at the leaſt on the times appointed by the Church.

ᵗ Omni benedictione cæleſti & gratia repleamur.

The end of this preſent petition tendeth to this,that as well the prieſt communicating Sacramentallie, as alſo the people ſpiritually (by
reli-

religious assiftance at this holy facrifice) may
be replenifhed with all celeftiall benediction
and grace, to carrie from this holie Communion, fruite profitable to their faluation.

Per eundem Chriftum Dominum noftrum, Amen.

Wherin we defire, that God for the loue of
his Sonne would both heare vs, & haue mercie on vs: as though God fhould feeme litle to
regard his Sonne, if he fhould not mercifullie
heare vs for his fake. And as if the Sonne afcend not to the Father, if our deuotions afcend not vnto him, and be accepted of him.

Of the three Croffes which are made at the three wordes aforefaid.

By the firft (which is made at *corpus*) is
commemorated the cold and ftiffe extenfion
of the body of Iefus Chrift: which according
to the faying of the prophet was fuch, that
they might denumerate all his bones. By the
fecond (which is made at *sanguinem*) the a-
boundat effufion of his pretious blood: whece
it followed, that all the humors being quite
exhaufted, his bodie was wholy parched and
withered. By the third (which is made at *omni*
benedictione) is defigned the fruite of his holie
paffion, from whence all benediction floweth
foorth vpon vs: for which caufe, the prieft
maketh the third benediction or Croffe vpon
him felfe.

CHAP.

CHAP. L.

Of the second Memento.

Memento etiam Domine.

AS before Confecration, mention was
made of the liuing, for fome in particular, but for all in generall: euen fo after Confecration, commemoration is made for the departed, for fome in particular, but for all in generall, faying. Remember alfo o Lord: to wit,
remember to comfort them, remember to
haue mercie vpon them, remember to deliuer
them, remember to take them out of their paines, and to glorifie them.

Famulorum famularumque tuarum.

Where they are called his feruants, that is
to fay, of his familie, becaufe whilft they liued
in their bodies, they were true members of
the Church (which is the familie, or houfe of
God) And alfo when they died, they died in
the fame Church, and therfore are rightlie called his feruants, or familie.

N. et N.

Thefe letters, put in this place of the Canon,
doe ferue for a marke to reduce particularlie
into memory, the names of thofe, for whom
the Prieft dooth fpeciallie pray, or celebrate
Maffe,

Maſſe, as his parents, benefactors, friendes, and others committed vnto his charge, for whom he prayeth ſecretly.

Qui nos præceſſerunt cum ſigno fidei.

Which ſigne of faith, is to haue bene regenerate of water and the Holie Ghoſt, and ſigned with the triumphant ſigne of the holy Croſſe, the peculiar marke or caracter of Chriſtians, whereby they are diſtinguiſhed from all Infidels. Signe of faith, to witt, for thoſe who before they departed, receaued the holie Sacraments, and were not ſeperated from the vnitie of the Catholique Church, by any note or marke of Hereſie. Signe of faith, in which wordes, as well noteth Gabriell Biell, is touched the deuotion and pietie of the departed, to wit, that when they were liuinge, there appeared in them euident ſignes, that they were both faithfull and true beleeuers.

Et dormiunt in ſomno pacis.

That is, are departed in peace of conſcience without mortall ſinne, and in the friendſhip and grace of almightie God. Who therfore are ſaid to ſleepe in peace; becauſe as thoſe that doe ſleepe in peace, awake againe: ſo thoſe that are departed out of this life in peace, ſhal ariſe againe. And as thoſe which depart out of this life without the ſigne aforenamed, are trulie ſaid to die: ſo they that depart with the ſame ſigne, are not ſaid to die, but

but rather to sleepe or to rest, then to be dead : for they are properlie said to be dead, which neuer shall be raised to the life of glorie.

Ipsis Domine.

To wit, to those, of whom before he hath made particular commemoration : taught so to doe by the Church, instructed by the holie Ghost, that the soules departed, are ayded by the suffrages, prayers, almes, and other workes of pietie, and principallie by the acceptable sacrifice of the Masse.

Et omnibus in Christo quiescentibus.

After particular commemoration of his frendes and parents, he maketh his generall prayer for all the departed, wherin he asisteth those, who haue no particular frendes to be mindfull of them. Who also are said to rest in Christ, because they died in Charitie : hauing yet some defectes to be purged, for that ether they haue not fullie satisfied for their veniall sinnes, or for the paine due to their mortall sinnes.

Locum refrigerij.

By the which is vnderstoode the kingdome of heauen, where all the Saintes doe day-lie draw out of the springes of the Lambe, the pleasant and coolinge waters of euerla-stinge comfort, after their long labours and torments, sustained ether in this life, or in
the

the fire of Purgatorie.

Lucis.

That is to ſay, ſuch a place, which needeth nether the lighte of the Sunne, nor of the Moone, nor yet of the Starres, becauſe the ſplendor of Gods preſence, doth face to face illuminate it, and the glorious Lambe of God, is their perpetuall lanterne.

Et pacis, vt indulgeas precamur.

In which place of light, moſt perfecte, full, ſecure, and ſempiternall peace doth raigne, where is nether faintnes, nor ſadnes: nor fraude, nor feare of foes: but one euerlaſting and ioyfull harmonie of voices in which place of peace, our Lord him ſelfe doth dwel, who doth gard and keepe it, ſo that nothing can enter therein, which may diſturbe theire peace.

Per eundem Chriſtum Dominū noſtrum.

To wit, into this moſt bieſſed citie, into this place of refreſhing, of pepetuall light, and of peace, we humbly beſeech thee, that the ſoules of them that are departed, hauing their offences forgiuen them by the vertue of this Sacrifice, may be brought to repoſe and dwel for euer, thorough him whom now we offer vpp vnto thee in their behalfes, Chriſt Ieſus. Amen.

Of the ceremonies vſed in this Memento.

In this Memento, three Ceremonies are

obſer-obferued. 1. The filent prayer of the Prieft, with his handes ioyned together. 2. The difioyning of them a funder. And 3. the conioyning of them againe together.

The 1. *Ceremonie, and its fignification.*

At the firft ioyning of his handes , he meditateth a while, and prayeth for his friendes departed. And by this may be vnderftood, the defcending of our Sauiour into Limbo Patrū, to comfort the foules of his deere friendes, who had long fate in darknes, & in the fhaddow of death.

The 2. *Ceremonie, and its fignification.*

At the difioyning or fpreading of his handes abroad, he prayeth for all the departed in generall. And by this may be vnderftood, how our Lord in triumphant & victorious maner, ledd foorth with him out of Limbo, all that company of holy foules.

The 3. *Ceremonie, and its fignification.*

At *Per Chriftum &c* he conioyneth them againe together. And by this may be vnderftood, that both they and we, as members of one body, fhall one day be infeperably vnited to our foueraigne head, Chrift Iefus.

Nobis

CHAP. LI.

Of the Commemoration of the Saints.

Nobis quoque peccatoribus.

The 1. Ceremonie, and its ſignification.

AT the recitall of theſe wordes, there are two ceremonies to be obſerued. The firſt, that the prieſt interrupteth his ſilence, which he vſed a litle before, repreſenting therby, how the good theife reprehended his companion, ſaying. We receiue worthie of our doinges, but this man hath done no euill. And preſently after, with contrition and ſorrowe for his ſinne, ſaid to Ieſus. Lord remember me when thou ſhalt come into thy kingdome. Luc. 23. 41.

The 2. Ceremonie, and its ſignification.

The ſecond, that in pronouncing the wordes aforeſaid, he ſmiteth his breaſt: expreſſing thereby that of the Centurion, and others who were preſent at the death of our Sauiour, who ſeeing what had hapned, were ſore afraid, ſaying. Indeed this was the Sonne of God. Mat. 27. 54. And the people who were preſent at this ſpectacle, departed ſorrowfull, and knocking their breaſts.

In ſaying, *Nobis quoque peccatoribus*, he knocketh his breaſt, becauſe as Alexander

Hales

Hales faith, albeit we ought at all times, from the bottom of our harts, to acknowledg our felues finners, yet that chieflie it is to be done in the time of the facrifice of the Maffe, which is celebrated in the remiffion and forgiuenes of finnes.

Famulis tuis.

In which wordes, there may feeme to be a certaine contrarietie, to wit, to be finners, and yet to be Gods feruants. But as becaufe of our procliuity & pronenes to finne, we may iuftlie affirme our felues to be finners, fo hauing bene contrite and confeffed, of thofe, wherein by frailtie we haue fallen, we are neuertheles bould and confident, to call our felues his humble feruants.

De multitudine miferationum tuarum fperantibus,

In the multitude of his mercies, not in our owne iuftifications, doe we proftrate our prayers before him. For holie Dauid, albeit fo great a kinge and prophet, yet that his prayer might be heard, he grounded it only in the mercie of God, faying. According to thy great mercie doe thou remember me, o Lord for thy goodnes. Pfl. 2.

Partem aliquam.

Titlemanus expoundeth this word *partem* a part (wherin we defire to haue fome part of the kingdome of heauen with the B. Saintes)

not

not for a peece, but for participation, for elſe
our petition were abſurd, if we ſhould thinke
that the kingdome of heauen , were deuided
amongſt the Saintes, by partes or peeces.

Et ſocietatem.

The learned doctor Gabriel Biel, explicating this woord , ſaith, that they are ſayed to
haue Societie, becauſe (in that place of beatitude (to each one in particular, the goodes of
all the Saintes are made common   Adde that
by the name of Societie, is inſinuated the ſingular peace, charitie, and vnitie of the B Saintes . And Alexander Hales verie well noteth,
that in the commemoration of the Saintes,
made before the conſecration of Chriſt, their
prayers and ſuffrages are implored: but in this
which is made after conſecration the Societie
of the Saintes is required . To ſignifie , that
before the comming of the kingdome of
Chriſt, we haue neede in this life of the ſuffrages of the Saintes , but after that the body of
Chriſt is conſecrated, that is , after this kingdome is manifeſted, we ſhall enioy their companie and ſocietie , nor ſhall any longer ſtand
in neede of their prayers or ſuplications.

Donare digneris.

And it is ſaid *Donare*, not *Reddere*, that is, to
beſtow or giue (of his bounty and liberality)
not to pay or render as a thing due in rigour.

Cum

Cum tuis ſanctis Apoſtolis & Martyribus.

So oft as there is any occaſion to ſpeake or make mention of the B. Saintes, firſt the A-poſtles are named: and next the Martyrs: the one, becauſe of the ſingular dignitie of their office, wherein they excelled all others: the o-ther, becauſe of their vnſpeakable patience in their tormēts, wherin they ſurpaſſed al others.

Cum Ioanne.

Amongſt the Saintes that are ſpecified in this part of the Maſſe, S. Iohn is firſt named. Some there be that ſuppoſe it to be meant of S.Iohn Baptiſt,who although he could not be named before amongſt the Apoſtles, yet may now be mētioned amōgſt the Martyrs.Others thinke it more probably, to be vnderſtood of S. Iohn the Euangeliſt, amongſt whom is In-nocentius tertius, ſaying, that although S. Iohn was mentioned in the firſt commemora-tion, yet that he is here againe rehearced in this, becauſe Chriſt vppon the Croſſe, com-mended his Mother to his Diſciple, the Mo-ther a virgin, to the Diſciple a virgin.

Stephano.

Next after S. Iohn,is named S. Steuen. The one excellent for the perogatiue of Apoſtle-ſhipp and virginitie: the other excellent for Martyrdome and virginitie. He was the very firſt that ſuffered for Ieſus Chriſt. In imitation of Chriſt,he payed for his enimies at the time

of

of his paſſion. To him was eſpeciallie deputed
by the Apoſtles, the charge of the deuout widdowes : In him ſhined the ſingular prayſe of
ſanctitie, of whom it is ſaid. Steuen full of
grace and fortitude, did great wonders & ſignes amongſt the people Of whom it is further
ſaid, that all that ſate in the councell behoulding him, ſaw his face, as it were the face of an
Angel. At the time of his diſputatiõ with the
Iewes, being full of the holie Ghoſt, looking
ſtedfaſtlie vp to heauen, he ſaw the glorie of
God, & Ieſus ſtãding on the right hãd of God.

Matthia.

S. Matthias was diuinelie elected by lot into
the Apoſtleſhip, to ſupplie the ſacred number
of twelue, diminiſhed by the diſloyal preuarication of Iudas : Hauing commiſſion to announce the goſpell in Aethiopia, he accompliſhed the ſame with exceeding labour. His
enimies attempted to ſtone him to death,
which not being able to take effect, he was in
the end martyred with a chopping knife.

Barnaba.

S. Barnabas was natiue of Cypres, and one
of the ſeauentie two diſciples of Ieſus Chriſt.
He was alſo by the ordonance of the Holie
Ghoſt, ſeperated with S. Paul, for the execution of the miniſtrie wherunto he was called.
He was put to death in the ſeauenth yeare of
the Emperor Nero. His bones were found in

O   Cypres

Cypres vnder a tree, hauing vpon his breſt the
goſpell of S. Mathew written with his hand,
as is before noted . To him and to S. Paul, is
attributed to haue bin the firſt Apoſtles of the
Gentils.

Ignatio.

S. Ignatius was companion of the Apoſtles,
diſciple of S. Iohn the Euangeliſt , and ſecond
ſucceſſor of S. Peter in the Biſhoprick of An-
tioch ; The footeman, or page of the glorious
mother of God , the Virgin Marie , and hir
Chaplin . Who as Dioniſius writeth of him,
had nothing elſe in his mouth, but *Amor meus*
crucifixus eſt. My loue is crucified. He was
condemned vnder Traian the Emperour of
Rome, to be deuoured with wild beaſtes. He
affirmed, that if they refuſed to hurt him, as
they had done other martyrs , he him ſelfe
would prouoke them , ſaying that he was
Chriſtes corne, and muſt be ground betwixt
the teeth of the Lyons. When he was dead,
the name of Ieſus was found written in his
hart, in letters of gould.

Alexandro.

S. Alexander was paſtor of the vniuerſall
Church, the ſixt pope from S. Peeter in the
ſeate of Rome . He gaue him ſelfe wholie to
aduance the worſhip and ſeruice of almightie
God , as his laudable inſtitutions doe verie
well witnes . He added to the Canon theſe
wordes

wordes *Qui prid e* &c. Hauing vertuouſlie ruled the ſpace of ten yeares in Rome, and conuerted Hernetus and Quirinus , he was there
martyred together with Eueutius and Theo-
dulus his Deacons , vnder Adrian the Emperor . Whoſe bleſſed bodie lyeth in S. Sabins,
vnder the high Aultar.

Marcellino.

S. Marcellinus was a Prieſt of the Church
of Rome in the time of the Emperor Dioclo-
ſian . He baptiſed Paulina the daughter of Ar-
temiras, keeper of the priſon of the city (who
S Peeter, the Exorciſt, deliuered of a malignant
ſpirit that poſeſſed hir) together with her father and mother, family, and neighbours, who
ran to ſee the miracle. For which he was moſt
ſtrangelie tormented, and in the end beheaded
by the ordre of the iudge Serenus, who could
nether bend nor moue him , from the holie
and inuincible reſolution of the obſeruation of
the Chriſtian faith and religion.

Petro.

This S Peter was ordained an Exorciſt in the
church of Rome , to impoſe (according to
the forme there obſerued) his handes vppon
thoſe which were vexed with vncleane ſpirits,
ether to caſt them out, to repreſſe them, or to
appeaſe them . Who for hauing diſpoſſeſſed
the keepers daughter , and aſiſted at the Baptiſme aforeſaid, performed by S. Marcellinus,

O 2   ſuffered

fuffered like martyrdome with him, and vpon
the fame day . Their holie foules. Doretheus
who beheaded them , faw clothed in moft
bright and fhininge garments, fett with moft
rich iewells,and carried vp into heauen by the
handes of Angells, wherupon he alfo became
a Chriftian.

Felicitate.

S. Felicitas was a noble woman of Rome,
who not onlie obfcured the luftre of all the
Ladies of hir time, but alfo far furpaffed them
in all vertu. She was mother of feauen fonnes,
who endured fundrie kindes of torments in
hir fight for the faith of Iefus Chrift, al which
fhe beheld with wonderfull conftancie, and
more then manlie courage , and gaue vnto
them many holfome admonitions and exhor-
tations . And a litle after fhee hir felfe followed them with the fame courage and conftancie. For which S. Gregorie faith, that fhe
fuffered eight times , 7. times in hir children,
and once in hir felfe. She made fuch proofe of
hir immoueable & inflexible refolution , that
all were filled with aftonifhment and admira-
tion.By the commandement of Publius, ruler
vnder Antonius Auguftus, fhe was commanded to be beheaded.

Perpetua.

Amongft the perfections where with S.
Perpetua was adorned , fhe is highlie p aifed,
for

for that ſhe alwayes ſtronglie reſiſted againſt the paſſions and prouocations of the fleſh, hauing vowed to God hir chaſt virginitie. She ſuffered martyrdome in Mauritanie vnder the Emperor Seuerus, wherby ſhe happilie arriuedto heauen, where ſhe gloriouſlie ſhineth with a double diademe. Tertullian and S. Auguſtin make honorable mention of hir in their writinges.

Agatha.

S. Agatha was amongſt the noble virgins of hir time verie famous, both for hir vertu & beautie, and for this cauſe was extreamlie loued of Quintianus gouernor of Scicily, euen to the attempting of hir virginall chaſtitie. But ſhee not induring anie breach nor blot in hir honor, ſtronglie withſtoode him. Whervpon he was ſo diſcontented, that his diſordered affection was changed into a maruelous hatred, and extreme deſire to reueng himſelfe by all the meanes he might poſſible deuiſe. After many inſupportable torments, ſhee was martyred, hauing firſt both hir breaſtes cut off by the commandement of the ſaid Quintianus, ruler vnder the Emperor Decius. In the time of hir impriſonment, ſhe was viſited by S. Peter the Apoſtle, and healed of hir woundes. Finallie this holy Virgin receaued in hir ſepulcher, a teſtimonie of hir ſanctitie by the handes of Angells.

Lucia.

Lucia.

S. Lucie was of a verie noble familie, and from hir infancie wholy giuen to pietie. Hauing by hir prayers made at the ſepulcher of S. Agatha, obtained of God the healing of hir mother, extreemelie afflicted with a flux of blood, diſtributed by hir conſent vnto the poore, that which ſhe had aſſigned for hir mariage. Wherupon he to whom ſhe was betrothed greatlie offended, brought hir before the Iuſtice for a Chriſtian. Paſcaſius Prouoſt of the citie, not being able, by infinit horrible torments, to diuert hir from hir religion, commanded hir throate to be cut.

Agnete.

S. Agnes was a Roman by birth, and borne of noble parents, exceeding beautifull, both of minde and bodie The gouernors ſonne of the citie, falling grealie in loue with hir, deſired to haue her for his wife, whom ſhe conſtanlie refuſed, ſaying that ſhe would haue none other, but Ieſus Chriſt to be hir husband. The Father of the young man, vnderſtanding that ſhe was a Chriſtian, thought by that meanes to conſtraine hir to marry with his ſonne. Which ſhe abſolutelie refuſing, he commanded hir to be led to the common brothell, or ſtewes. But God ſo prouided, that hir haire grew ſo thick and ſo longe, that it couered hir all ouer, and ſeemed to
adorne

adorne hir more then hir apparell. In the ſaid
brothell houſe where ſhe was put, an Angell
of our Lord came vnto hir, to defend hir that
ſhe ſhould not be abuſed or defiled. She was
caſt in to a great fire to be burned, but the
flames had no powre to touch hir chaſt bodie.
At the laſt Aſpaſius cauſed hir to be beheaded.
She ſuffered in the yeare 317. S. Ambroſe
wrote of hir.

Cecilia.

S. Cecilie was alſo of the linage of the noble citizens of Rome, in the time of the Emperor Marcus Aurelius. She was who'ie deuo-
ted to the honor of God, and to his diuine ſeruice. She was married againſt hir will to Val-
lerian a citizen of Rome. Whom ſhe warned
in the firſt night of hir mariage, that he ſhould
not touch hir, for that ſhe was committed to
an Angell of God, who would preſerue hir
from all pollution, and ſharplie reuenge the
wronge,which he ſhould doe hir. Whereunto
he willinglie accorded, and was conuerted to
the faith by the exhortaion of S. Vrban, of
whom he was baptiſed, toge her with one of
his bretheren. Afterwards perſeuering conſtantlie in the faith, they were all three martyred by the fire and the ſwoord. S. Cecilie
had hir head cut off And being dead was foũd
to haue an hayre cloth vnder hir pretious habits of goulden tiſſue.

Ana-

Anaftafia.

S. Anaftafia, was the daughter of a noble citizen of Rome, called Pretextus. She was wonderfull charitable to the poore, amongſt whom ſhe libeially diſtributed all hir ſub-ſtance. Wherupon Publius hir husband, who was an Infidel, was greatlie offended, and cauſed hir ſtreightlie to be reſtrained in a moſt hideous priſon. And not being able to diuert him from hir faith, cauſed hir to be burned a liue. During hir impriſonment ſhe receiued ſundrie conſolatorie letters from S. Chriſo-goꝛus, which, together with hir anſweres, are inſerted in the eccleſiaſticall hiſtorie of Ni-cephorus.

Et omnibus ſanctis tuis.

To auoide prolixitie, the prieſt comprehen-deth in generall all the Saintes, after the ſpe-ciall commemoration of thoſe which are ex-preſſed in the Canon. Alwayes inſiſting to be admitted vnto their number, and to come with them vnto euerlaſting glorie, by imita-tion of their vertues. And therfore procee-deth, ſaying.

Intra quorum nos conſortium, non aſtima-tor meriti, ſed veniæ.

In which wordes the Church doth not ſimplie denie God to be the eſteemer of me-ꝛits, but the ſence and meaning is, that God will not barelie reward euerie godlie man ac.

cording to his merit, but of his goodnes and liberallitie, will add to him aboue his deser-uing: nor rigorouslie punishe the defectes of him that sinneth, but alwayes reward the one aboue his merit, and punishe the other lesse then his desert.

Quæsumus largitor admitte, per Christum Dominum nostrum.

Not to be refused in his request, he maketh and concludeth it thorough Iesus Christ. For what exterior shew soeuer our workes may haue, they are not agreeable to God, but by his Sonne woorking in vs. Who hath so greatlie loued vs, that he would descend from heauen vnto earth to be our Mediator, and finallie to place vs amongst his Saints.

Of the ioyning of the priestes handes.

In saying, *Per Christum Dominum nostrum.* He ioyneth his handes together. By which ceremonie vsed at the commemoration of Saints, may be vnderstood the same that before was said concerning the soules departed, to wit, that thorough the merits of Christ our Lord, who is our head, we hope to be ioy-ned with him, and his Saints, in euerlasting glorie.

Per quem.

For as much as the confection of the holie Eucharist is attributed to Iesus Christ, who is the authour of this holie institution, ther-

fore the prieft giueth thankes and prayfeth
God the Father, for that by him he hath created the matter, to wit, the bread and the wine,
vnder the formes whereof, he doth exhibit
vnto vs, trulie and reallie, his bodie and blood
in foode and nourifhment of our foules.

Hæc omnia, Domine, femper bona.

To wit, all the Hoftes, which the Church
doth immolate thorough the whole worlde.
Which if we confider the fenfible qualities,
are of infinit number, but if the fubftance, all
is one body, and all is one blood, which is dailie made prefent in this holy Sacrifice, by him,
by whom as faith S. Iohn, all thinges were
made, and without him, was made nothing
that was made. Iohn. 1.

Creas.

Here a queftion may be moued, why the
Prieft doth not make the figne of the Croffe
at the word *Creas*, as well as at the other wordes following *Sanctificas, viniças*, &c. Wherof Alexander Hales, giueth a verie fufficient
reafon, faying that the figne of the Croffe is a
reprefentation of our Lordes paffion: and becaufe the creation of man was no caufe of his
paffion, but the fall of man was therby to be
repayred, therfore when fanctification, viuification, and benediction are mentioned, the
figne of the Croffe is made, but when creation
is named, the prieft doth not then make the
figne

signe of the Crosse, because the creation of
man was not painefull to our Sauiour, but
his redemption And S. Thomas in his exposition of the Masse faith, that this was ordayned by the admirable prouidence of almightie God, to signifie, that man had not that by
nature in his creation, which since he hath
obtayned by the Crosse of Christ, in his redemption.

Sanctitficas, viuitficas, benetdicis.

These three wordes may be cōsidered three
maner of wayes. They may ether be referred
to the bread and wine. Or to our Sauiour. Or
to our selues. Yf you consider them as spoken of the bread and wine, then it is most easie to conceiue their sense. Dost sanctifie, to
wit, according to their sacramentall causes.
Viuificate, by conuerting them into thy flesh
and blood. Blesse, by pouring downe and mul-
tiplying thy graces vpon them. If you refer
them to Christ, then are they thus to be vnderstood, to wit ; those creatures which before
were but earthlie, voide of life, and of all benediction, are by the blessing of Christ, made
heauenlie liuelie, and euery way most blessed.
If we applie them vnto our selues, then may
they thus be taken, to wir, that this sacred
Host is sanctified in respect of vs (that it may
be our sanctification from all sinnes) viuificated, that it may be the life of our soules (to
O 6 quicken

quicken vs in fpirit to newnes of life.)Bleffed,
that we may by the fame attaine the aboundance of all fpirituall grace and perfection.

Of the three Croffes which are made at the three wordes aforefaid.

As touching the three Croffes which are
made in this place vpon the Hoft and the Chalice together, they are made to fignifie vnto vs,
that our redemption wrought by Chrift by the
vertu of his Croffe , was with the confent of
all the bleffed Trinitie . Or , according to Albertus Magnus, three Croffes are made in this
place, to fignifie that all thinges are fanctified,
viuificated , and bleffed , by the vertu of the
Croffe and paffion, of our Redeemer.

Et praftas nobis.

The thing which in thefe wordes, we defire
of God may be giuen vnto vs , is the pretious
bodie and blood of Chrift his Sonne , for our
refection : who lying hid vnder thefe fpecies,
giueth him felfe to vs to eate , that fo he may
be in vs, & we in him. And Titlemanus faith,
that this holie Hoft is giuen vs , to our vtility
and health, it is giuen vs in meate , it is giuen
vs in drinke, it is giuen vs in life, it is giuen vs
in nourifhment, it is giuen vs in preferuation,
it is giuen vs in defence , it is giuen vs in remiffion of our finnes , it is giuen vs for the
obtayning of good thinges , it is giuen vs a-
gainft the affaultes of our enimies , it is giuen

vs

vs for the subduing of our flesh, it is giuen vs in commemoration of the death of Christ, and of all his benefits.

Per ipsum, & cum ipt so, & in ipt so.

Then vncouering the Chalice, bowing his knee and houlding the Host in his right hand, and the Chalice in his left, he maketh three Crosses, from side to side of the Cha ice, saying. *Per ipsum*, as by the Mediator be wixt God and man. *Et cum ipso*, as euery way equal with the Father. *Et in ipso*, As consubstantiall and coeternall, both with him and the holie Ghost Againe, *per ipsum*, by whom thou hast created all thinges. *Et cum ipso*, by whom thou gouernest all thinges created. *Et in ipso*, in whom thou consummatest all thinges.

Est tibi Deo partri † omnipotenti.

Not called Father onlie by name, honor, and veneration as we cal our elders and betters fathers, but by nature and origen, so that trulie and properlie the diuine generation appertayneth vnto him.

In vnitate spiritus † sancti.

That is to say, in the communion of the Holie Ghost, who is the knot and loue of the Father and the Sonne; in whom they communicate as in one common gift, proceeding from both.

Omnis honor & gloria.

Be all honor, as to our Lord, and al glorie as,
io

to our God . Where , in the fame order that
God the Father doth fend his graces and blef-
finges vnto vs , which is by the meanes of
Chrift his Sonne : euen fo in the fame order all
honor and glory returneth againe by the mea-
of Chrift vnto the Father , and that euermore
in the vnitie of the holie Ghoft.

Of the fiue Croffes which are made at the fiue wordes aforefaid.

The 1. *Reafon.*

As touching thofe three which are made
with the Hoft ouer the Chalice , at thefe wordes *Per ipfum &c.* diuers thinges may be fignified by the fame. Firft they may fignifie, the
three howres , wherein our Lord and Sauiour
hunge vpon the Croffe , in moft vnfpeakable
paine aliue.

The 2. *Reafon.*

According to S. Thomas, thefe three Croffes are made , to fignifie the triple payer of
Chrift vpon the Croffe. Firft , Father forgiue
them. Secondly . My God why haft thou for-
faken me . Thirdly , Into thy handes I commend my fpirit.

The 3. *Reafon.*

The other two Croffes , which he maketh
betwixt the Chalice and his breafte , at thefe
wordes. *Eft tibi Deo Patri omnipotenti &c.* doe
fignifie , the mifterie of the blood and water
which

which issued out of the side of our B. Sauiour, hanging dead vpon the Crosse, and the two Sacraments, which were instituted in vertue of the same, to wit, Baptisme, and this B. Sacrament of the Altar. According to the testimonie of S. Iohn. One of the soldiears with a speare opened his side, and incontinent there came foorth blood and water. Iohn 19. 34.

The 4. Reason.

At the wordes. *Omnis honor & gloria*, the Host is held aboue, and the Chalice beneath, and both a litle eleuated. Which Ceremonie doth verie aptlie signifie the death of our Sauiour, to wit, how in his passion, his blood was truly seperated from his body, and consequently also his blessed soule.

Of other Ceremonies performed after the short eleuation.

The Priest hauing performed this short eleuation, layeth the Host downe vppon the Corporall, couereth againe the Chalice, and then adoreth.

The 1. Ceremonie, and its signification.

First, the Host is laid vpon the Corporall, because Ioseph and Nichodemus, beging of Pilat the body of Iesus, tooke it downe from the Crosse, wrapped it in a fine sindon, and after buried it.

The 2. Ceremonie, and its signification.

And because they rouled a great stone before

fore the doore of the fepulcher, therfore the
Prieft with the Palle couereth the Chalice. And
becaufe thofe holie men worfhipped, the bodie of Chrift in the fepulchre, at their departure, therfore the Prieft adoreth our Lord in
this holy Sacrament.

The 3. Ceremonie, and its fignification.

This done the prieft lifteth vp his voice and
pronounceth on high thefe wordes faying.
Per omnia fecula feculorum. And the people
anfwere. *Amen.* Our Doctors here doe fay,
that this lifting vp of the voice of the prieft,
reprefenteth the ftronge crie of our Lord and
Sauiour, whē he yealded vp his fpirit into the
handes of his Father. And that the anfwere
of the people, fignifieth the lamentation and
pittie of the deuout wemen which were prefent at this fpectacle. In this maner Innocentius tertius interpreteth the fame. Becaufe Iefus (faith he) crying with a high voice, rende-
red vp his fpirit, therfore the prieft lifteth vp
his voice faying. *Per omnia fecula feculorum.*
And becaufe the women lamenting bewailed
their Lord, all the quyre, as lamenting, doe
anfwer, Amen.

                                        C H A P.

CHAP. LII.

Of the end of the ſecret part of the Canon.

Per omnia ſæcula ſæculorum.

World without end.

BY the wordes them ſelues, are commonlie vnderſtood, one of theſe two thinges.
Ether that all honor and glory, appertaineth
to God, world without end. Or that the Sonne
doth liue with the Father and the holy Ghoſt,
world without end. Againe, *Per omnia ſæcula
ſæculorum,* that is, thoroughout all ages of the
world, for *ſæculum.* is taken for a time ſome-
what long: and ſo is called *ſeculum* of this
worde *ſequor,* to follow, becauſe time followeth time.

Oremus. Let vs pray.

The Prieſt hauing gotten as it were, a
good opoitunitie, hauing now before him,
the Lord & Maker, both of heauen and earth,
and that according to his corporall preſence,
he exhorteth all the people hartely to pray,
ſaying. *Oremus.* Let vs pray.

*Præceptis ſalutaribus moniti, & diuina in-
ſtitutione formati.*

Admoniſhed by wholſome precepts, and
formed by diuine inſtitution.

And

And therfore the Prieſt ſayeth that it is by
precept, and deuine inſtitution, that wee
are admoniſhed to ſay this prayer, becauſe
both our Lord inſtituted the ſame, and alſo
commanded his Apoſtles to vſe the ſame, ſaying. Pray alwayes and be not weerie. Againe.
Pray without intermiſſion. Which prayer,
Chriſt him ſelfe taught his Apoſtles to ſay in
the holy ſacrifice of the Maſſe, as S. Hierom
witneſſeth. Hier. li. 3. contra Pelagianos.

Audemus dicere.
We dare to ſay.

The reaſon why we heere affirme, that wee
are bould to ſpeake vnto the maieſtie of God
almighty, is becauſe that this ſelfe ſame prayer
which we poure foorth before God, the ſelfe
ſame prayer proceeded out of the mouth of
God : ſo that in this prayer, we recommend
our ſelues vnto God, with no other thin the
verie wordes of God. For as S. Gregorie well
ſaieth, it were verie vnmeete, that vpon the
holie Euchariſt, any prayer ſhould be recited of
the ſchollars compoſing, and that ommitted
of the Maſters making.

The prayſes of the Pater Noſter.

This prayer for many cauſes, doth very far
excell all other prayers. For the authoritie of
the teacher, for breuitie of wordes, for ſufficiencie of petitions, fecunditie of myſteries,
vtilitie, efficacie, and neceſſitie. For the authoritie

ritie of the teacher, because as we said before,
it proceeded out of the mouth of almightie
God. For breuitie of wordes, because it is easilie learned, and soone recited. For sufficiencie
of demandes, because it comprehendeth the
necessities of both liues. For fecunditie of
mysteries, because it contayneth innumerable
sacraments. In vtilitie, because Christ being
our aduocate, with the Father for our sinnes,
we praying vnto him, doe pronounce and vse
the verie wordes of our aduocate. In efficacie,
because as S. Aug. saith, it taketh away our
veniall sinnes. In necessitie, because as S. Clement saith, all Christians are bound to knowe
it, and often to rehearse and say it. Lastly
this prayer aunciently was held in so great reuerence, that it was not permitted but to
such as were baptised, nether to write, nor to
pronounce the same.

Pater. Father.

I will here set downe for this first point, a
right worthie consideration of Leo Magnus,
sayinge. Great my beloued is the gift of this
sacrament, and this gift exceedeth all giftes,
that God should call man his sonne, and man
name God his Father. Hence also S. Aug. admonisheth the rich and noble of this world,
not to wax proude, or contemne the poore &
ignoble, because they pronounce and say that
together to God our Father, which they can
neuer

neuer trulie fay, vnles they acknowledge
them felues to be bretheren.

Nofter. Our.

As by the word (*Pater*) we vnderftand
the grace of adoption: fo by the word (*nofter*)
we vnderftand brotherlie vnion, For as S. Cyprian faith, our Lord who is the mafter of peace and vnitie, would not that when any one
prayeth, he fhould pray for him felfe onlie,
and fay, My Father, not giue me my dayly
bread, nor forgiue me my trefpaffes, nor leade
me not into temptation, nor deliuer me from
euil: but our Father, giue vs our dailie bread,
forgiue vs our trefpaffes, leade vs not in temptation, and fo of others.

Qui es in cœlis.

Which hart in heauen.

1. The prieft in faying that God is in heauen, doth not inclofe or confine God with
in heauen, but endeuoreth to draw him which
prayeth, vp from earth to heauen. 2 In af-
firming our Father to be in heauen, we are put
in minde that we are ftrangers here in earth,
and far from our proper countrie and home,
which is in heauen.

Sanctificetur nomen tuum.

Hallowed be thy name.

The name of God, hath in it felfe no neede of fanctification: but becaufe here in earth
it is not worthelie fanctified as it deferueth,
and

and that by many , and euen almoſt hourlie,
it is moſt ſinfullie prophaned , by exerceable
blaſphemies, imprecations, deteſtations, cur-
ſinges , ſwearinges , forſwearinges and the
like; therfore we pray, that the ſame may be
honored, prayſed, exalted and ſanctified of all
in the world.

Adueniat regnum tuum.

Thy Kingdome come

The kingdome of God in which he doth
raigne , is the Church militant on earth , and
the Church triumphant in heauen. Wherfore
by thy kingdome come , is vnderſtood, kingdome to kingdome,the militant to the triumphant,that theſe two may be vnited and made
one kingdome. This likewiſe doth reprehend
all thoſe perſons , who would prolong this
worldlie life, whereas the iuſt do hartily pray,
that that kingdome of God would ſpeedelie
come.

Fiat voluntas tua.

Thy will he done.

The will of God is taken two maner of
wayes. The one , his will and decree as it is
eternall . The other,the ſignes of his will,
which are temporall . And theſe are fiue , to
wit, precept, prohibition, permiſſion, coun-
ſail , and operation: theſe latter are not alwayes fulfilled, for which cauſe we pray daily
that they may be fulfilled,ſaying. *Fiat voluntas*
tua,

tua, to wit in all thou commandeſt, in all thou forbideſt, in all thou permitteſt, in all thou counſelleſt, in all thou workeſt.

Sicut in cœlo & in terra.

In earth as it is in heauen.

By heauen, is vnderſtood the heauenlie ſpirits, to wit, the Saints and Angels, For the bleſſed Angells, ſo ſoone as they conceiue the conception and minde of almighty God, doe incontinentlie, with inexplicable delight and readines, tranſport them ſelues to accompliſh the ſame. And therfore we pray that the will of almightie God may be fulfilled, *ſicut in cœlo, & in terra.* To wit, as by Angels in heauen, euen ſo by men in earth.

Panem. Bread.

Four ſortes of bread are neceſſarie for vs. Three whilſt we are pilgrimes in this life, and the fourth in the life and world to come. To wit, Corporall, Spirituall, Sacramentall, and Eternall. Of the firſt it is written, man liueth not by bread only. Of the ſecond, My meat is to doe the will of him that ſent me. Of the third. He that eateth this bread vnworthelie, is guiltie of the body of our Lord. Of the fourth. I am the bread of life which came downe from heauen.

Noſtrum Quotidianum.

Our dayly.

Our, not myne, ſaith S. Chriſoſtom, becauſe

cauſe all whatſoeuer God giueth vs, he giueth not to vs alone, but alſo to others by vs; that of that which we haue receiued of God, we alſo giue part therof vnto the poore. Againe our bread, to wit, got by our true labours, for all that which we eate vniuſtlie gotten or ſtolen, is not ours, but other mens bread. Againe, our bread, to wit, the ſpirituall foode of our ſoules, as true Catholique doctrine, Sacraments, wholſome Ceremonies, and the like: not others, that is, the doctrin and ceremonies of Infidells or Heretiques. And this our bread is called daylie, becauſe we daylie ſtand in neede thereof.

Da nobis. Giue vs.

This doth Chriſt teach vs, that we doe not onlie pray that bread be giuen vs, that we may haue to eate, but, as S. Chriſoſtom ſaith, that what we eate, we may receiue from the hand of God. For, to haue to eate, is common both to the good, and to the bad, but to acknowledg it from the hand of God, is proper, or belongeth only vnto the good.

Hodie. This day.

This day, to wit, in this preſent life, as S. Aug. expoundeth the ſame. Which we ought to account but as one day, it is ſo frayle and of ſo litle laſting:

Et dimitte nobis.
And forgiue vs.

Three

Three maner of wayes we offend and trefpaffe, whereof we craue of God forgiuenes.
Againft God. Againft our felues. And againft
our neighbour. Becaufe we haue offended a-
gainft God, we fay, *Et dimitte*. And becaufe
we haue offended againft our felues, we fay,
nobis. And becaufe we haue likewife offended
againft our neighbour, we fay, *Sicut & nos
dimittimus debitoribus noftris*.

Debita noftra.
Our trefpaffes.

Our trefpaffes are called *Debita, Debtes*, becaufe they make vs debtors of paine, which
muft of neceffitie be paid, ether in this life,
or in the other. Againe finnes or trefpaffes are
called dettes, for that finne, being the wealth
and fubftance of the diuel, a man which committeth finne, is made a dettor to the diuell:
euen as he is made a dettor, which vfeth or
houldeth an other mans monie.

Sicut & nos dimitimus debitoribus noftris.
As we forgiue them that trefpas againft vs.

In this requeft we aske to be forgiuen, vpon
condition, to wit, as we forgiue others: he
therfore that asketh to be forgiuen, and doth
not himfelfe forgiue, requireth of God not to
be forgiuen. By reafon whereof, who foeuer
is in hatred or malice, is more hurt, then holpen by this prayer, vnles at the very fame prefent he haue a purpofe to forgiue.

Et

Et ne nos inducas in tentationem.

And leade vs not into tentation.

After we haue required forgiuenes of ſinnes paſt , we demand to be preſerued from thoſe which we may commit for the time to come, which, we call by the name of temptation. Concerning which we craue of almightie God, not that we may not be led to temptation, but, that we may not be led , into it, that is, ſuffered to fall into it.

Sed libera nos à malo.

But deliuer vs from euill.

Vpon theſe laſt wordes Cardinall Bellarmin hath verie learnedlie noted , that our Lord with great wiſdome teacheth vs to demaund to be deliuered from all euill , and commeth not to particulars, as to pouertie , ſicknes and the like . For that oftentimes it ſeemeth that a thinge is good for vs, which God ſeeth is euil for vs: and contrariwiſe euell for vs, which he ſeeth to be good for vs. And that therfore according to the inſtruction of our Lord we demaund , that he vouchſafe to deliuer vs from that, which he ſeeth and knoweth to be euill for vs , be it proſperitie , or aduerſitie , well, or woe . The Fathers of the Greeke Church, commonlie vnderſtand by the name of Euill, the diuell , as S. Chriſoſtom , Cyrillus , Euthimius, S. Germanus, Tertulianus, and otheis. Yea and ſome great Saintes of God , neuer

P   would

would call the diuell by any other name . As
amongft others S. Catharin of Sienna.

Amen.

After the anfwere of the afiftants, the Prieft
faith, Amen: which importeth a great confidence, that God will giue them their demand:
euen as if, hauing obtained , he fent the that
by the Priefts meanes which they defiered.

Or more briefly, thus.

Our Father which art in heauen , hallowed
be thy name. Becaufe thou art our Father. Thy
kingdome come, Becaufe thou art our Kinge.
Thy will be done in earth as it is in heauen,
Becaufe thou art our Spoufe. Giue vs this day
our daylie bread, Becaufe thou art our Paftor.
And forgiue vs our trefpaffes , as we forgiue
them that trefpaffe againft vs, Becaufe thou art
our Iudge. And leade vs not into tentation,
Becaufe thou art our Captaine. But deliuer vs
from euill , Becaufe thou art our phifition.
Amen.

Of the Priefts refuming the Patin.

By the roundnes of the Paten , as before
we faid , is fignified charitie . And the hiding
and couering thereof duringe the Sacrifice
(wherein the mifteries of the death and paffion of our Sauiour are reprefented) fignifieth,
the flight of the Apoftles , who at the firft
through the great affection and charitie which
they bore to their Lord and maifter, promifed

to

to die at his feete, rather then they would euer
forsake him: yet as soone as he was in the handes of his enimies, they all forsooke him, and
hid them selues.

*Libera nos, quæsumus Domine, ab omnibus
malis, præteritis, præsentibus, & futuris.*
Deliuer vs. o Lord we beseech theee, from all
euills past, present, and to come.

The priest in resuming the Patin as afore-
said, repeateth the prayer made by the asistants at the conclusion of our Lordes prayer.
Which is nether in vaine nor superfluous, because it explicateth the same more particularlie. Wherfore here there are named three
sortes of euills, from the which we haue great
neede to pray to be deliuered, to wit, from
all euills, past, present, and to come, tempe-
stes, souddaine and vnprouided deathes &c.
All which because they are punishments due
to our sinnes, we here pray to be deliuered
from them.

Et intercedente beata.
And the blessed Marie interceding.

The Virgin Marie first is here called, Blessed, for so the woman in the gospel witnessed
of hir, saying. Blessed is the wombe that bare
thee and the pappes that gaue thee suck. Or
blessed, to wit, in the generations both of heauen and earth. Of heauen, to whom she bare
their restorer. Of earth, to whom she brought

foorth their redeemer.

Et gloriosa.

And glorious.

Next she is said to be glorious, becaufe she is the feate of the kinge of glorie, of whom he taking flesh, sate in hir as in his feate : Or glorious, becaufe she dwelleth on high, where she sitteth glorioustie on the righte hand of hir Sonne. Or glorious, becaufe she is most glorioustie assumpted, both in soule and bodie, and highlie exalted far aboue all human and Angelicall vertues,

Semper Virgine.

Alwayes virgin.

Alwayes, to wit, before hir deliuerie, in hir deliuerie, and after hir deliuerie. A virgin, in body, in minde, in profession, in obseruation.

Dei Genitrice Maria.

Marie Mother of God.

This blessed and glorious virgin, is fayd to be mother of the Sonne of God, wherupon it followeth, that she hath one Sonne common with God ; O wonderfull mysterie, he hath not a Sonne, wherof Marie is not the mother: she hath not a Sonne, wherof God is not the Father.

Cum beatis Apostolis tuis, Petro.

With thy blessed Apostles Peter.

S. Peter is next named, becaufe commandement was giuen to the holy wome by the Angell,

gell, to carrie the good tidinges of our Lordes resurrection (which the priest by & by goeth about to represent vnto vs) to the Disciples, and in especial to S. Peter: He hauing neede of particular consolatiō, because lately before he had denied his master, and had now bitterly wept and done austere pennance for the same.

Paulo & Andrea.

Paul and Andrew.

After our Lady and S. Peter, S. Paul and S. Andrew are next named for some speciall perogatiues. Gabriel Biel saith, that to obtaine the gift of peace these four, albeit recited before, are here introduced againe, because these aboue others, were most configurat to the passion of Christ, in vertu wherof peace is giuen vnto vs.

Et omnibus Sanctis.

And all Saintes.

By which wordes the intercession of other Saintes is not ommitted, but in the commemoration of these few, and those the most eminent, the suffrages of all are required. For so are all vnited to God, and so doe all desire one thinge, that in one all are in some sort included, and in one all are neglected.

Why the priest signeth him selfe with the Paten.

That the Priest signeth him selfe with the Paten, it is done, to signifie that the cheife of the priestes and pharises, signed and healed the stone of the sepulcher, setting soldiears and watchmen to keeepe the same.

Da propitius pacem.
Grant mercifully peace.

Hauing prayed for our deliuerance from euils, next we craue for perfect peace: to wit, in the remission of sinne, perfect peace in the tranquillitie of conscience, and perfect peace in amitie with our neighbour: because this perfect peace, is the holy aud sacred band of all human societie.

In diebus nostris.
In our dayes.

To wit, in the time of this life, according as Titlemanus expoundeth the same. And this we craue, after the example of king Ezechias, that we may liue in the feare of God, & obseruation of this holy commandementes, without seeing the opressions and incomodities, which the vncertaine change of worldlie thinges, may vnexpectedly bringe vpon vs.

Vt ope misericordia tua adiuti.
That ayded by the helpe of thy mercy.

That our petitions which we offer and present to almightie God, may take the better effect, it is most necessarie, that we haue his mercifull helpe and asistance here vnto, without the which we doe confesse, that we cannot, as we ought, ether beginre, continue, or end, nor eu.robtaine the thinge which we desire.

Et a peccato ſimus ſemper liberi.

We may both be alwayes free from ſinne.

The thinge wherunto we principally require the ayde of his mercie,is, to be freed frō our ſinnes, becauſe ſinne hath this propertie, that it allwayes bringeth three euills with it.

The firſt is,it maketh vs of free men,bond men,for as our Sauiour ſaith,he that committeth ſinne, is the ſeruant of ſinne. Secondlie,it alienateth vs from Gods holy grace. Thirdly, it iuſtly procureth his wrath againſt vs.

And hence it is that S. Bernard ſaith,that ſo long as in any creature there is power to ſinne, it is ſecure in no place, nether in heauen, nor in paradiſe, nor in the world ; For in heauen fell the Angells, euen in Gods preſence. In paradiſe fell Adam from the place of pleaſure: in the world fell Iudas, from the ſchoole of our Sauiour.

Et ab omni perturbatione ſecuri.

And ſecure from all perturbation.

Nexr, to be ſecure from the perturbations, tumultes and troubles of the world, becauſe from thence proceedeth the matter of ſinne, and hinderance that whē we approach to this moſt holy Communion,we come not in ſuch puritie as is fit and requiſite.

P 4 Of

Of fundrie ceremonies performed by the priest in this part of the Maffe.

The 1. Ceremonie, and its fignification.

Firft he putteth the Paten vnder the Hoft (which as we faid before, by its roundnes, reprefenteth Charitie.) The Hoft therfore layed vpon the Paten to be broken and diuided; fignifieth, that Chrift of his loue and Charitie, expofed his body to fuffer death for our redemption.

The 2. Ceremonie, and its fignification.

Next he vncouereth the Chalice. By the Chalice, is fignified the fepulcher. And the vncouering of the fame, is done to fignifie how the Angell of our Lord remoued away the ftone from the doore of the fepulcher.

The 3. Ceremonie, and its fignification.

After this, he deuideth or breaketh the Hoft into two partes; which fignifieth the feparation of the holie foule of our Lord and Sauiour, from his bleffed bodie: the one defcending into hell, and the other remaynting in the Sepulcher. Wherof Innocentius tertius yealdeth another reafon; faying that therfore the Prieft breaketh the Hoft, that in the breaking of bread we may knowe our Lord, as the two difciples knew him in breaking of bread, to whom he appeared the day of his refurrection as they went to Emaus.

P rr

Per eundem Dominum noſtrum Ieſum Chriſtum Filium tuum.

Thorough the ſame our Lord Ieſus Chriſt thy Sonne.

In diuiding the Hoſte he ſaith , *Per eundem Dominum noſtrum*. To wit , vnto whom all power is giuen both in heauen earth . *Ieſum*, Sauiour , for he commeth to ſaue his people from their ſinnes. *Chriſtum*, Anointed aboue all his fellowes, with the oyle of gladnes . *Filium tuum*, Naturall and onlie begotten.

Theſe wordes ended , the part of the Hoſt which he houldeth in his right hand, he layeth vpon the Paten , and from the part in his left hand, he breaketh off another litle prrticle, & ſo the Hoſt is deuided into three partes.

The hoſt thus deuided into three ſeuerall partes , repreſenteth vnto vs the ſtate of the Church in three ſeuerall places. The part held in the right hand (which is no more deuided but remayneth entire) repreſēteth the Church triumphant, ſignified by the right hand, which hath paſſed ouer all hir troubles, and hath now no more to ſuffer.

The other which is helde in the left hand, and is againe deuided, doth ſignifie the eſtate of the Church militant (vnderſtood by the left hand) part wherof remayneth in this life, and part in Purgatorie, both which are ſubiect yet to ſuffer.

P 5   This

This part held in the left hand, is next con-ioyned to that which lieth vpon the P en,and was before helde in the right hand: signi-fie, that thofe which are in purgatorie, shall infallibly after a while, haue their part and fruition in glorie, and be conioyned with the Church triumphant.

The part subdiuided from the fecond, held in the right hand and put into the Chalice,fig-nifieth thofe which yet remayne in this pre-fent life (who by doing penaunce, for their finnes, may obtaine mercie and remiffion thorough the merits of Chrift before their de-parture) and therfore the part which reprefen-teth them, is not laid with the other, but is put into the facred blood contained in the Chalice.

And let it here be noted, that this third part of the holy Hoft, is held ouer the Chalice with two fingars: to wit, with the thumbe, which is interpreted Force, and vertu: and with the fecond,named by the Latins *Index*, interpre-ted difcretion of vnderftanding. To declare that this diuine myfterie ought to be confi-dered with force of Faith, and with difcretion of vnderftanding.

Qui tecum viuit & regnat in vnitate fpiri-tus Sancti Deus.

Who liueth and raigneth with thee in the vnitie of the holy Ghoft God.

In

In the ſubdiuiſion of the ſecond part as aforſaid, he ſaith. *Qui tecum viuit* (inceſſantly in all eternitie.) *Et regnat* (with all power and maieſty.) *In vnitate* (in eſſentiall identitie of the Holy Ghoſt.) *Spiritus Sancti Deus* (The third perſon the Holie Trinitie.

Per omnia ſæcula ſæculorum.

Woﬂd without end.

Hauing by ſundrie deuout ceremonies ſet before vs the death and paſſion of our bleſſed Sauiour, he beginneth now not onlie by ſignes, but alſo by wordes, to ſet before vs the ioy of his reſurrection : for which cauſe he lifteth vp his voice ſaying. *Per omnia ſæcula ſæculorum.* And the people anſwere. *Amen.* The Prieſt doth therſore eleuate his voice in this place not only to haue the conſent of the people, but alſo to repreſent the gladnes which the Apoſtles and Diſciples had, when they vnderſtood the ioyfull newes of the reſurrection. For as they were in great feare and ſorrowe, to ſee their Lord and maſter in the handes of his enimies, and afterwards to ſuffer his death: ſo were they filled with great ioy, when they ſaw him reſtored againe to life, *Gauiſi ſunt Diſcipuli viſo Domino* The Diſciples reioyced, hauing ſeene our Lord.

Amen.

The people anſwere by this Hebrewe word that they doe firmely & ſtedfaſtlie ſo beleeue.

Pax † *Domini ſit* † *ſemper vobiſ* † *cum.*

The peace of our Lord be alwayes with you.

To ſhew this more euidently, the Prieſt
ſaluteth the people with the ſame woordes
wherwith our Lord ſaluted his Apoſtles, at
his reſurrection, ſaying. *Pax vobis.* Now there
are three ſortes of peace right neceſſarie for
vs, to wit ſpirituall, temporall, and eternall:
and according hereunto, the Prieſt maketh
the ſigne of the Croſſe three times in pronouncing the wordes aforeſaid The ſpirituall
peace, is the repoſe and tranquilitie of conſcience, which is obtained by the meanes of
a virtuous and innocent life. The temporall
peace is, that it would pleaſe almightie God,
ſo to bleſſe vs and our labours, that we may
eate our bread in peace and quietnes: that is
to preſerue vs, and all ours, from warres, miſ-
fortunes, ſickneſſes, ſutes, wrongfull moleſta-
tions, detractions, diffamations, & all other
ſortes of troubles and vexations. The peace
which is eternall, is the chiefe and principall
of all the reſt, which ſetteth vs free from all
the cares and labours of this life, and bringeth
vs, from mortalitie, to immortalitie: from
corruption, to incorruption: from feare, to
felicitie: from vexaton to glorification: and
finally, to the cleare viſion and euerlaſting
fruition of God him ſelfe. He therfore of his
infinit mercie, giue ynto vs, both the ſpirituall
and

and the temporall peace in this world: and peace euerlasting in the worlde to come.

Et cum spiritu tuo.

And with thy spirit.

The asistants for answere desire to the priest the same peace which he hath wished vnto them, to the end that being vnited by the bond of this celestiall benediction, they may mutuallie receiue the grace which they desire.

Of that part of the Host which is put into the Challice.

This done, the priest putteth one litle part of the Host into the Chalice: to shew vnto vs hereby, that our Lordes body, is not without his blood, nor his blood, without his body, nether body and blood, without his holy, and liuelie soule. Secondlie, to shew, that but one Sacrament is made, of the species, both of the bread and wine. Thirdlie, to shew, that as he ioyneth the bodie to the blood; so we being conioyned to the same body thorough the merits of the same blood, are purged from our sinnes: and herupon it is that he immediatlie asketh the remission of sinnes, saying. *Agnus Dei qui tollis peccata* &c.

Hæc commixtio.

This commixtion

This commixtion of the bodie and blood of our Lord, is not according to their true and real essences (in which sence, they are ne-

uer

uer feperated) but according to their exterior,
or Sacramentall formes, vnder which, the bodie and blood of Chrift is trulie contayned. For
manie thinges which appertaine to the onlie
fpecies, by the vfe of fpeakinge, is attributed
to that which is contayned vnder the fpecies.

*Et confecratio Corporis & Sanguinis Do-
mini noftri Iefu Chrifti.*

And confecration of the body and blood of
our Lord Iefus Chrift.

Not that by this immiffion, the bodie and
blood of our Lord Iefus Chrift, is ether made
holie, or confecrated: but that the confecration firft made, by vertu of the facramentall
formes, now taketh its effect in the minde of
the receuer. And therfore it followeth.

Fiat accipientibus nobis.

Be to vs receiuing it.

To wit, vnto vs Priefts, who receiue it facra-
mentally, and to all others who receiue it reallie or fpirituallie by the meanes of the Prieft,
who is as it were the hand and mouth of the
mifticall body of Chrift, as by which nourifhment is drawen and imparted, to all the feuerall members of the bodie.

In vitam aternam. Amen.

Into life eternall.

To wit, by confernation of the fpirituall
life, here in this world, which is done by daylie augmentation of grace; wherewith our
foule

ſoule is ſuſtained , leaſt thorough defect therof, it decline and fall away by euill deſires and
hurtfull deedes, and afterwardes come vtterly
to looſe the euerlaſting life in the world to
come .

CHAP. LIII.

Agnus Dei.

Lambe of God.

THe Prieſt hauing put the third part of the
Hoſt into the Chalice, as before we haue
declared , next hee couereth the ſame , and
knocking his breaſt , ſaieth twice ; Lambe of
God which takeſt away the ſinnes of the
world, haue mercie vppon vs. And once Lamb
of God which takeſt away the ſinnes of the
world, graunt vs thy peace. And therfore Agnus Dei is ſaid, the Chalice being couered: becauſe Chriſt appeared to his Apoſtles the doores being ſhut, and gaue them powre and authoritie to remit ſinnes.

As touching the woord it ſelfe. *Agnon* in
Greeke , ſignifieth as much as gentle or meek
in Engliſh . And Chriſt is here called a Lamb.
becauſe a Lambe hurteth nothing, nether man
nor breaſt .

Againe Agnus is called *ab Agnoſcendo* , becauſe

cauſe amongſt a great flock and multitude by his only crie and bleating, he is acknowledged by his mother. And euen ſo Chriſt the Lambe of God, hanging vpon the Croſſe, by his voice and cry, was acknowledged by his mother.

Qui tollis peccata mundi.

Which takeſt away the ſinnes of the world.

Vpon which wordes Theophilactus ſaith. *Non dixit qui tollet, ſed qui tollis: quaſi ſemper hoc faciente.* He ſaith not, who will take away, but who doth take away, as daily and continuallie doing the ſame. For he did not only then take away our ſinnes (as ſaith Ludolphus) when he ſuffered, but alſo from that time vnto this preſent, he doth dailie take them away, although he be not dailie crucified for vs.

Miſerere-nobis.

Haue mercy on vs.

Haue mercie on vs, to wit, by taking away our ſinnes, becauſe S. Iohn (whoſe woordes theſe are) hath aſſured vs, that he is the ſame Lambe, who truly taketh away the ſinnes of the world. And Algerus ſaith, that with this faith we adore the Sacrament as a thing deuine, and we both ſpeake to it, and pray to it, as hauing life and reaſon, ſaying. Lambe of God &c. Thus he.

Agnus Dei.

Lambe of God.

Lambe of God, ſaith Biell, which ſuckedſt
thy

thy mother in the ſtable: followedſt hir flying into Egipt: and heardedſt hir bleating, ſeeking thee in the Temple

Qui tollis peccata mundi.

Which takeſt away the ſinnes of the world.

Originall, by Baptiſme. Mortall, by Pennance. And Veniall, by the vertu of this holie Euchariſt.

Miſerere nobis.

Haue mercie on vs.

Flying vnto thee for pardon for our ſinnes paſt. For victorie againſt temptations preſent. And for preſeruatiō from ſinnes to come. Further, beſides the former expoſition, in theſe wordes are plainly teſtified, two notable verities of Chriſt our Sauious: the one of his humanitie, the other of his diuinitie. Of his humanitie, in theſe wordes. *Agnus Dei &c.* Lambe of God, that is to ſay, ſent of God as a moſt innocent Lambe, to be offered vpp in ſacrifice for our ſaluation. Of his diuinitie, when he adeth. *Qui tollis peccata mundi,* which takeſt away the ſinnes of the world: becauſe to take away ſinne, is proper to God, and to none other.

Agnus Dei qui tollis peccata mundi.

Lambe of God which takeſt away the ſinnes of the world.

This Agnus Dei is ſaid or recited the third time: becauſe this Lābe of God not onlie was

acknow-

acknowledged of others, but alfo him felfe
acknowledged others, namelie, his heauenlie
Father: his bleffed mother: and alfo vs. He
acknowledged his Father when he faid. Father into thy handes I commend my fpirit. He
acknowledged his mother, when he faid. Woman behould thy fonne. And he acknowledged vs, when faid. Father forgiue them they
knowe not what they doe. So that *Agnus Dei*
thrice repeated, is as much to fay, as. Lambe
of God which didft acknowledg thy Father,
haue mercie vpon vs. Lambe of God which
didft acknowledg thy mother, haue mercie
vpon vs. Lambe of God which didft acknowledg vs, graunt vs thy peace.

Dona nobis pacem.

Grant vs thy peace.

The diuell, that ould perturber of peace, did
euer labour to breake and take away this triple peace, to wit, betwixt God and man: Of
man in him felfe: and betwixt man and man.
For firft he brake the peace betwixt God and
man, when he feduced our firft parents to
tranfgres the commandement of almightie
God. Secondlie, he brake the peace of man
within him felfe, when leauing him confounded with the fight of his owne fhame, he
fought for leaues to couer his nakednes.
Thirdlie, he brake the peace betwixt man and
man, when thorough malice he incited one
                                    brother

brother to murther the other. This triple peace therfore the prieft prayeth for, to wit, peace betwixt God and man: peace of man within himfelfe: and peace betwixt neighbours, that is, betwixt man and man.

Why we aske mercie and peace for the liuing, and repofe or reft for the departed.

The reafon why we demaund mercie and peace for the liuinge, and repofe or reft for the departed, is to fignifie the true and proper place of forgiuenes, to be in this worlde: as contrarie, the other worlde is the place of iuftice and punifhment. Againe in this world we are in continuall warre, as holic Iob faith. *Militia eft vita hominis fuper terram*. The life of man vpon earth is a warfare. And for this caufe we iuftlie aske for our felues peace, but as touching the departed, they are in peace although they are not in repofe; for they are in peace with all theire former enimies, the world, the flefh, and the diuell (for otherwife they were not in ftate of faluation:) but they are not as yet in repofe, but in paynes and torments, vntill they fhall haue fullie fatisfied for all their finnes & offences, for which they remayne indetted to almightie God: and for this caufe we do rather wifh the repofe, the peace.

And Reft is therfore added thrice, becaufe there is wifhed to the foules departed a triple or theefould reft. One from the afflidion of paines paine : an other for the beatifying of the foule : and the third for the glorifying both of the foule and body .

Domine Iesu Christe.

Lord Iesus Christe .

To wit , most pittifull, mercifull, louing, gentle , and beninge Lord Iesus.

Qui dixisti.

who saidst .

Being by thy passion to depart and leaue this world.

Apostolis tuis .

To thy Apostles.

Called by thee to the knowledg of the faith, sent by thee to the preaching of the faith : and, who suffered for thee, for the confession of the same faith

Pacem relinquo vobis .

I leaue you my peace.

To the end that they might firmelie remayne in peace, lest terrified and affrighted with miseries , they might fall from the faith .

Pacem meam do vobis.

I giue you my peace .

Giuinge vs thy peace , and taking to thy selfe in steede thereof, all our euils. O change of incomparable charitie!

Ne respicias peccata mea.

Behold not my sinnes .

To

To wit perſonall, where with I haueing offended thy maieſtie, am vnworthie to obtaine at thy handes the peace of thy Church, vnworthy to offer vp thy ſacred bodie to thy Father, and vnworthy to take vpon me to reconcile ſinners vnto thee.

Sed fidem eccleſiæ tuæ .

But the faith of thy Church.

Wherein thou haſt eſpouſed hir vnto thee as thy ſpouſe: wherin thou haſt ſanctified hir in the lauer of the word of life:wherin leſt ſhe ſhould fayle,thou haſt for euer confirmed hir.

Eamque ſecundum voluntatem tuam.

And according to thy will.

To wit, will moſt amorous, out of which thou vouchſafedſt to take frayle fleſh: will moſt pittifull, out of which thou vouchſafedſt to die: will moſt bountifull out of which thou vouchſafeſt to giue thy ſelfe in this holy Sacrament,in meate for her loue, redemption and comfort.

Pacificare & coadunare digneris.

Vouchſafe to pacifie and vnite it together.

That pacified in good, preſerued from euill counited in charitie, and gouerned both within and without by thee, ſhe may be accounted worthy of the communion of ſo excellent a foode.

Qui

Qui viuis & regnas Deus per omnia
secula seculorum

Who liueft mightelie: and raigneft, wifely:
God, confubftantiallie: world without end,
fempiternallie.

Of the Priests kissing the pax, saying.

Pax tecum.

Peace be with thee.

The 1. Reason.

Innocentius tertius faith, that after our Lord
had faluted his Apoftles, he faid againe vnto
them *Pax vobis*, Peace be vnto you, and then
breathed vpon them faying. Receiue yee the
holy Ghoft. Which to fignifie vnto vs, the
Prieft in the Maffe kiffeth the Pax (which is reuerently held vnto him by him which ferueth
at the Aultar.) And becaufe the loue of God
is diffufed in our hartes by the Holie Ghoft,
which is giuen vnto vs, therfore the kiffe of
peace is diffufed in the Church, amongft all
the faithfull.

The 2. Reason.

By this ceremonie we are admonifhed to
haue perfect loue & concord with our neighbours. And that if we haue any enimies, we
endeauour to kiffe them, as we kiffe the Pax,
to wit, to reconcile our felues vnto thē in fuch
coniunctiō of perfect loue, that we kiffe them
and embrace them as our deareft frendes.

The

The 3. Reason.

Againe this kisse of the Pax , serueth vs for three thinges . First, to shew that Iesus Christ hath appeaf d the wrath and anger of his Father towardes vs . Secondlie, that we doe all beleeue in one and the same God , and doe sweare to maintaine one Christian doctrin. Thirdlie , that we professe to loue christianlie one another, purposinge to reconcile vs to all those, who haue any way offended vs.

The 4. Reason.

This custom certainlie first came from our Lord him selfe , for it is not probable that Iudas would euer haue bene so hardie as to kisse his master , were it not , that this was the custome of the house of our Lord , and a common thinge amongst the Apostles, to vse this signe of loue when they returned from some iornie, as well towardes their master , as one of them towardes another . The which they haue practised euer since , and exhorted other Christians to doe the like . as we may see in the last chapter of the epistle to the Romans. 1. and 2. to the Corinthians, and 1 of S. Peeter saying. Salute one another with an holie kisse.

Nether is there any of our Doctors, who haue expounded the misteries of the Masse , that affirme not this ceremonie to haue come from the Apostles , and to be founded vpon the places of scripture before alleadged The
which

which is euidentlie to be prooued out of the
Liturgies of S. Iames, of S. Bafil, and of S.
Chrifoftom. Out of the 3. cap. of the Eccle-
fiaftcall Hierarchie of S. Denis. Out of the
2. and 8. booke of the Apoftolicall conftitu-
tions of S. Clement. Out of the 2. Apologie
of Iuftin Martyr, and manie others. Laftlie
one principall reafon of the inftituion of
this ceremonie, was, the dignitie of this
moft holie Communion, to the which none
ought to prefent him felfe with hatred and
rancour, but firft to be thoronghlie reconciled to his brother.

Pax tecum.

The prieft in kiffing the Pax faith. Peace
be with thee, which by this figne of a kiffe
I reprefent vnto thee.

Why the Pax is not giuen in the Maffe for the dead

In a Maffe of *Requiem*, the pax is not giuen, becaufe fuch a Maffe is principallie faid
for the foules in Purgatorie, amongft whom
there is no difcorde nor diffention. But the
fame is giuen, when Maffe is faid for the liuing, which oftentimes be at debate and difcord, to the end to reconcile them to peace
and concord.

Domine.
Lord.

Here the Prieft hauing his eies and intent,
fixed

fixed and bent towards the bleſſed Sacrament, ſpeaketh vnto our Lord Chriſt, reallie and trulie preſent vnder the viſible formes, ſaying. Lord.

Ieſu Chriſte. Ieſu Chriſt.

Sauiour of all mankinde, and anointed of the Father with the plenitude & aboundance of the Holie Ghoſt.

Fili Dei viui.

Sonne of the liuing God.

Sonne of the liuing God, naturall, conſubſtantiall and coeternall.

Qui ex voluntate Patris.

Who by the will of the Father.

Who by the will of the Father, moſt liberal, bountifull, and moſt mercifull, ſending thee in the fullnes of time vnto vs for our redemption.

Cooperante ſpiritu Sancto.

The Holy Ghoſt cooperating.

The Holy Ghoſt cooperating, who as he hath with thee and the Father one eſſence, ſo both in will and worke, is vnſeperable and vndeuided.

Per mortem.

By the death.

To wit, the moſt bitter, painfull, and opprobrious death of the Croſſe, which thou patientlie induring, didſt thereby make thy

Q

ſelfe

felfe obedient to the wil of thy Father.

Tuam. Thy.

Thy, to wit, put in thyne owne power, becaufe thou hadft powre to lay downe thy life. and power to take it againe,

Mundum viuificasti.

Haft giuen life to the world.

Haft giuen, fpirituall life to the world, for thou art the true bread which cameft downe from heauen to giue life to the world, all the whole world for one onlie finne, being depriued of life.

Libera me.

Deliuer me.

Deliuer me, (offering this facrifice) as al-fo all other faithful people for whom it is of-fred, that we may be in perfect libertie from all finne.

Per hoc facrofanctum corpus &
fanguinem tuum.

By this thy holy body and blood.

Holie aboue all holies : holy becaufe it was made in the wombe of the moft holie virgin, by that high artificer the holie Ghoft: and holie, becaufe it was vnited to the holy word.

Ab omnibus iniquitatibus meis.

From all myne iniquities.

That is frō all my finnes, wherwith I haue defiled and polluted my foule, made after the
image

image of the holie Trinitie.

Et vniuerſis malis.
And from all euills.

To wit, ether of body or ſoule, preſent or future, and to be endured ether in this life, or in the life to come.

Et fac me
And make me.

And make me who of my ſelfe am not able to doe any good deede, nor yet ſo much as to thinke any one good thoughte, vnleſſe I be aſſiſted and enabled by thee.

Tuis ſemper inherere mandatis.
Alwayes to cleaue to thy commandements.

Allwayes, that is to ſay, that at no time I tranſgreſſe thy holy commandements. Or alwayes, that is, that I obey and fulfill them al, leaſt offending in one, I be made (as the Appoſtle ſaith) guiltie of all.

Et a te nunquam ſeparari permittas.
And neuer to ſuffer me to be ſeperated from thee.

To wit, nether in this worlde by ſinne, nether in the worlde to come, by that horrible ſentence to be pronounced againſt the reprobate. Depart yee curſed into euerlaſting fire.

Qui. Who.
Who, by thy diuine eſſence.

Cum

Cum eodem Deo Patre.

With the fame God the Father.

Of whom all paternitie both in heauen and earth is denominated.

Et cum Spiritu Sancto.

And with the Holy Ghoft.

The knot and bond of charitie, both of the Father, and the Sonne.

Viuis.　Liueft.

For as much as one is the life, diuinity, and effence, of the Father, the Sonne, and the holy Ghoft.

Et regnas.

And reigneft.

Both in heauen and in earth, as abfolute Lord ouer all the inhabitants, both in the one and in the other.

Deus.

God.

True, naturall, and vndeuided.

In fecula feculorum. Amen.

World without end, Amen.

Infalliblie, immutablie, and eternallie without all end. Amen.

Perceptio corporis tui.

The receiuing of thy body.

The receiuing of thy bodie, which verelie and trulie lyeth hid and veyled ynder this diuine and dreadfull Sacrament.

De-

Domine Ieſu Chriſte.

O Lord Ieſu Chriſt.

O Lord Ieſu Chriſt, O Lord who haſt created me, O Ieſu who haſt redeemed me, O Chriſt who ſhalt iudge me.

Quod ego indignus.

Which I vnworthy.

Vnworthie, for my manifould and ſundrie ſinnes committed. Vnworthie, for my great defect and want of feruóur and deuotion.

Sumere præſumo.

Preſume to take.

Not confiding in myne owne iuſtice, but in in thy great benignitie, mercie, and bountie. Which haſt promiſed not to quench ſmoking, flax, nor to breake a ſunder a bruſed reede.

Non mihi proueniat in iudicium &
condemnationem.

Be not to me ro iudgement and condemnation.

Which the Apoſtle threatneth vnto all thoſe who approache vnworthely to the ſame, becauſe they diſcerne not our Lordes bodie: to the end that none which are dead, doe preſume to take the meate of life.

Sed pro tua pietate.

But for thy goodnes.

By the which thorough thy onlie goodnes thou haſt exalted me to the ſtate of prieſt-

Q 5   hood

hood : hitherto haſt patientlie borne with
my offences : and mercifullie expected my repentance .

Profit mihi ad tutamentum mentis.

Let it profit me to the ſauegard of ſoule.

That ſo it preſerue me for time to come,
that I neuer conſent in minde to ſinne , nor
any way offend thy gratious preſence within
my ſoule.

Et corporis.

And body.

That nether by the way of my bodie , or
gates of my ſenſes , I euer admit death into
my ſoule , nor make the members of my bodie conſecrated vnto thee , weapons of ſinne
to procure the death of ſoule and bodie.

Et ad medelam percipiendam.

And to the receiuing of cure.

Qui viuis & regnas &c.

Who liueſt and raigneſt.

To the receiuing of medecine, to wit , of
thee , who art the true phiſitian both of ſoule
and body , and onlie canſt cure the diſeaſes,
both of the one and the other.

Panem cœleſtem accipiam.

I will receiue the celeſtiall bread.

Then hauing adored, he riſeth vp to take
the healthſome Hoſt , ſaying . I will receaue
&c. To wit, I a poore pilgrime in this world,
will

will receaue the viaticum and food of this frayle life, in the ſtrength whereof I wil walke to the mount of God. I ſick, will receaue the celeſtiall bread which fortifieth and corroborateth the hart of man. I hungrie and ſtarued, will receaue the bread, which who ſo eateth, ſhall neuer hunger more. I diſquieted and anxious, will receaue the bread which eſtabliſheth the hart, and calmeth the ſtormes of a troubled conſcience. I feeble and lame, will receaue the bread, being inuited of that great kinge, vnto the ſupper whereunto all the feeble and lame were brought in. In all ſinfull & vncleane, wil receaue the bread which only can make cleane that which was conceiued of vncleane ſeede, and of ſtones can raiſe vp ſonnes to Abraham.

The celeſtial bread, not made of the graine of the earth, but of the virgins blood, The celeſtiall bread, which refreſheth the Angells with beatitude. The celeſtiall bread, which deſcendeth from aboue to nouriſh the hartes of his poore ones, aſpiringe and ſighinge after the celeſtiall ioyes The celeſtiall bread, which changeth the receauer, though a ſinner, into a celeſtiall creature, and a Saint.

Et nomen Domini inuocabo.

And will call vpon the name of our Lord.
That is, will inuoke or call the name of our Lord vpon my ſelfe and by the meanes of this

celeſtiall

celeftiall bread, will fuppe with Chrift, that
he may fhew mercie vnto me now inhabi-
ting in heauen, as he did vnto them that fup-
ped with him on earth. Or I will call vpon
the name of our Lord, that he may call me
a finner vnto him, place me amongft the
number of his elect,and for euer reconcile me
vnto his Father

What the Prieft doth before receiuing of the hoft.

This done, the Prieft a litle inclininge his
bodie, and vniting all his cogitations as much
as is poffible, doth deuoutlie recollect him
felfe,and directeth, not onlie the corporal eies
of his bod.e,to the outward fpecies & formes
of the Sacrament,but much more the inward
eies of his faith to our Lord Iefus Chrift,
trulie contayned vnder thofe vifible formes:
whom with all reuerence, feare, deuotion,
charitie, affection of mind and foule, he is to
receiue.

Domine.

Lord.

The Prieft therfore, being readie to receiue, and harbour within his foule, this facred Hoft,firft fayth, Domine, Lord. Which
word of it felfe doth clearlie fhew, what maner of houfe it ought to be, and how it ought
to be decked and adorned,wherin fo facred a
gueft ought to be lodged: for a Lord, ought

to

to haue a lordlie lodging : and a noble perſonage, a noble habitation. For, *Talis hoſpis, ta-*
le hoſpitium: ſuch a Lord, ſuch a lodging.

Non ſum dignus.

I am not worthy.

Next conſidering him ſelfe to be a miſerable creature, & an earthlie veſſel of clay, he
ſaith, I am not worthie. To wit, of myne owne
preparation , knowinge that thou haſt ſaid,
that when we haue done all that which is
commanded vs , we ſhould ſtill confeſſe our
ſelues vnprofitable ſeruants . Yea which is
more, although he ſhould burne with Sera-
phicall charitie, yet may he truly ſay he is not
worthie.

Vt intres ſub tectum meum.

That thou ſhould.t enter vnder my roofe.

Darkned with the obſcuritie of ſinnes, rui-
nous for defect of vertues , ſtirred to vnlaw-
full deſires , ſubiecte to paſſions , repleate
with illuſions, proane to euill, and procliue to
vice, finallie a wretched child of Adam , vtterlie vnworthie of the bread of Angels.

Sed tantum d.c verbum , & ſanabi-
tur anima mea.

But ſay the word only , and my ſoule
ſhall be healed.

As thou ſaidſt the worde to the ſick of the
palſie, willing him to take vpp his bed and
walke, and he incontinentlie aroſe and wal-

Q 5   ked,

ked. As thou faydft the word to the woman,
fick of the iffue of blood, who onlie touched
the hemme of thy garment, and fhe was immediatlie healed. As thou faidft the word to
the faithfull Centurion, and his feruant was
immediatelie cured:

Corpus Domini noftri Iefu Chrifti.
The body of our Lord Iefus Chrift.

The body of our Lord Iefus Chrift, offered vpon the Aultar of the Croffe for the finnes of all the world in expiation. The bodie
of our Lord Iefus Chrift, giuen vnto vs vnder
this venerable Sacrament for our viuification.
The body of our Lord Iefus Chrift, to be re-
seiued of me for the obtayning of future glorification.

Cuftodiat animam meam.
Keepe my foule.

Preferue and keepe my foule, to wit from
relapfe into finne, leaft, I become contume-
lious againft my Sauiour Chrift. Keepe my
foule, to wit, by corroborating, foftering,
and fortifying me daylie more and more in
the fpirituall life. Keepe my foule, to wit, at
the dreadfull hower of my departure, foorth
of the clawes and iawes, of the fierce, deuou-
ring, and infernall Lions.

In vitam æternam.
To life eternall.

That as the breade miniftered by the Angell

gel to the prophet Helias ſo fortified him,
that in the force thereof he walked vp to the
mountaine of God, Horeb. And as the bread
which deſcended from heauen, brought the
people of Iſraell thorough the deſert into the
land of promiſe: euen ſo, ô gratious Lord, I
humblie beſeeche thee, that this heauenlie
bread may be my true viaticum, to lead me
thorough the deſert of this worlde, to that
bleſſed and ſupernall countrie, promiſed to all
thoſe that faithfullie ſerue thee, Amen.

Of the prieſtes receauing of the Chalice.

As before the receiuing of the bodie of
our Lord, the prieſt (to acknowledg his own-
ne inſufficiencie) prepared him ſelfe thereunto by prayer and humilitie: euen ſo proceeding to the receauing of the blood of our
Lord, he doth againe by prayer and humilia-
tion of him ſelfe, acknowledg his owne in-
dignitie, ſaying.

Quid retribuam Domino.

What ſhall I rendar to our Lord.

What ſhall I (duſt and aſhes) handie worke
and workmanſhip of my Creator; frayle, vnworthie, and vile man, the loweſt and leaſt of
all his ſeruantes, render vnto our Lord; who if
I haue but one good thought (where with to
render thankes vnto him) the ſelfe ſame
thought is ſent of him, the ſelfe ſame thought
proceedeth from him.

Q 6 Pro

Pro omnibus.

For all.

For all thinges, whoſe number and immenſitie, doth far exceede all humane ſenſe &
vnderſtanding. For as Hugo ſaieth, if thou
ſhouldeſt looke into the whole world, thou
ſhalt finde no kinde of thinge which doth not
liue to doe thee ſeruice.

Quæ retribuit mihi.

Which he hath giuen me.

Not onlie to all in generall, but to me in
particular: to me I ſay his creature, his gift of
mightie and maruelous Creation; his gift of
carefull and Fatherlie conſeruation : his gift
of gentle and patient expectation : his gift of
celeſtiall and diuine inſpiration : his gift of all
giftes, his pretious bodie and blood for my
refection. Neuer am I able o my Lord to come
out of this dett, albeit I had as many liues to
ſpend for thy ſake, as I haue ſeuerall droppes
of blood within my bodie.

Calicem ſalutaris accipiam.

I will take the Chalice of ſaluation.

Accipiam I will take, being drie and thirſtie for lack of the humor of heauenly grace.
I will take, being parcht and withered for
want of the dew of diuine benediction. I will
take, being dead and vnfruitful, for lacke of
the fruites of good life. I will take, which am
a ſtranger and pilgrime in this world, and
haue

haue as yet a longe and labourſome iorney, to my celeſtiall habitation.

Calicem The Chalice, that is the blood of Ieſus Chriſt in the Chalice, the blood which in his laſt ſupper he gaue to his Diſciples. The blood which Longinus pearcing his ſide, ran foorth aboundantlie out of his glorious breaſt. The blood, which in his glorious reſurrection (to conſerue the integritie of his nature) he moſt miraculouſlie reaſſumed. The blood which he commanded vs to take in memorie of his paſſion, ſaying. Drinke yee all of this, ſoe often as you doe this, doe it in remembrance of me.

Saluaris Of ſaluation So called, becauſe it contayneth in it Chriſt, the author of our ſaluation Or of ſaluation, as greatlie wiſhing and deſiring our ſaluation, which none may ſay ſo trulie as our Sauiour Chriſt, becauſe neuer any ſo greatlie deſiered and ſeriouſlie ſought the ſame as he. Or of ſaluation, by reaſon of the effects, becauſe it effected our ſaluation, when ſhed on the Croſſe, it reconciled vs to God.

Et nomen Domini inuocabo.
And will call vpon the name of our Lord.

To the end that ſacred blood may come vpon me to my benediction, which the wicked and perfidious Iewes asked to come vpon them, to their deſtruction and damnation,
ſaying.

faying. *Sanguis eius fuper nos , & fuper filios noftros* . His blood be vpon vs , and vpon our children .

Laudans inuocabo Dominum.

Prayfing I will inuocate our Lord.

Prayfing him for the exhibition of fo great a benefit , who did not onlie fhed the fame his pretious blood for vs , but alfo gaue the fame in drinke vnto vs. And who but moft vngratefull, will not laude our Lord for fuch a benefit?

Et ab inimicis meis faluus ero.

And I fhall be fafe from mine enimies.

For this moft pretious blood of Iefus Chrift, hath many moft fingular effects and operations . It giueth grace , it giueth glorie, it taketh away our finne , it fortifieth our frailtie, it calleth Angells to vs, and driueth the diuels from vs: and as Lyons , breathing foorth fire, fo depart we from this table; being made terrible vnto them.

Sanguis Domini noftri Iefu Chrifti.

The blood of our Lord Iefus Chrift.

The blood of our Lord Iefus Chrift , which is the fountaine and lauer of our emundation and fanctification . The blood of our Lord Iefus Chrift , which is the price of our redemption and reparation. The blood of our Lord Iefus Chrift , which is to the worthie receauer, the chalice of all benediction.

Cuſto-

Cuſtodiat animam meam

Keepe my ſoule.

Keepe my ſoule in innocencie of life and puritie of hart, leaſt with Iudas I crie, *Peccaui tradens ſanguinem iuſtum.* I haue ſinned betraying the innocent blood. Keepe my ſoule, from that ſmitinge and plague of our Lord, which ſmote al the firſt borne of Egipt, whoſe poſtes of their houſes were not ſprinkeled with the blood of the Lambe. Keepe my ſoule in ſpirituall force & vigor, that in vertu of this blood, I may vndertake to fight againſt diuells and infernall furies, like as the Elephant is encouraged to fight at the ſight of blood.

In vitam æternam.

To life euerlaſting.

According to the promiſe of our Sauiour him ſelfe, ſaying. He that eateth my fleſh and drinketh my blood, hath life euerlaſting, and I will raiſe him vp at the latter day, to wit, from a temporall death, to a perdurable, euerlaſting, and eternall life.

Of the prieſtes giuing the holie Sacrament to the aſſiſtants, when any be to communicate.

This done, the prieſt (as Innocentius ſaieth) communicateth to the people, inſinuating, that Chriſt after his reſurrection, did eate with his Diſciples, as S. Luke teſtifieth,

fieth, faying. Iefus tooke bread and brake, and
reached vnto hem.

And here let the Chriftian receauer vnderftand, that fo much difference as there is be-
wixt heauen and earth, betwixt the Creator,
and the creature, fo much difference is there,
betwixt this facred viand, and al others which
euer at any time God gaue to man. For in this
diuine Sacramēt, there is to drinke, there is to
eate: there is wine, and there is mylke: there
is bread, and there is water. Drinke for thofe
that are drie : meate for thofe that are hungrie wine for great ones: and mylke for litle
ones: bread to fortifie , and water to refrefh.
Finallie, in this diuine Sacramenr, our Lord
doth nourifh vs with him felfe, with his own,
true, and proper fubftance, as well diuine, as
humane. What could he doe more for vs?
What banquet, what feaft, could he prouide
more exquifite, or more noble for vs?

Quod ore fumpfimus Domine.

That which we haue taken with our
mouth , o Lord.

Where firft let it be noted , that the Prieft
fpeaketh in the plurall number , faying.
Which we haue receaued &c. fignifying hereby, that he did not confecrate this Sacrament
onlie for him felfe, but for the whole myfti-
call bodie of Chrift, whereof he is a part, and
as it were the mouth of this body.

PNYA

Pura mente capiamus.

Les vs receiue with a pure minde.

Free from all spot and pollution of sinne, from al spiritual drowsines and tepidity, with full faith, loue, and feruent deuotion , to the strengthning of the soule, and to the spirituall sustentation of all good actions.

Et de munere temporali.

And of a gift temporall.

To wit , as touching the visible formes, which of thy gentle gift, and bountifull liberallitie, we haue receaued.

Fiat nobis remedium sempiternum.

Let there be made vnto vs a remedy eternall.

To wit , against all diseases both of soule and bodie, that in our last end, fortified with this viaticum, we may be brought to the true beatifying and sempiternall securitie , both of the one and the other.

Corpus tuum Domine quod sumpsi.

Thy body o Lord which I haue receiued.

Vnder the species of bread , thy true body, thy naturall bodie , the same which was borne of the virgin Marie , laid in the manger, adored of the Sages, borne into Egipt, apprehended, whipped, crowned, and crucified of the Iewes.

Et sanguis quem potaui.

And blood which I haue drunk

Which

Which I haue drunke vnder the ſpecies of wine, thy very true and proper blood, the ſame blood which thou didſt ſhed being circumciſed, the ſame which thou didſt ſweate in the garden, the ſame which thou didſt ſhed being ſcourged, the ſame which ran out of thy handes and feete being nayled, the ſame which guſhed out of thy moſt holy ſide being peirced.

Adhereat viſceribus meis.

Cleaue vnto my bowells.

The bowells of our ſoule, are hir powers, ſuch are our vnderſtanding, our will &c. And here we pray that, to theſe powers of our ſoule, this pretious foode may ſo adhere, that it doe not preſentlie paſſe thorough our mindes, like as ſome liquid corporall meates paſſe thorough the ſtomack, leauing behind them no ſuccour nor nouriſhment, but ſo to cleaue, to our bowels, that it make its aboade & ſtay in our ſoules.

Et praſtavt in me non remaneat ſcelerum macula.

And grant that there remaine not in me, ſpotts of wickednes.

By this ſpott of wickednes, may be vnderſtood the guilt of veniall ſinne, or temporall paine remayning in the ſoule, from the which he prayeth to be releaſed, for that exiſting and remayning in the ſoule, it cannot be admitted:

ted to the ioyes of the bleſſed , although it be
adorned with grace and charitie.

Quem tam pura & ſancta.
W hom ſo pure and holy.

Pure, by reaſon that it purifieth the minde,
from all impure cogitations . And holie , becauſe it is ſanctification in it ſelfe , and alſo
ſanctifieth the receauer , repleniſhing him
with all aboundance of grace and ſanctification.

Refecerunt ſacramenta. Qui viuis &c.
Sacraments, haue refreſhed.

For this holie Sacrament, refreſheth the
bowells of the ſoule of the worthie receauer:
it refreſheth the vnderſtanding by the illumi-
nation of knowledge : it refreſheth the will,
by inflammation of loue : and it refreſheth
the memorie , by excitinge it to the reme-
moration of the paſſion; and by leauing a certaine ſpirituall ioy and ſweetnes in the whole
man .

Of the waſhing of the endes of the prieſtes
fingars after receauing.

The 1. Reaſon.
After the receauing of the holie Euchariſt , the prieſt waſheth the endes or tippes of
his fingars : for it were moſt vnworthie, that
the handes which haue handled that incorruptible body , ſhould touche a corruptible
body,

body, before they were firft dilligentlie, wa-
hed and cleanfed.

The 2. Reafon.

The triple wafhing of the prieftes handes,
the firft before he begin Maffe, the ;fecond
after the Offertorie, and the third now after
Communion, or as Innocentius faieth, in the
begining, in the mideft,& in the ending,doth
infinuate the clenfing of thoughtes, of words
and of woikes. Or the purging, of originall,
mortall, and veniall finne. And this laft ablu-
tion, may properlie be referred to the ablu-
tion of Baptifme,the forme whereof Chrift in-
ftitured after his refurrection, faying. Going.
therfore teache yee all nations,baptiiing them
in the name of the Father, and of the Sonne,
and of the holie Ghoft. he that beleeueth, and
is baptifed, fhall be faued. Marc. 16. 16.

Of the returne of the prieft to the right hand of the Aultar.

Let vs now come to the laft point, which
is of the returne of the prieft, to the right end
of the Aultar, after the Communion. This
is not done for fuperftition, as if the prayer
were better at one end, then at the other, as
fcoffing heretiques doe calumniate, but to
fignifie fome fpeciall myfterie comprehended
in the holie Scripture, to wit, the finall conuerfion of the Iewes. This Hugo de fancto
Victore, auoucheth moft clearlie faying.

His

His completis &c. Theſe thinges accōpliſhed, the prieſt returneth to the right end of the Aultar: ſignifying, that in the end of the world, Chriſt ſhal returne to the Iewes, whom now he hath reiected, vntill the fulnes of the Gentils be entred in, for then the remainder of Iſraell, according to the Scriptures, ſhall be ſaued. This he. li. de ſpecial. miſ. obſer. cap. 4.

Of the Anthem or poſt Communion.

The 1. Reaſon.

It is more then manifeſt, that the cuſtome and vſe of reciting a hymne, or Canticle in the end of the Maſſe, is come vnto vs, from Chriſt him ſelfe, and his Apoſtles: for after our Lord had communicated his bodie and blood to his Apoſtles, the Scripture preſentlie addeth. *Et hymno dicto, exierunt in montem Oliueti.* And an hymne being ſaid, they went foorth vnto mount Oliuet. This is moſt euidentlie to be ſeene in the Liturgie of S. Iames, wherin you ſhall find theſe four pſalmes following, to haue bene ſonge in this part of the Maſſe. *Dominus regit me. Benedicam Domino in omni tempore. Exaltabo te Deus meus rex.* And *Laudate Dominum omnes gentes.*

The 2. Reaſon.

Theſe Pſalmes, Canticles, and Hymnes aforeſaid, were ſonge in the primitiue Church during the time of the holie Communion, in which time the Chriſtians did communicate

cate verie often, yea euerie day, as diuers hi-
ftories doe teftifie: For which caufe the number of Communicants being very great, the
Church retayned thefe longe Anthiemes,
very agreable to the feruent deuotion of that
time. But fince the Chriftians ceafing to
communicate euery day, and the number of
communicants much decreafing, fo longe
Canticles were not thought expedient, and
therfore in place thereof, are faid thefe fhort
Anthiemes after the Communion. Which is
the reafon and caufe, that moft now at this
day, doe call them by the name of the poft-
Communion.

The 3. Reafon.

Mifticallie, according to Innocentius, the
Anthiem which is recited after the Communion, doth fignifie the ioy of the Apoftles for
Chriftes refurrection. According as it is written faying. The Difciples therfore were glad
when they fawe our Lord. And therfore, in
high Maffe, the fame is founge reciprocallie,
to infinuate, that the Difciples did mutuallie
recite one to another the ioy of the Refurrection; As S. Luc. teftifieth, that the two Difciples to whom our Lord appeared in the way
to Emaus, went back into Hierufalem, & they
found the eleuen gathered together, and thofe
that were with them, faying. That our Lord
is rifen indeed, and hath appeared to Simon.

Luc.

Luc. 24. 34.

Dominus vobiſcum.

Our Lord be with you.

According to ſome theſe ſeuerall ſalutations of the prieſt to the people, doe repreſent vnto vs, the ſeuerall apparitions of our Sauiour to his Diſciples. Or the promiſe of our Lord made vnto them, touching the ſending of the holie Ghoſt.

Et cum ſpiritu tuo.

And with thy ſpirit.

The propertie of Chriſtian charitie is, that euerie one ſhould be carefull, not only for him ſelfe, but alſo for his neighbour. For this cauſe the aſiſtants anſwere the Prieſt, in recogniſſance of that which he hath done for them by his prayers, that God may be with his ſpirit, to guide him by the inſpiration of his diuine grace wherſoeuer neede is; for the execution of this his ſacred function.

Of the laſt Collects.

The 1. *Reaſon.*

Theſe prayers are made after Communion in the end of the Maſſe, to giue vs to vnderſtand, that ſubſequent prayer is as neceſſarie for vs as precedent: becauſe we are admoniſhed, to pray alwayes without intermiſſion. Luc. 18.

The

The 2. *Reafon.*

Of thefe Colleets, or thankfgiuinges, we are admonifhed in fundry places of the holy fcripture to doe the fame, as Colof. 3. faying. All whatfoeuer you doe in word or in worke, all thinges in the name of our Lord Iefus Chrift, giuing thankes to God & the Father thorough him. Befides it is moft conforme to reafon it felfe, that receiuing fo great a benefit from God, we fhould render due and conuenient thankes vnto him for the fame. And what greater benefit could we poffiblie receiue at his handes, then the moft pretious bodie and blood of our Sauiour Iefus, for the health and nourifhment of our foules and bodies?

The 3. *Reafon.*

Mifticallie the Colleets fignifie, how the Apoftles and Difciples, after the Afcenfion of our Lord, perfeuered in prayer. As alfo the prayers of Iefus Chrift our head, who maketh dailie interceffion vnto his Father for vs.

Dominus vobifcum.
Our Lord be with you.

The Colleets being ended, the prieft faluteth the people the fecond time, faying. Our Lord be with you. As if he fhould fay. The time to let you depart is now at hand : but albeit you depart from the temple of our Lord, yet depart not away from our Lord, but fo leade your liues that his holie grace neuer depart

part away from your soules. And the people make answere saying.

Et cum spiritu tuo.

And with thy spirit.

And with thy spirit , praying , that in all wayes wherin the Priest wisheth our Lord to be with them, in the same sorte our Lord may also euer be, and abide with him.

Of *Ite Missa est.*

Depart, Masse is ended.

This was ordayned to be said , to let the people knowe that the Masse was ended, and so to giue them leaue to goe away : becauſe they are, not to depart till Masse be ended, and vntill they haue receaued the prieſtes benediction .

The word *Missa* is in this place diuerslie expounded by our learned Doctors . Some conſider it adiectiuelie , and vnderſtand for the Subſtantiue, *Hostia, aut oblatio*, and ſo they interpret it thus, *Ite Missa est , scilicet , Hostia est oblatio*. Goe, or depart, the Hoſt, or oblation is ſent for you, that is to ſay, is preſented or offered vp to God in your behalfes.

Others conſider it ſubſtantiuelie , ſomtimes referring it to the myſterie which hath bene celebrated: and ſomtimes to the people who haue aſiſted at the ſame . When it is referred to the miſterie, the ſenſe is . *Ite Missa est dicta aut peracta* . Depart yee, Masse is ſaid

R   or

or ended: which expofition in the opinion of
many is the moft proper , and moft familiar.
If one would referre it to the people , *Miſſa*,
importeth as much as *miſsio* , and *miſsio* , as
much as *dimiſsio*, that is to fay, to let depart,
to difmiſſe , or fend away the people , and fo
the fenſe according to this interpretation is.
Goe your wayes , licence or permiſſion is giuen you to depart. For as by this world Miſſa
Maſſe , they vnderftand commonlie and properlie , the great and diuine myfterie of all
Chriftians : fo when it is ſaid vnto them *Ite
Miſſa eſt*, they vnderftand preſently that Maſſe
is ended , and that leaue is granted them to
with draw them ſelues.

Innocentius the third faieth , that this Sacrifice, that is the holie Hoſt , is called *Miſſa*,
quaſi tranſmiſſa, as fent betwixt. Firft from the
Father to vs, that it may be with vs. And then
to the Father from vs , that it may intercede
with the Father for vs . By the Father to vs,
by his Incarnation : from vs to the Father, by
his paſſion . In the Sacrament by the Father
to vs by fanctification: and by vs againe to the
Father by oblation.

Of the laſt benedıction.

This done , the Prieſt kiſſeth the Aultar,
and then with his handes eleuated, geueth the
laft benediction vnto the people : fignifying
that laft benediction, which Chriſt, Afcending,

ding, gaue vnto his Difciples : for as S. Luke
fayeth. He brought them foorth abroade into
Bethanie, and lifting vp his handes he bleffed
them And it came to paffe, whiles he bleffed
them, he departed from them, and was carried into heauen. And for this caufe (in a
highe, or folemne Maffe) after the laft falutation which the prieft maketh vnto the people,
the Deacon, with a highe voice, pronounceth
Ite miſſa eſt, depart, it is fent, or, afcended, for
you. And the people prefentlie with gratula-
tion, doe anfwere fayinge, *Deo gratias,* giuing thankes to God, and imitating herein
the Apoftles of our Lord, who as the fame S.
Luke faieth, adoring, went back into Hierufalem with great ioy, and they were alwayes in
the temple prayfing and bleffing God.

It may likewife fignifie the miffion of the
Holie Ghoft, which our Lord fent downe
from heauen vpon his Apoftles ; accordingly
as he had promifed them, faying. You fhall
receaue the vertu of the Holie Ghoft coming
vpon you.

S. Aug. maketh mention of this benediction, and houldeth, that the prieft by the
fame offereth the people vnto God, and leaueth them to him in protection. In the eccle-
fiafticall hiftorie of Ruffinus is recited, that it
was made with the hande, and he further-
faieth that him felfe was bleffed in this maner
by the Heremites of Egipt,

2 R   Final-

Finallie, *Ite Miffa eft.* is fayd, vpon folemne and feftiuall dayes, and that in figne of fpirituall ioy and iubilation.

Benedicamus Domino, vpon the weeke daies, and dayes of faft, in the which the fonges of ioy doe ceafe in the Church, and is to admonifh vs, that we ought to begin all our actions in him, and to finifh them thorough him.

The office ordayned for thofe which are dead *in* the faith of Iefus Chrift, endeth by this prayer *Requiefcant in pace*, to obtaine vnto them reft and repofe.

To the two firft, the afiftants anfwere *Deo gratias*. In thankfgiuing for the accomplifhment of the holie myfteries of the Maffe, to the end that they may not be blamed of ingratitude, as were the nine Lepers mentioned in S. Luke, who returned not thankes, nor magnified Iefus Chrift, for the recouery of their health, and healing.

To the prayer made by the prieft for the remedie of the foules departed, anfwere is made Amen; which is as much to fay. Be it fo as hath bene requefted, and our Lord vouchfafe to giue them euerlaftinge repofe (as he hath promifed them) in Abrahams bofome.

Of the Gofpell of S. Iohn.

This gofpell all Chriftian people haue euermore held in wonderfull reuerence; for it hath bene accuftomed to be reade vnto
                                                them,

them , not onlie in the end of the Maſſe , but
alſo after the ſicke bath receaued the B. Sacrament, and the Extreme vnction, when children are Baptiſed, and when women are chur-
ched: the which goſpell , the very Panims
them ſelues haue much admired , for as S.
Aug. teſtifieth , a certaine philoſopher , and
Platonick , haueing read the ſame , was in ſo
great admiration therof , that he ſaid it was
worthie to be written in letters of gould, and
to be placed by Chriſtians in all their Churches in the moſt eminent places.

Finallie , the prayſes of this goſpell can neuer be ſufficientlie expreſſed , and eſpeciallie
where it is ſaid. *Et verbum caro factum eſt &*
habitauit in nobis. For reuerence wherof as
we dailie ſee , the prieſt falleth downe on his
knees , at the pronunciation of the ſaid wordes . I will brieflie recite certaine examples concerning the efficacie of the ſame;
In Aquitania there were two poſeſſed of
the diuell , both beggars ; and the one
perceauing that more was giuen to his fel-
low then to him , he ſaid in ſecret to a
prieſt . If thou wilt doe what I ſhall tell thee,
to wit , that thou wilt reade in my fellowes
eare , the goſpell , *In principio erat verbum,*
(but yet ſo as I heare not the ſame) knowe for
certaine the diuell ſhall be driuen out of him.
But the prieſt vnderſtanding the craft of the
diuell , pronounced the ſaid goſpell out a
lowde

lowde. And when he faid. *Et verbum caro factum eſt & c.* prefentlie the euill fpirits flew from them, and both were difpofeſſed and deliuered of the diuell.

It is alfo declared, that the diuell him felfe faid vnto a certaine holie man, that there was a certaine worde of the gofpell, verie dreadfull to the diuels. Who asking what that word was, the diuell would not tell. When the holie man had recited diuers authorities, the diuell anfwered to euery one, that it was not that. At the laſt being asked if it were that, *Verbum caro factum eſt* He anfwered not, but with fearfull cryinge foorthwith vaniſhed.

For conclufion (gentle Reader) I will clofe vp this difcourfe with the wordes of a godlie writer, and not with myne owne, faying. Let no man fuppofe, hauing heard in this expofition, that this Sacrifice is fufficientlie explicated, leſt perhaps in extollinge the worke of man, he doe extenuate fo diuine a Sacrament. For in this diuine office there are fo many myfteries inuolued, that no man, vnles diuinelie infpired, is able or fufficient to explicate the fame. I therfore herein, haue done diligentlie what I could, not fufficientlie what I would. The onlie recompenfe which for this labour I looke for from men, is, that they would vouchfafe before the mercifull iudge (who beit beſt knowes with what intention of hart I wrote this treatiſe) to ſhed foorth their deuout prayers vnto him for my ſinnes. Beſeeching him, that if it profit not many, yet it may profit ſome, or at the leaſt me alone, though neuer ſo litle. Make this petition for me, and I ſhall hould my ſelfe aboundantly paid for my paynes.

FINIS.

APPROBATIONES.

Perlecto hoc libro cuius titulus eſt *A Deuout expoſition of the holy Maſſe*, à Domino Ioanne Heigham cópoſito, nihil in eo reperio, quod fidei aut bonis moribus contradicat, quin potius multa notaui quæ ad conſolationem & deuotionem Catholicorum excitandam conducere poſſunt.

IOANNES NORTONVS
S. Theol. Doctor.

Continet hic liber deuotam explicationem ceremoniarum & mysteriorum sacrosanctae Missae, ad fidelis populi eruditionem, vt sacrificio piè afsistere discant: nec sese intromisit author in materias sublimes aut quaestiones controuersas, sed omnino deuotionem & affectus inflammationem spectauit: quod ita fecit, vt nihil dissonum rectae fidei aut sanis moribus, sed omnia solida & pia & proficua pijs mentibus collegerit. Ita lecto libello testor

F. *Leander de S. Martino*
Benedictinus Sacrae
Theol. Licentiatus.

Horum testimonio subscripsi, & eundem librum vtiliter excudi posse censui. Actum Duaci 15. Iulij 1612.

GEORGIVS COLVENERIVS
S. Theol. Doctor & Professor, & in Academia Duacena librorum Censor.